Brian Gibbons presents the idea of multiplicity as a way of understanding the form and style of Shakespeare's plays: composed of many different codes, woven together in a unique pattern for each play, rather than variations on the fixed notion of comedy or tragedy.

The method of this book is comparison, using an imaginative range of texts and a variety of new approaches, and there is lively discussion of modern stage performance. The study selects plays from different phases of Shakespeare's career. Comparison with major works by Spenser, Sidney and Marlowe is an important feature, while Shakespeare's re-use of his own previous work further demonstrates his artistic decision-making in action and suggests how he himself saw his own earlier plays and poems.

Far from reducing the plays to a formula, Brian Gibbons shows how criticism can make articulate what popular audiences have always instinctively known, that the plays' sheer abundance and variety is their strength. This is an original book: it is scholarly, yet straightforward and lively, and it engages an issue of central interest.

SHAKESPEARE AND MULTIPLICITY

SHAKESPEARE AND MULTIPLICITY

BRIAN GIBBONS

CAMBRIDGE
UNIVERSITY PRESS

Published by the Press Syndicate of the University of Cambridge
The Pitt Building, Trumpington Street, Cambridge CB2 1RP
40 West 20th Street, New York, NY 10011-4211, USA
10 Stamford Road, Oakleigh, Melbourne 3166, Australia

First published 1993

Printed in Great Britain at the University Press, Cambridge

A catalogue record for this book is available from the British Library

Library of Congress cataloguing in publication data

Gibbons, Brian, 1938–
Shakespeare and multiplicity: Brian Gibbons.
p.   cm.
Includes bibliographical references and index.
ISBN 0-521-44406-3
1. Shakespeare, William, 1564–1616 – Criticism and interpretation.
1. Title.
PR2976.G48   1993
822.3′3 – dc20   92-42706 CIP

ISBN 0 521 44406 3 hardback

TAG

To my best friend and collaborator

Contents

Acknowledgements

The shape of this book reflects my fascination with the variety of interest Shakespeare offers, and the sheer newness of his work. I argue that we can demonstrate directly from the plays their author's critical intelligence at work, both in his eclectic use of the work of others and his re-use of his own previous writings. 'Shakespeare' in this sense is by no means an invisible poet.

Though it has been long in meditation, this book has finally come together quite quickly, and I am most grateful to two institutions, The Folger Shakespeare Library, where I held a Fellowship in 1989, and The Huntington Library, where I was Andrew W. Mellon Fellow in 1990, for giving me space to think at just the right time, and for the stimulus of good company. Speaking of good company, I count myself fortunate to work in a field where intellectual exchange can be so generous and agreeable. I owe a special personal debt to Andrew Gurr, who read and criticised a draft of the whole manuscript, an act of sheer generosity I will not forget. I am extremely grateful to Mick Hattaway and to the anonymous readers for Cambridge University Press for the spirit as well as the substance of their generous suggestions and shrewd criticism. The inadequacies and errors that remain are all mine. Leo Salingar, whose study *Shakespeare and the Traditions of Comedy* I find indispensable, kindly presented me with supplementary notes about Eliza-bethan views of Native Americans for chapter 2. As to published scholarship and criticism, I have done my best to record acknowledgements in notes and in the bibliography, and I apologise for any omissions.

I thank Sarah Stanton for the prudence and tolerance with

which she has treated this project. For help in Zürich I am grateful to Vreni Bühler and Marianne Kaempf, and in Münster to Lydia Remke, Gabriele Sieweke and Oliver Rachner.

A version of chapter 2 was originally a lecture delivered in 1980, subsequently published in *Shakespeare Jahrbuch-West* 1987. Chapter 6 was published in *Fann'd and Winnowed Opinions, Essays Presented to Harold Jenkins*, ed. John W. Mahon and Thomas Pendleton (Methuen, London, 1987). Material in chapter 5 was first published in my article in *The Huntington Library Quarterly*, spring 1991. I extend my thanks to the editors and publishers concerned for permission to reprint.

CHAPTER I

Introduction

There is a sense of great abundance in Shakespeare's plays – so much so, indeed, that in every generation there are interpreters who cut and simplify, unable to cope with the wealth of ideas and experiences in the plays, or supposing their audiences incapable of doing so. I believe, on the contrary, that abundance is a great strength of Shakespeare's plays, that they are designed deliberately to expand the mind – to generate a sense of concentrated vigorous life in emotions and ideas, to promote as multiple an awareness as possible of differing facets of a story; and that this aim, already discernible in Shakespeare's earliest work, is at the core of his development, and of his power and distinctiveness as an artist.

My aim in this book is to take some examples which focus on Shakespeare's art of translating – or better, transfiguring – material into the three-dimensional language of theatre. Each new Shakespeare play is to a certain extent a 'reading' of material from other books and plays – and, it should be stressed, this usually includes plays he had himself already written. The plays he used as sources offered a visual dimension, presenting their narratives not only in words but in practicable stage action and stage images, and these Shakespeare noted with care; yet even when he read the most unpromising kinds of prose chronicle his dramatist's instinct for selection is evident: he had an eye for the telling action no less than the telling phrase: he made a narrative visual as well as verbal, and his plays, when acted, present stage metaphors which can equal those in the spoken text.

Following his method of composition as I do here means

I

seeing Shakespeare's plays in terms of multiple codes woven
together in complex designs, often involving eclectic mixing of
generic elements (here Shakespeare was in accord with sixteenth-century Italian theory and practice[1]), so that each play
is a unique answer to the particular challenge he set himself on
that occasion. It is necessary to take account of the stories
themselves, as well as the way his dramatic designs shape them
to concentrate on central issues: the exceptional individual and
extreme experience, and – no less profound concerns – communal life, cultural structures and imperatives, and the relation of
story to history, and to myth.

In each chapter I take a different bearing on Shakespeare's
art of theatre, and aim to follow the implications of his designs
in a variety of different genres, whether or not the consequences
seem disconcerting or otherwise unfamiliar. I deliberately use a
variety of approaches and ideas – an eclecticism of method
prompted by Shakespeare's own eclecticism, for this is the key
feature of his constructional method, of his attitude to subject-
matter, to dramatic structure, genre, style.

Shakespeare had an excellent memory, yet when he recalled
previous work – whether his own or other people's – he always
did so with fresh ideas in mind, and he persistently set himself
challenges, reshaping available theatre styles and ceaselessly
inventing new ones. He was always ready to look with fresh eyes
at familiar material or techniques – he recreated Falstaff in *The
Merry Wives*, he shaped the same novella material into extraordinarily different forms in *Much Ado* and *Othello*; and he
varied it again in *Cymbeline*.

In *The Comedy of Errors*, Shakespeare subverts the academic-
ally solemn doctrine of the three unities, and in doing so reveals
his alertness to the debate about the future of the drama in
Elizabethan England, to which Sir Philip Sidney had lent his
eloquent weight on the side of conservative orthodoxy. In
Polonius' list Shakespeare parodies academic pedantry: 'tragedy, comedy, history, pastoral, pastoral–comical, historical–
pastoral, tragical–historical, tragical–comical–historical–pastoral' (*Hamlet*, 2.2.364–5). This reduces the matter of genre to
just four fixed terms, absurdly supposing that any variant may

be accommodated by a simple mechanical permutation. Polonius' clumsy effort here may result in nonsense, but Shakespeare himself took the subject of genre most seriously: he was highly conscious of artistic decorum in dramatic form, style and genre, except that, from the outset, his creative imagination displays great power in creating new dramatic shapes, choosing eclectically among a diverse and wide range of traditions.

My choice of plays for sustained discussion is intended to be exemplary rather than exhaustive. It includes examples of the major genres in which Shakespeare worked. I have chosen some plays which, though less famous, seem to me especially interesting in themselves, and to throw fresh light on Shakespeare's artistic evolution. Allusions in the later plays to the earlier works can suggest what their imaginative and technical significance was for Shakespeare himself as he reflected on his artistic development. For this reason Shakespeare's early, middle, and later phases are represented.

While the chronological order of Shakespeare's earliest plays is still a matter for contention, it is accepted that by 1596 he had produced *The Taming of the Shrew*, *Titus Andronicus*, *King Henry VI* (*Parts 1, 2*, and *3*), *King John*, *King Richard III*, *The Comedy of Errors*, *The Two Gentlemen of Verona*, *Love's Labour's Lost*, *Romeo and Juliet* and *A Midsummer Night's Dream*; the question of which came first is disputed – *Titus Andronicus*, *The Taming of the Shrew*, *1 King Henry VI* and *The Two Gentlemen of Verona* have each their recent supporters.[2] The problem of establishing a chronology is partly due to the lack of conclusive external evidence, but there is also the difficulty of making comparisons between works as unlike as these. Indeed, though the twelve plays are early works, each shows confident independence in its handling of Elizabethan dramatic conventions, while the sheer range of different genres and styles which Shakespeare explores in them is unequalled.

This body of work, which Shakespeare had achieved by 1596, provided him with source material so rich that he was able to return to it again and again for inspiration, and at the same time it served as a handbook of solutions to technical problems of play-making. As an assertion of versatility it challenged rival playwrights; at the same time it was a demonstration to acting companies and audiences of his ability to reshape the kinds of play already established on the Elizabethan stage, and it held out the promise of new kinds of play altogether.

Questions of style and genre are important because they can influence, indeed partly predetermine, a good deal of the affective as well as the intellectual scope of a play. The plays I choose for discussion are of diverse kinds, which tradition has been content to label tragedy, comedy, history; but inspection of that tradition – of stage interpretation as well as critical reception of the plays – shows that very often, over-rigid assumptions about genre and style have reduced and distorted the dramatic and intellectual experience the plays can offer. I invoke the idea of multiplicity as a way of accounting for the generic mingling which is so pronounced a characteristic of Shakespeare and which has proved such a barrier to neo-classical critics.

My method is comparison, I study Shakespeare's re-use of his own earlier work – its importance as a source seems to me profound – and I study his use of plays, poetry and prose by others. However, while I attend closely to Shakespeare's art of transfiguring in relation to his active development as an artist, I also use another quite different approach, one that is non-chronological: I ask what is revealed – on both sides – when one particular work is placed beside another. I ask: what does one see in Shakespeare when he is placed beside Spenser, or Sidney; but also: what do we learn of Spenser, or Sidney, when we turn to them after Shakespeare.

Dr Johnson made an important distinction when he declared that Shakespeare's first concern was theatrical, not literary, in writing his plays – 'He sold them not to be printed but to be played'[3] – although there is no better witness than Johnson to the effect on the solitary reader of a Shakespeare play. In the following pages I am much concerned with Shakespeare's verbal text, but I also endeavour to relate the verbal text to the other elements of theatre-language, the codes that together constitute the sign-systems of live performance – especially those involving the body. It is from the interplay of the verbal and non-verbal codes that a play, as distinct from a non-dramatic narrative, is composed. Because they are not only verbal, these interconnections have tended to be overlooked.

I have concentrated on instances where Shakespeare worked very closely with specific texts – including his own previous work – when making a new play, because in these cases his artistic decision-making can be identified with particular clarity – he becomes visible as an artist. In many respects, even so, 'Shakespeare' remains invisible: his medium, drama, is a performance art in which the writer's self-expression is displaced on to invented figures, the 'persons of the play', and these figures take on further independence when impersonated variously by actors. It is a fact of live theatre that there will be differences between one performance and another even with the same cast of actors.[4] Shakespeare's response is to make a virtue of necessity, devising robust dramatic designs woven from matter so substantial that they generate repeatedly diverse interpretations; and this multiple-faceted quality is a great source of their narrative interest and energy.

The special quality of live performance which Shakespeare stresses is suspense. If he compares great men making history to actors performing a play, it is because they both confront the risk of live performance. They must perform well, but the occasion always has an element of unpredictability: so in *Julius Caesar*, immediately Caesar falls to the knives of Cassius and his friends, Cassius imagines how the theatre will perpetuate the live performance of their much-rehearsed scene:

> How many ages hence
> Shall this our lofty scene be acted over
> In states unborn and accents yet unknown!
> (3.1.111–13)[5]

Shakespeare's audiences, ages hence, do indeed still see the lofty scene, as Cassius correctly prophesies; but what history and theatre commemorate is not his success, as he anticipates, but his tragedy.

I value the live performance, and I devote some space to

discussion of live performances. Since 1969 I have been exploring Shakespeare with students through theatre-workshop classes, sometimes with full performances as spin-offs, and my approach partly derives from this experience, as well as from going to the theatre.

Acting versions, however, are normally abbreviated, sometimes drastically so, and often contain further changes: to the words, or to the number and order of scenes, to the staging, to the narrative, depending on the playing place, the occasion, audience, company size. This common theatrical practice is apparent from the unauthorised early Quarto editions of several Shakespeare plays, but it is significant that Shakespeare or his company took the trouble to publish fuller, more literary Quarto editions for these plays. It should be emphasised that no play of Shakespeare's survives in its original manuscript. There are only printed editions. There is no direct access to what Shakespeare wrote. It is uncertain what changes would have been made (and with what degree of consistency) to the authorial fair-copy when it was prepared for the use of the 'bookholder' (or prompter) in the Shakespearean playhouse. The practice with regard to prompt-books in later historical periods is that detailed practical performance notes are recorded, but, as William B. Long argues,[6] evidence is lacking of such detailed marking-up in Elizabethan playhouse 'books'. Thus although certain printed texts of Shakespeare plays show signs of playhouse adaptation, they leave many questions of performance unanswered. Nor is one able to recover 'the original performance', since any performance involves features unique to that occasion – the voicing of the speeches, physical action, and audience collaboration – which are not recorded. Much, therefore, remains uncertain or unknown, and so it is fortunate that all of Shakespeare's play-texts do contain many implicit as well as explicit directions for staging and performance, and these provide some guidance for critical as well as stage interpretation.

For many plays there is relatively little textual instability because there is only the Folio text; for several of the best-known plays, however, there are both Quarto and Folio versions, between which there are variations involving not only words and lines but whole speeches and scenes. This is the case, famously, in *Hamlet* and *King Lear*.[7] In my discussion of *King Lear* I confine myself to the earlier complete version, the Quarto, as I wish to concentrate on Shakespeare's direct reworking of earlier plays. Throughout this book I base my discussion on the earliest edited Shakespeare play-texts – up to and including the First Folio – and responsible modern editions based on them.

I take it for granted that Shakespeare anticipated diverse emphases in stage interpretation of his plays, and I imagine he welcomed the fact; but at the same time his play-texts have proved to be both ample and sturdy enough in conception, practical design, and written substance, to accommodate very various emphases without losing an overall dynamic shape. Indeed it is the common experience that to work on Shakespeare under rehearsal conditions is to become aware of ordering principles deeper than those explicit in the verbal text. As Emrys Jones shows in his classic study *Scenic Form in Shakespeare* (Oxford, 1971), Shakespeare's constructional unit is the scene, and within the scene the sequence of speakers creates strong formative patterns. Experience of rehearsal and performance shows that minor changes may be made within scenes without altering the design as a whole, while the fixed order of the scenes guarantees a basic sequence, ensuring that predetermined patterns of repetition and variation of different kinds must be woven, so that it takes heavy cutting or the transposition of whole scenes to disrupt these patterns. Such robust methods of composition secure the narrative and give firm guidance about performance; yet far from inhibiting the performers, they also positively enable a certain space for improvisation in the moment of playing.

The plays I have chosen for discussion mostly involve representation of the past, and from the perspective, whether unobtrusive or evident, of Shakespeare's own time. Shakespeare's Romans reflect certain immediate concerns of his culture, and indirectly reflect Elizabethan ideas of the past (contrast the Romans in Dryden's *All For Love* or Shaw's *Caesar and Cleopatra* or Howard Brenton's *The Romans in Britain*). In 1610–11, very near the date of Shakespeare's *Cymbeline*, Sir Walter Raleigh, imprisoned in the Tower of London, wrote in the Preface to his *History of the World*:

I know it will bee said by many, That I might have beene more pleasing to the Reader, if I had written the Story of mine owne times; having been permitted to draw water as neare the Well-head as another. To this I answer, that who-so-ever in writing a moderne Historie, shall follow truth too neare the heeles, it may happily strike out his teeth ... It is enough for me (being in that state I am) to write of the eldest times; wherein also why may not it be said, that in speaking of the past, I point at the present, and taxe the vices of those that are yet lyving, in their persons that are long since dead; and have it laid to my charge? But this I cannot helpe, though innocent.

To Raleigh it is evidently an accepted commonplace that one might write a history, even of remote times and places, to provide an oblique critical commentary on current events. He declares that it is certainly too dangerous and too difficult to write the history of the present.[8]

The majority of Shakespeare's plays have settings remote in time and place, but they are scattered with deliberate anachronisms which, like his allusions to acting and theatre, are locally enlivening – as when in the ancient Greece of *A Midsummer Night's Dream*, King Theseus watches an entertainment by his subjects, every one of whom is manifestly an Elizabethan tradesman, or in the remote Vienna of *Measure for Measure*, where the suburbs are populated with Jacobean London low-life. Yet behind such incidental features is a much larger scheme in which Shakespeare pays only intermittent respect to having set the action in some remote time and place, otherwise representing the narrative in terms of his own culture. This gives him the freedom to shift the point of view, now viewing the past from an Elizabethan perspective, now adopting the historical context to throw a defamiliarising light on the Elizabethans – inviting recognition of their present time of live performance itself in relative, historical terms.

In Shakespeare, theatre is not only a mode of representation, it is a language for perception and thought; a language made up of many voices, perspectives, many codes, brought to bear on major issues. Each of Shakespeare's plays burgeons with ideas. His presentation of the past involves reflecting the present, and this is also true in a special sense, to which he draws attention: since theatre is a performance art, a play can only be staged in the present, and spontaneous audience response, unique to that occasion, is a part of any performance. Again, neither actors nor spectators are immune to the broad influence of their own social and political context, so that the same play-script will be perceived in different ways in different historical periods or cultural situations. In the USA, *Julius Caesar* in the nineteenth century[9] was seen especially in terms relevant to that society, of republicanism and the phenomenon of political assassination, and *Hamlet* in the Paris of Sartre reflected current existentialist ideas – indeed photographs of the actor Jean-Louis Barrault as Hamlet seem now more a visual epitome of the period than a representation of a Shakespearean character.[10] In such apparently anachronistic applications of Shakespeare, later generations are in a sense being true to Elizabethan practice, for while the large majority of Shakespeare's plays have settings remote in time and place, the Elizabethan actors usually performed in modern dress. In the earlier part of the sixteenth century it was the fact that religious morality drama was customarily performed in contemporary terms that had made it so susceptible to politicisation,[11] and this led, menacingly, to its complete suppression. The stage history of Shakespeare's plays in later centuries shows how variably the plays have been and continue to be interpreted, according to prevailing cultural conditions: thus an audience today at a performance of Shakespeare's *Troilus and Cressida* contemplate a multi-layered narrative, one depicting the ancient world, but doing so partly in Elizabethan terms, and one which must in turn be represented by today's actors and to some degree in today's accents, thereby invoking a present-day perspective[12] on the Elizabethans as well as on the ancient culture of 'windy Troy'. The reflection offers an audience an oblique, defamiliarised view of their own time and place.

Georg Lukacs in his study *The Historical Novel* defined the genre of historical novel in terms equally applicable to historical drama. Invoking the light of Hegel – 'the historical reality represented must be made clear and accessible to us ... so that we ... may find ourselves at home therein'[13] – Lukacs commended Scott's historical fiction as a form of critical realism, for its ability to represent the minute particulars, the detail of ordinary life and of ordinary men's lives, as the 'real social and economic basis' from which historical necessity arises (p. 65), while he saw Scott's leading figures concentrating in themselves the salient positive and negative sides of the historical movement concerned. The protagonist, according to Lukacs's model of the historical novel, should be a type, a synthesis of general and particular, in whom is embodied 'the complex interaction of concrete historical circumstances ... with the concrete human beings ... who have been very variously influenced by them, and who act in an individual way' (p. 64). Detail in the narrative will not be 'local colour' but positively serve as 'a means of achieving historical faithfulness', making clear 'the historical necessity of a concrete situation' (p. 65).

Recently emphasis in literary theory and practice has shifted to the multiplicity of perspectives from which events can be interpreted, to the problematic nature of the ideal of 'historical faithfulness' – of objective recording of fact. Thus Hayden White asserts that 'every representation of the past has specifiable ideological implications'.[14] History may refer to reality in a different way from fiction, but both are narratives, and the act of reference may be problematised by stressing its rhetorical status.

The issues and approaches outlined here will be familiar from their reflection in contemporary post-modernist historical fiction: for example John Fowles, *The French Lieutenant's Woman*, Julian Barnes, *Flaubert's Parrot*, Gabriel García Marquéz, *One Hundred Years of Solitude*, or Salman Rushdie, *Midnight's Children*; and also in poetry: Geoffrey Hill, *Mercian Hymns*; and drama: Tom Stoppard, *Travesties*, or Caryl Churchill, *Top Girls*. In such works different historical moments are juxtaposed by unexplained time-shifts, often involving abrupt changes of style –

realism, surrealism, and the absurd. Historical figures in post-modern fiction tend to be used not so much to hide the joins between fiction and history but rather to stress the fissure between them. There is stress on texts as texts, whether oral and popular or written, historical or fictional. There may be unexplained gaps and discrepancies, an absence of narrative closure, humorously playful metafictional elements.

Such self-consciousness about the rhetorical structure of texts (in this widely inclusive sense) is bound up with the question of verifiability of the content and hence about the inherent relativity of history itself. This is apparent in post-modern self-conscious citation of, and allusion to, other literary and historical writing. All this reinforces a sense of significance as something generated intertextually – of writing, like history itself, seen as referring as much to other texts as to the extratextual world, of a general anxiety about borders between the two. In this way intertextuality and post-modernism are closely associated.[15]

In a post-modern historical novel such as Salman Rushdie's *Midnight's Children* the problematic nature of history is exhibited in a dazzling variety of narrative and stylistic perspectives: the narrator is Indian, the text is in English. From the perspective of English culture its literary ancestry seems plainly to include the ironically self-conscious, parodic–ludic English novel, Sterne's *Tristram Shandy*, though Rushdie himself has claimed that his own native culture's oral tradition is the prime inspiration for his digressive, multiple narrative.[16] Certainly, however, Rushdie's concern with the diversity of historical records, with the cultural and ideological implications informing their rhetorical structures, and their variable transmission through time and across cultural barriers, is characteristic of post-modernism, especially when expressed in a humorous, parodic and ironic manner – as when, with cheerful insouciance (p. 163), he compares his moment of inspiration, hearing 'a headful of gabbling tongues, like an untuned radio', to that of Moses, or Mohammed, or Joan of Arc.

This dense allusiveness to other texts is more than mere quotation, and it is not satisfactorily to be explained in the terms of W. J. Bate's *The Burden of the Past and the English Poet* (Cambridge, Mass., 1970), or the thesis of Harold Bloom, *The Anxiety of Influence* (New York, 1973). Rushdie mixes realism with the fabulous and the surreal in the tradition of his native culture's oral narratives (though he acknowledges Swift and Rabelais too), but he himself is well aware that 'when you look at the old narrative and use it, as I tried to do, as the basis of a novel, you become a post-modernist writer'.

The observation, familiar among art-historians and from the work of Wölfflin,[17] that all works of art owe more to other works of art than they do to nature, has since the 1960s been given a specifically linguistic reinterpretation and anti-scholarly thrust by Roland Barthes – for example his 1977 essay 'From Work to Text'.[18] There Barthes wished to assert the primacy of in-numerable codes – linguistic, cultural, generic, formal – as playing so diversely in the text, or the 'plural' text, that they cannot be the individual contribution of an author; moreover, that without the prior existence of these codes no work would be readable. The text is to be recognised as held in the web-like system of codes which Barthes here calls 'the intertextual'. This (now widespread and familiar) idea of intertextuality would replace the concept of the author as father and owner of his work with that of the Text, which 'reads without the inscription of the Father' (p. 161). Paul Auster in his post-modernist novel *New York Trilogy* incorporates pastiche of the detective novels of Raymond Chandler but also the stylistic feel of Beckett's prose, and drops teasing allusions to *Don Quixote*, *Moby Dick*, Poe, Whitman and Hawthorne. He even includes an elusive writer called Paul Auster, presumably in ironic homage to Barthes. (If the author comes back into his text, says Barthes, he does so no longer privileged, paternal – 'the I which writes the text, it too, is never more than a paper-I'. One might think of Alfred Hitchcock in an earlier generation, appearing in walk-on parts in his own movies.)

The relevance of the developments of post-modernism and deconstructionist theory to the interpretation of Shakespeare's plays is indirect, but today's readers and spectators, like theatre directors and designers, will be more or less influenced by this intellectual and cultural climate, by the terms of the present dialectic. To move from the familiar, from present-day postmodernism, to Shakespeare's plays and the cultural context of the Renaissance, requires some care, but it can also prove illuminating. Renaissance culture may have been deeply respectful of sources, as is implied in the neoclassical doctrine of imitation, which required a certain conservatism in writers – at least in learned writers;[19] on the other hand the irony and playfulness of an Ariosto or a Rabelais imply a developing recognition, also, of the importance of originality in the artist.[20] In Elizabethan English writing, rhetorical systems were valued for their importance in generating variation,[21] and they were learned and put into practice as systems for seeing as many diversities – and from as many different points of view – as possible. While there are obvious differences between formulations of the Renaissance and of today, there is also significant continuity, a shared interest in certain issues.

My own choice of approach and selection of texts for this book has evolved at the same time as the post-1960s developments described above, but I am aware of more influence from certain novels, plays and performances than from exclusively theoretical writing. I have no single axe, theoretical or ideological, to grind. I try to focus on specific texts and to maintain a rational method of comparison; I also aim to be specific in identifying certain Elizabethan literary and theatrical contexts which seem to me illuminating in exploring Shakespeare's treatment of history and story, his transfiguring of prior texts, historical and fictional. These are questions which interest me: I do not claim to hold the key to all the mythologies.

I begin, in chapter 2, with *Cymbeline*, a play in which Shakespeare is concerned with evolution – the evolution of Britain from its origins, and his own more personal evolution as a dramatist. The appearance of Spenser's *The Faerie Queene* in 1590, the same year which saw the performance of Shakespeare's own first version of epic in dramatic form, *King Henry VI*, suggests that Shakespeare would have read Spenser with particular interest. My argument is that in *Cymbeline* Shakespeare recalled Spenser much more intensively than scholars have supposed, and that this is consistent with a general feature of *Cymbeline*, Shakespeare's use of retrospective allusion: in *Cymbeline* his self-conscious, critical re-use of themes, motifs and images, both verbal and theatrical, from his own previous work, shows how important that work continued to be for him – so that he maintained a kind of internal critical debate with it. He seems anxious to preserve motifs and images as kernels of thinking (as theatrical hieroglyphs, as it were) and to find new ways of combining them in a multi-layered discourse, a new kind of drama intended to be as inclusive as possible, and which seems in significant respects original in its absorption of Spenserian influence.

Chapter 3 explores in general Shakespeare's use of sculptural effects in his presentation of the human body and notices the conviction with which Shakespeare specifies certain visual theatre images. They are sparingly but decisively deployed – something often overlooked or underestimated by theatre producers as well as by critics. There is a visual text which must be honoured, as well as a verbal text. To explore such sculptural effects also reveals Shakespeare's tenacious memory and eclectic use of his own previous work, progressively important as source-material in the later plays, where it is deployed to increasingly complex, teasingly multiple effect. The chapter also traces a particular motif, the silent and inert human body, as theatrical and cultural sign in a variety of contexts, and to various effect, across the broad span of his work. Shakespeare's non-dramatic poem *The Rape of Lucrece*, which may predate any of his theatrical presentations of the unconscious female body, presents this motif with imaginative intensity, and it continued to inspire him to the end of his career.

In chapter 4, I go on to consider the formal and thematic connections between one early Shakespeare comedy and one early tragedy, which when read in the light of the later *King Lear* display some remarkable likenesses. It is questionable whether works so assured in their different modes as *King Henry VI* or *The Comedy of Errors* or *Titus Andronicus* or *The Taming of the Shrew* should be thought of as 'early' in any sense except the merely chronological, but the term 'early' is often used pejoratively to suggest a Shakespeare still prone to indulgence in excessive elaboration and artifice, on the one hand, and extremes of violence and crudeness on the other. It is doubtful whether Shakespeare's development is best understood in terms of his discarding complex patterning, or whether his maturity is best characterised as subduing extremes of violence. Granted that his changes and new discoveries, especially in the arts of characterisation, are made with unexampled pace, nevertheless for critics to use the comparison between Shakespeare's 'early' and his post-1600 'mature' plays to argue that he outgrew a taste for paradox, word-play, conceits, and extremes of action and experience, is to over-simplify the real texture of those so-called 'early' Elizabethan works just as it over-simplifies the 'mature' Shakespeare. Placing an early play of Shakespeare beside a late one can startlingly increase understanding of both; it can also reveal continuity, at deep levels, in his thinking about his material and his technique.

Chapter 5 opens with an account of Shakespeare's use of Whetstone's play *Promos and Cassandra* in writing *Measure for Measure*. In Whetstone Shakespeare found a version of the story already prepared for practical performance on an Elizabethan stage and with topical issues in mind. I then examine the interplay of verbal and visual metaphors in *Measure for Measure*, and the play's continuing receptivity to topical applications. This issue emerges with particular clarity in relation to *Measure for Measure*, since the play combines a number of issues of social and political debate so central to Western society that they have remained persistently important, outside the theatre, up to the present day. Shakespeare provides a dramatic form which has several potential centres, structural and thematic. This has made the play highly adaptable, and has allowed *Measure for Measure* to be related to topical contexts which could scarcely have been anticipated at the time it first appeared in 1604. Because *Measure for Measure* in the first place is based on traditional folk-tales which encode deep cultural issues, and yet represents them in complex social, political and psychological terms – because, that is to say, it was in the first place detached,

as well as engaged, in its presentation of a Jacobean present –
it is always being rediscovered as topical, and too outspokenly so
– as I demonstrate by reading certain issues in recent British
history in the play's terms.

Reading Sidney's *Arcadia* in the light of *As You Like It*, in
chapter 6, alerts one to Shakespeare's critical intelligence as well
as his imaginative interest in problems of translating pastoral
and romance narratives into a play, and in finding theatrical
equivalents to these highly non-dramatic modes. Sixteenth-
century heroical romance relies on highly structured narratives
with conventionalised motifs, and pastoral is an essentially
subtle and ambivalent mode which invites self-conscious skill in
its readers to match its own elusive wit and style. Elizabethan
theatre might seem to be a somewhat inhospitable medium for
such bookish modes, theatre being an art of live performance,
an art of presence, of physical action. Shakespeare in *As You Like
It* plays with such seeming antitheses in a dazzling paradoxical
display which dissolves such superficial contrasts: the written
word itself, in the form of Orlando's poems, being incorporated
into the action as literary leaves stuck on stage trees, while the
physical stage action itself is rendered somewhat insubstantial
by Ganymede's being only the substitute for Rosalind, while
Rosalind herself finally, in the epilogue, is made to vanish into
air.

In chapter 7 the complexities and perplexities of Shakespeare's last love tragedy, *Antony and Cleopatra*, are explored. The
story, as Shakespeare found it in Plutarch, could only be made
into a play by trenchant adaptation. I argue that Shakespeare
as a playwright was bound to find particular interest in
analogous models already in Elizabethan dramatic form, and
designed for an Elizabethan stage, and that his memory of
Marlowe played a significant part in the making of the play.
One can also put the comparison in reverse, and find that to
consider the dramatic working of Marlowe's *Tamburlaine* and
The Tragedy of Dido Queen of Carthage in the light of Shakespeare's
Antony and Cleopatra is invigorating.

In conclusion, in chapter 8, I discuss the mode of multiplicity,
the mingling of different generic and stylistic elements, as a

characteristic of Shakespeare's from the beginning to the end of his career, as it is seen particularly in the presentation of love–idealism; and I suggest that it is wholly characteristic of his consummate skill, his independent search for a style answering to a given subject, and his sense of humour, that he should write two comedies – *The Comedy of Errors* near the beginning, *The Tempest* near the end of his career – which comply, technically, with the academic rule of the unities, while creating a more mischievous sense of confusion and disorientation than almost any of his other works.

CHAPTER 2

Fabled ' Cymbeline'

The lightning look, the birding cry, awe from the grave
ever-flowing on the times
(James Joyce, *Finnegans Wake*)

In 1589, one year before the publication of Spenser's *The Faerie
Queene*, Books 1–3, Puttenham published *The Arte of English
Poesie*. Puttenham begins by offering a short history of human
cultural evolution, describing what the original phase of human
existence was like, a time 'before any civil society' when the
people 'remained in the woods and mountains, vagarant and
dispersed like the wild beasts, lawlesse and naked, or verie ill
clad'. He offers a remarkably clear view of culture as a human
construction: thus it was poets who were the first to bring 'the
rude and savage people to a more civill and orderly life', poets
'were the first that instituted sacrifices of placation'; furthermore 'all the rest of the observances and ceremonies of
religion' were 'invented and stablished by them', and it was by
their chaste and austere lives that poets developed the power to
'receave visions, both waking and sleeping, which made them
utter prophecies'. What is no less striking is Puttenham's basic
assumption that human culture as a whole is a process of
evolution: 'there was no art in the world till by experience
found out', and as Greek and Latin literature became an art
only after 'studious persons' created 'a method of rules &
precepts', then, he asks, 'Why may not the same be with us
aswel as with them'. This reflects a more general Elizabethan
trend towards the interpretation of cultural and social history in
evolutionary terms. The topic of the origins of human culture
grew in fascination as a result of the discoveries and colonisation

in the New World, while the monarchy had its own interest in historical, fabulous and mythological versions of British history; these different elements can be seen in Spenser himself, and in Shakespeare's later plays, particularly *Cymbeline*.

In Act 4 of *Cymbeline* Shakespeare presents a version of prehistoric Britain. With the cave he represents a stage of human history too irretrievably remote to have left historical record – a stage fascinating to poets concerned with cultural origins. Shakespeare mediates this primitive phase through the presence of Belarius who knows civilisation. The episode presents the audience with a kind of fantastic journey into the remote national past, from a modern perspective. In their cave-dwelling in the mountain wilderness the royal brothers and their surrogate father have to reenact the stages through which their aboriginal ancestors passed in evolving the simplest human culture. They have to hunt to get meat (and presumably to clothe themselves). They have fire, and have learned to cook: their diet is meat and root vegetables and herbs (see 4.2.49–50). They learn tribal history from their bard (Belarius) by oral transmission. Their values are based on honesty, courage, and physical aptitudes. They evolve simple manners and rites: hospitality, the hunt, fighting, prayer, burial of the dead. These latter are poignant in the stoic austerity with which they exclude so much that Christian rite provides. By framing the scene with a self-consciousness about the Jacobean Christian perspective from which these fable episodes are seen, Shakespeare ensures that for the first Jacobean audience consciousness of the historical gap between their own civilisation and pre-Christian Britain becomes part of the experience of the play. For audiences in subsequent centuries the experience will be more complex, for they will be conscious of the gap between themselves and the Jacobean age, and between their perspective on primitive culture and that of Jacobean audiences in 1610. Shakespeare presents his own age as itself a historical phase: this is an inevitable consequence of the design of *Cymbeline*.

In 1590, the same year as *The Faerie Queene*, Books 1–3 was published, Thomas Hariot's *Brief and True Report of the New Found Land of Virginia* was reprinted. It included John White's pictures of the Indians he had seen during the 1585 expedition to Virginia, with additional engravings of Picts, to show that they had been as savage as the natives of Virginia. The natives of the New World were seen as providing evidence for an evolutionary development of human society. Christopher Hill describes this as 'a notable contribution to historical imagination, which was used by Vico'.[1] One year after *Cymbeline*, in 1611, John Speed's *Historie of Great Britaine* used four of these engravings to illustrate 'Ancient Britaines', and John Speed explained that the savage appearance he believed characteristic of the early Britons and their neighbours the Picts would have changed as 'civilisation' increased.[2]

Elizabethans whose duties had brought them into close contact with the Irish recognised in them an alien culture, only slightly more advanced in the temporal scale than the Red Indians. A recognition that immense distances of time, in terms of cultural development, could coexist with small geographical separation in terms of space, clearly quickened the imagination of those Elizabethans interested in history and ideas of human cultural evolution. To Spenser and Camden the native Irish society of their own time also suggested comparisons with early barbarians – Britons, Gauls, Goths, Huns, and Scythians – described by the authors of classical antiquity. Arthur B. Ferguson notes[3] that Raleigh recognised the wicker-and-leather boats of the Britons, spoken of in classical writings, in similar structures used in the Ireland of his day.

In his *View of the Present State of Ireland*,[4] Spenser shows a concern to distinguish history from traditional legend and mythology when Irenius is rebuked for relying on Irish chronicles, 'which are most fabulous and forged', the nation being 'so antique, as that no monument remaineth of her beginning... but only bare traditions of times and remembrances of bards, which use to forge and falsify everything as they list to please or displease any man'. Irenius replies that, unlike the Irish themselves who deeply believe them, he himself would compare their chronicles to cultural practices recorded from other societies and historical periods, such as language, manners and customs, rites and ceremonies, 'monuments of churches and tombs', and he concludes that although the chronicles are unreliable, partly through 'ignorance of art and pure learning' (scrupulous concern for evidence, presumably) 'yet there appeareth amongst them some relics of the true antiquity, though disguised'.

In this connection it is interesting to recall some remarks of Francis Bacon published in Latin in 1609, the year before *Cymbeline*, in *De Sapientia Veterum* (*The Wisdom of the Ancients*).[5] Francis Bacon was deeply interested in the analysis of history as a means of deriving lessons to be applied directly in his own times. Writing of the origins of fables in the remote past of human history, Bacon insists on the subtle and complex care needed in reading these seemingly naive if not sometimes downright absurd stories. 'The most ancient times', writes Bacon,

(except what is preserved of them in the scriptures) are buried in oblivion and silence: to that silence succeeded the fables of the poets: to those fables the written records which have come down to us. Thus between the hidden depths of antiquity and the days of tradition and evidence that followed there is drawn a veil, as it were, of fables, which come in and occupy the middle region that separates what has perished from what survives.

Bacon goes on to develop the proposition:

in the old times, when the inventions and conclusions of human reason (even those that are now trite and vulgar) were as yet new and strange, the world was full of all kinds of fables, and enigmas, and parables, and similitudes, and these were used not as a device for shadowing and concealing the meaning, but as a method of making it understood ... For as hieroglyphics came before letters, so parables came before arguments.

Bacon observes that although the fables have an air of simplicity, as of 'sacred relics and light airs breathing out of better times', few of them were invented by the poets who recited them: they are delivered 'not as new inventions but as stories already received and believed'. Bacon stresses that there is variegated stuff in fables and a complex means of transmission, requiring the reader to sift sceptically, to recognise different kinds of code:

And what if we find here and there a bit of real history underneath, or some things added only for ornament, as times confounded, or part of one fable transferred to another and a new allegory introduced? Such things could not but occur in stories invented (as these were) by men who both lived in different ages and had different ends, some being more modern, some more ancient, some having in their thoughts natural philosophy, other civil affairs.

These are recognisably modern ways of thinking about the remote historical past and about the different kinds of evidence about it which have come down to us, which the discovery and preliminary exploration of the New World evidently stimulated. They seem to me to throw an interesting light on *Cymbeline*, since the play's presentation of the many codes of theatre stresses the question of how its hieroglyphs, letters, parables and fables are to be interpreted.

I believe that Shakespeare designed *Cymbeline* to create, in part, the impression of a Fable in Bacon's terms, where the narrative is clearly heterogeneous, being partly based on the written records of British chroniclers but also including a history written by a god and delivered personally during the play, a number of popular myths and national legends, and folk-lore motifs of wide European provenance. These elements are related to different cultural and religious phases in the nation's past, but there are discrepancies of tone and anachronistic clashes between content and style, as well as abrupt disjunctions in the narrative; all this creates an effect like that in fables, handed down through generation after generation. Although the end of *Cymbeline* clearly affirms providential deliverance – 'Howsoe'er 'tis strange…Yet it is true' – corresponding with a Spenserian design of Christian grace intersecting with providential process in national history, nevertheless *Cymbeline's* calculated artful intricacies set the audience teasing problems of understanding and interpretation, and at certain points deceive them as well as certain of the characters. Such difficulties seem to be deliberately and ironically reflected in the puzzle left by Jupiter himself on the breast of the dreaming hero, a riddle on the face of it so absurd that the unfortunate soothsayer, who earlier in the play gets an augury hopelessly wrong, manages to make his interpretation, fitting it to events which by then have already been unravelled, yet still cannot make it sound plausible. His interpretation is in the worst tradition of allegorical exegesis, depending on extracting an excruciating pun from the words 'mollis aer'. It is the very last pun of many in the play.

The hint of absurdity in solving of the final riddle leaves an audience with a last tinge of that uncertainty which is a palpable undercurrent throughout the play. This uncertainty is increased by odd and elusive patterns of many kinds which surface and submerge too quickly in the course of a performance to be fully grasped, and although the major patterns do finally come out clearly, the question of their real nature and their pervasive yet intangible presence remains a secret or at least a submerged feature of the play, inseparable from the deceptive and illusory medium of drama. The explicit ritual elements in *Cymbeline* implicitly remind, or warn, an audience, of the relation of drama to magic and religion, and the folk-lore motifs in the play (especially those associated with the role of Cloten) assume a magical view of experience. Deception, mistaking and misinterpretation are the very stuff of *Cymbeline*; we may notice that the audience is particularly sensitised to these things, and that this may not be inappropriate in a play concerned, in many senses, with history.

Cymbeline is unique, even among Shakespeare's remarkably various works, for the heterogeneity of styles it employs and the strangeness of the story it tells:[6] the extraordinary frequency with which Shakespeare makes apparent allusions to his own earlier work indicates that he wishes an audience to take a highly alert interest in the way this particular story is told, his intricate narrative surprising them but also deceiving them in ways which underline its strangeness. Not least among the signs of Shakespeare's full imaginative commitment is the fact that the allusions to his own works seem to constitute a kind of oblique, perhaps ultimately even secret, commentary on his personal history as a writer: it is a history within a history. Anyone with a good knowledge of Shakespeare's *Lucrece*, *Romeo and Juliet*, *King Henry V*, *All's Well*, *Othello*, *King Lear* and *Antony and Cleopatra* would certainly be visually reminded of them at one time or another during a performance of *Cymbeline*, but they would also be surprised at the new twists or unexpected changes Shakespeare makes when re-using the material. In the episode, for instance, where the sleeping Imogen is spied upon by the intruder Iachimo, Shakespeare makes Iachimo compare himself to Tarquin approaching Lucrece to rape her: yet having thus awakened the audience's expectations he at once distorts the echo and radically alters the outcome of the story, without quite severing its associations. The instance is characteristic of *Cymbeline*.

Surveying the play from a distance we can see that Shakespeare has ransacked theatre high and low, recent and ancient, to present a whole variety of styles and genres through which a history can be told, (and this constitutes a small history of theatre in itself), from folk-plays, miracle plays, popular romances and their Elizabethan descendants, like *Mucedorus*, to pageantry and its offshoots, from the court masque, such as Daniel's *Thetys' Festival*, with its allusions to Milford Haven,[7] all the way down to crude extravaganzas like those of Heywood at the Red Bull.[8] In terms of the representation of historical periods Shakespeare offers a dramatic narrative which presents a Jacobean audience with a mirror of its own contemporary *haute couture* in manners and topical allusions (including court taste for Gothick medievalism and Augustan classicism, the investiture of the Prince of Wales in 1610, and Shakespeare's recent work seen in court performance), while also relating it to the cultural past in the European Renaissance in Italy, beyond that to the medieval world of chivalry, thence to ancient Rome and Brutan Britain, and beyond that again to the primeval wilderness of prehistory, which is staged in the central part of the play.

Shakespeare makes alterations from the chronicle sources in *Cymbeline* but he also freely invents or appropriates fictional material to form a history of Britain that makes palpable its components of myth, recorded fact, legend, folk-tale, romance, his own earlier plays and poems, and miracle.

He gives the audience a guide through these time-warps in the form of his heroine Imogen, whose dream and subconscious life are as important as her waking life, in which, indeed, she twice suffers a kind of death in the course of the play before, at last, reassuming a name which is not only her own but that of the very first queen of Britain, the consort to the great-grandson of Aeneas (if that story were to be believed).[9]

In this sense we might consider *Cymbeline* a cultural history, public and private or, to use the play's own favoured terms, 'outward' and 'inward', of Britain, and its style self-consciously alerts an audience to the discrepancies between these elements (rather than concealing them) in order to create the effect of fable – as I hope to show.

Cymbeline is concerned in a profound sense with origins, and in this sense may properly be called a historical play; it also shows how the way a history is told will determine, to no little extent, what it tells and to what effect. It alerts us to the fictional as well as the factual possibilities of the content of narrative histories, for although the word 'history' can mean 'a formal record of the past, as recorded in writings or otherwise ascertained' (OED sb 3) it also means 'a relation of incidents real or imaginary' (OED sb 1), and in fact Shakespeare's readiness to change the material he found in the chronicles can often be shown to accord with another sense of 'history' – that is, 'a study of the formation and growth of communities and nations' (OED sb 3).

In his free rearrangement of material from the chronicle histories of Britain and in fictional additions to them Shakespeare very obviously aimed to please the king, who was also patron of his company of players and commanded them to perform at court. In *Cymbeline* Shakespeare gives the king two sons and a daughter like James I, but he had to change the chronicles to do so; he also set certain episodes near Milford Haven, to make an allusion to the great-grandfather of James and also to the investiture of his eldest son Henry as Prince of Wales,[10] and this involves the inventive adaptation of a whole romance tale of stolen royal children being educated in manners, arms and arts in a Welsh mountain cave – and one without even a library. Shakespeare also incurs the minor absurdity of having to represent Milford Haven as the chief port for continental travel, rather than Dover. To emphasise the legendary British military taste for 'damned close-run things', and to compliment James I's oldest friend, James Hay, knighted at the investiture of the Prince of Wales in 1610, Shakespeare transfers from Holinshed's history of Scotland[11] the account of how a husbandman called Hay and his two sons turned a rout of a Scottish army into victory over an entire Danish army. It is all the more remarkable that Shakespeare chooses this improbable story, has his hero Posthumus stop a fleeing courtier and give him a stirring epic account of it (even more incredible in the telling than Agincourt) but then shows the courtier react in total disbelief and continue his cowardly flight from the battle.

In thus stressing the play's location in a remote period of history and in failing to conceal – even actively exaggerating – minor absurdities, Shakespeare may have partly had in mind the need to foil any attempts at dangerous political application in other areas of the play. The history of Ben Jonson's *Sejanus*, 1603–4, in which Shakespeare acted, was a warning of the dangers of presenting political themes which might become all too topical.[12] Would it have been possible in the Jacobean court, one may wonder, to take offence at the story of a king of Britain under the influence of a favourite who employs sexual and necromantic charms for purposes of high treason? Could the picture of a Britain beset by a dangerously aggressive Rome, or of Italian courtiers using slander and treachery to demoralise Imogen and Posthumus, be interpreted topically? Is the idea of the heir to the throne, symbolically associated with Tudor values, exiled from court, and having to be nourished for his health's sake away from court on stoic austerity and warlike attitudes, calculated to please Puritan opposition groups?

Would Shakespeare be able to say of *Cymbeline*, as Hamlet says of the *Murder of Gonzago*, that it offers no offence, 'no offence i'the world'? Apparently no royal displeasure was expressed, which suggests that Shakespeare's company got the emphasis 'right'; but this is not to rule out the possible ironic and critical elements in *Cymbeline*. In view of the fact that James I was often unfavourably compared with his Tudor predecessor Elizabeth I, there was always a potential for irony in presenting Tudor material in the Jacobean period. On the other hand, Jacobean panegyric followed James's own wishes in stressing his Tudor ancestry, and the investiture of his eldest son as Prince of Wales offered to strengthen the idea of continuity from the Welsh Tudors (that the court masque *Thetys' Festival* of 1610 also features Milford Haven confirms that this was so understood). James was happy also to be seen as the second Brutus,[13] uniting once more the whole island under his single monarchy, so that a play about remote British history might safely offer to follow *King Lear* and *Macbeth*, both of which, despite their potentially ambivalent treatment of the past, and their touching on serious topical issues, had not caused the king apparent displeasure.

It is worth noting a number of possible ways in which *Cymbeline*, so close to it in date, reflects or is reflected in the court entertainment, *Prince Henry's Barriers*, of 6 January 1610, which inaugurated the public career of Prince Henry, James's son and heir. Prince Henry expressed a strong interest in history, and the theme of the *Barriers* reflects that interest, seeing Henry's destiny as ruler over the reunited empire of Great Britain and promoter of the cause of militant Protestantism abroad. The entertainment begins with a speech by the Lady of the Lake, prophesying the revival of Chivalry to coincide with the resurrection of the ancient empire of Great Britain, already embodied in the present monarch, James I, his heir Prince Henry, and their court, the audience assembled before her. A resurrected Merlin appears and sonorously lists the English monarchs who cultivated peace – thus complimenting King James I. He then gives a second list commending those who waged war – and this warlike stance corresponded to Prince Henry's own ambitions. Merlin's warlike and aggressive speech is tactfully modified right at the end in deference to the peace policy of James I himself, acknowledging that Agincourt and the Armada, great victories and patriotic symbols though they may be, should not incite Britain to provoke war, but should inspire her to be valiant if neighbour princes attack:

> give them all their due
> And be prepared if they will trouble you.
> He doth but scourge himself his sword that draws
> Without a purse, a counsel and a cause.   (323–6)

Then attention is directed to a cave; within it lies the sleeping figure of Chivalry: he is awakened by the sound of the name Meliadus, representing Prince Henry. Chivalry then declares to King James that his son Prince Henry

> Shall second him in arms and shake a sword
> And lance against the foes of God and you.

The scenes were designed by Inigo Jones, and they express his conviction that the introduction of Renaissance classical architecture into England was a revival of ancient British architecture. The first scene of the *Barriers* depicted ruins which the text, by Ben Jonson, says are ancient British but which Inigo Jones took from engravings depicting Roman ruins, among which are identifiable Roman monuments; the scene is, as Roy Strong[14] remarks, 'a phantasmagoria depicting the empire of Great Britain in decay in terms of Nova Roma'. In the main scene the architecture of the Goths from the intervening centuries is shown standing alongside classical British architecture depicted in terms of a triumphal arch, a column reminiscent of Trajan's column, and a tomb resembling a Renaissance tomb by Michelangelo.

How might all this be connected to Shakespeare's *Cymbeline*? It has the same thematic images. Here too is the simultaneous presentation of Gothic, classical Roman and Renaissance Italian culture; here is Chivalry sleeping in a cave and waking to revive the honour and fortune of the nation; here is emphasis on ancient Britain as manifesting classical Roman piety and virtue. Here Gothic symbolises decay, and the renewal of hope in the present Jacobean moment; and here is a difficult balancing act between James's peace policy and Prince Henry's Protestant militancy. Here is deliberate stress on Britain's glorious isolation, defended by God and the sea, carefully ignoring the humiliating invasions of Caesar and William of Normandy.

The point is, however, that *Cymbeline* contains far more material than a straightforward compliment to royalty requires, and this produces a multivalency in place of a court entertainment's perspectival focus on the monarch himself. The play refuses this. It is in the elaborate ingenuity of the narrative that Shakespeare, for good or ill, far outgoes any of his previous designs.

In common-sense terms we might acknowledge that Shakespeare, wishing to compliment the king's foreign policy of peace-seeking and his current negotiations with Papal Rome, and also wishing to allude to his Tudor and Brutan allegiances, found in the story of Cymbeline's peace with imperial Rome a fit analogy, though a thinnish subject for a play; but common sense does not serve to explain[15] the decision to fill out the chronicle material with stories derived partly from Boccaccio and Frederick of Jennen, which seem emphatically restricted to the merchant class and concerned with the personal domain of sexual and psychological experience. It has been persuasively argued by L. G. Salingar[16] that the changes Shakespeare makes to these stories as he transfers them to *Cymbeline* indicate that he is relating them to a version of a medieval miracle play, *Oton*.

Oton has scenes in Heaven, Rome, Burgos, Granada, and somewhere in Barbary. It concerns the interwoven public and private faith of its hero, Oton, who wagers on his wife's fidelity, is deceived into believing her unchaste and in despair joins the national enemy, the infidel Saracens. The virgin wife is advised by the Virgin Mary, who descends to her accompanied by music, to make a journey in disguise. Later her husband is ordered by God, who descends to him from heaven, to return to Rome. After being a prisoner he there confronts his deceiver and defeats him in single combat, and everyone is finally reconciled. The relevance of this romance to *Cymbeline* (first suggested by J. P. Collier) seems indisputable, although the Arden edition's editor J. M. Nosworthy says it has none.

Another analogue to which scholars have allowed only minor

importance is Spenser's *The Faerie Queene*, on the strength of a direct reference to Cymbeline in two stanzas in canto 10 of Book 2. Yet Spenser published the first three books of his romance epic of British history in terms of holiness, temperance, and chastity in 1590, when Shakespeare was completing his first tetralogy of history plays. Shakespeare must have read Spenser with the greatest interest on this account alone. When Spenser names Kimbeline he tells in the same breath, and with the most marked emphasis, that Christ was born during his reign. Holinshed mentions this fact in more oblique as well as subdued terms, so that, scholars suppose, Shakespeare may have owed to Spenser the association of Cymbeline with the birth of Christ. Yet if one reads Spenser's account of the reign of Cymbeline in its full context of canto 10 as a whole one may think that Shakespeare's memory of Spenser, and use of him, in *Cymbeline*, was a good deal more significant than scholars have allowed especially when the use of *Oton* is taken into account.

I would stress the wider importance of canto 10 of Book 2 for the whole design of *Cymbeline*. I believe it furnished Shakespeare with a literary model for the shaping of historical chronicle material into a compact and patterned form, expressive of a mythical but also a religious idea of providence in history. Shakespeare and Spenser both made use of Holinshed and Geoffrey of Monmouth, and accepted their schematic division of British history; but from Spenser Shakespeare could absorb a literary mode of transforming prolix and disproportioned chronicle into a symbolic drama using a complex dialectic between historical causality and miraculous religious intervention. To show Britain's political and religious evolution to a present moment of triumph, through miracle, as Shakespeare does in *Cymbeline*, but nowhere else, suggests the influence of Spenser.

It is worth examining canto 10 in detail. In the three preceding stanzas (43–6) Spenser records how Britain was well ruled by Cassibalane:[17]

> Till the prowd Romanes him disquieted,
> And warlike Caesar, tempted with the name
> Of this sweet Island, neuer conquered,

> And enuying the Britons blazed fame,
> (O hideous hunger of dominion) hither came. (47)

The language here: 'tempted', 'sweet', 'hideous hunger', interprets Caesar's assault as a sexual attack on a virgin Britain. In the next stanza (48) Spenser tells how fiercely she resisted, only succumbing finally through an act of treachery. Caesar imposes tributary status on Britain, and Spenser begins the story of British patriotic resistance to paying tribute, celebrating the line of resistance heroes culminating in Arthur, who frees Britain from the Roman yoke. The first resistance hero is Kimbeline, and Spenser names him immediately after Arthur and in connection with Christ's birth:

> this land was tributarie made
> T'ambitious Rome, and did their rule obay,
> Till Arthur all that reckoning did defray;
> Yet oft the Briton kings against them strongly swayd. (49)

> Next him, Tenantius raigned, then Kimbeline
> What time th'eternall Lord in fleshly slime
> Enwombed was, from wretched Adams line
> To purge away the guilt of sinfull crime:
> O joyous memorie of happy time,
> That heauenly grace so plenteously displayd;
> (O too high ditty for my simple rime). (50)

Perhaps Shakespeare took the hint in that last line; the point is certainly important. According to Spenser the struggle for British freedom, which begins with Kimbeline and ends with Arthur, is associated with the spiritual freeing of mankind which comes with Christ: Christ's birth and the first step towards British national rebirth in Arthur coincide. But furthermore, the motif of betrayal is crucial in all these stories: Kimbeline, according to Spenser, meets his death in battle with the Romans at the hands of a disguised traitor. Three stanzas later Bonduca, type of British female heroism, repeats the resistance of Kimbeline, like him meets defeat through treachery, but commits brave suicide rather than surrender. In the story of Bonduca (much of which appears to be Spenser's invention, perhaps because the providential pattern was so important to him) the sexual analogy for the struggle between Britain and Rome is repeated. Courageous, and inspiring the divided kingdom to unity, she is betrayed, her captains being corrupted by a Roman general's bribes; nevertheless, spiritually untarnished, she preserves her integrity, choosing death rather than surrender: Spenser's commendation suggests the typological anticipation of Christ and Arthur (Shakespeare could add Lucrece):

> She triumphed on death, in enemies despight.　(56)

The Spenserian model could well have suggested to Shakespeare the relevance and mythical aptness for *Cymbeline* of an intrigue plot concerning the treacherous sexual approach to, and betrayal of, the British heroine by a Roman whose further treachery leads to a kind of death for both hero and heroine and brings them both to a decisive British–Roman battle in disguise. Further details could be added, but there is a larger analogy still, which supports the case for seeing *Oton* and Spenser as congenial twin models for the design of *Cymbeline*.

Spenser's canto 10 of Book 2 gives, in a comparatively brief space, the whole history of Britain. It is (we are to imagine) set out in two books, and Arthur and Guyon read one each, side by side, in Alma's castle. The two books offer two simultaneous versions of history, one in the horizontal perspective of men, names, and recorded events, in time, the other a fable encoding a religious vision. Arthur reads the first, a chronicle history, based on Geoffrey of Monmouth, but with additions from other chronicles and from Spenser's imagination (stanzas 5–68). Simultaneously, we are to imagine, Guyon reads the history of faeryland (70–6), the mythological and fabulous analogy to the chronicles. The providential design which emerges only slowly and with difficulty in the chronicle read by Arthur is repeated in Guyon's book in religious and fabulous affirmatory terms; both books end in saluting the achievement of national unity and Christian grace in the unfinished present. Arthur, devout and inspired by his reading, shows that he has responded to the scheme of providence working mysteriously through time: 'How brutish is it not to understand' (69.7).

Because of its emphatic shape and relative brevity, Spenser's whole chronicle history leaves a strong impression in the mind, nowhere more so than at its beginning, where Spenser describes the origins of Britain from times before it even took identifiable shape but

> was saluage wildernesse,
> Vnpeopled, vnmanurd, vnprov'd, vnpraysd   (5)

The name it finally got, 'Albion', was given it by mariners afraid of the dangerous white rocks all along the southern coast: thus at its birth Britain is both virgin white and defiantly independent in spirit, Spenser's mythopoeic treatment declares: the white cliffs were made a sea-mark warning ships to keep off, and this myth is recalled in *Cymbeline* 3.1. Spenser says that only later did mariners land when on fishing voyages and begin 'further to inuade'. This was as well for them, for 'farre in land a saluage nation dwelt / Of hideous Giants and halfe beastly men' (7). These aboriginal inhabitants, remembered in fable, are described as both brutish and physically heroic, seen from a Christian and chivalric perspective:

> That neuer tasted grace, nor goodnesse felt,
> But like wild beasts lurking in loathsome den,
> And flying fast as Roebucke through the fen,
> All naked without shame, or care of cold,
> By hunting and by spoiling liued then;
> Of stature huge, and eke of courage bold,
> That sonnes of men amazd their sternnesse to behold.   (7)

A similar perspective is offered in the Welsh mountain episodes in *Cymbeline* where the outlaws display heroic physical fortitude and hunting skill, but lament their half-beastly state as cave-dwellers: their cave, unlike the gates of monarchs, is too low for giants (3.3.5)! As the young exile complains:

> We are beastly: subtle as the fox for prey,
> Like warlike as the wolf for what we eat;
> Our valour is to chase what flies. Our cage
> We make a choir, as doth the prison'd bird,
> And sing our bondage freely.   (3.3.40–4)

So here in *Cymbeline* Shakespeare shows a 'saluage nation'
dwelling, but this time they are the repository of British honour,
the precondition for national rebirth, and the Christian
anticipation hinted in their language witnesses to a Spenserian
mode in which they are presented. Spenser's scheme of British
history gives boldly emphatic form to what it takes from the
chronicles. First, chaos, thence brutal giants, replaced by Brutus
bringing the simplest unity and rule. After Brutus' line comes
Mulmutius Dunwallo, who reimposes unity and is the first to
give law. Spenser records of these 'sacred lawes' that some men
say they were revealed to Mulmutius 'in vision' (39.1).
Shakespeare's Cymbeline boasts of Mulmutius his ancestor. Is it
a coincidence that Britain's destiny in the play is revealed in a
vision (5.4) by a Jupiter clearly identified with law and justice?
The fact that there are other possible sources for the descent of
Jupiter at the end of *Cymbeline*[18] does not exclude a memory of
Spenser, when taken with the other strong emphases shared by
Shakespeare and Spenser. This is not to insist that Holinshed or
Geoffrey are not in Shakespeare's mind, but rather that the
particular shaping and selective emphasis made in *Cymbeline*
may have an artistic, literary source in Spenser.

Spenser's second phase of British history which begins with
Mulmutius seems to end badly with Caesar's conquest; but
Kimbeline begins the next phase, which for Spenser is the
decisive one, where British uprisings evolve a new sense of
Christian patriotism culminating in Arthur's delivering Britain
into freedom. Spenser's scheme of providential history could be
succinctly expressed in the words of Jupiter in *Cymbeline*:

> Whom best I love I cross; to make my gift,
> The more delay'd, delighted.   (5.4.101–2)

The phase begun by Kimbeline and climaxing in Arthur is
succeeded by that which culminates in the Elizabethan present,
an independent nation-state, having secured a Protestant
victory over the sea-borne invasion of the Spanish Armada, and
now advancing the cause of the true Church against Rome. The
militant Protestantism of Spenser's epic had its supporters in
James I's Britain, but Shakespeare cannot firmly be allied to

them. Nevertheless Spenser's history of Britain perceives, or inscribes, its aboriginal state in terms of its present-day cultural and religious values, of tasting grace and feeling goodness, and a similar concern animates Shakespeare's depiction of savage times and wildernesses in his Jacobean British plays *King Lear*, *Macbeth* and *Cymbeline*. All three are concerned with historical evolution towards the present day under James, but at the same time all three represent cultural regression, uncovering the most barbarously primitive at the heart of a recognisably present-day centre of power and culture at court. Spenser's frequent dispatch of his hero or heroine to wildernesses or desert places allows for psychological or spiritual self-exploration, for inward temptation as well as outward threat. These features of romance are of central interest to Shakespeare too, often calling out his subtle artistry in deception, while showing how the encounter with the wilderness, the forest, can be an encounter with buried aspects of the self, uncovering layers of cultural and psychic history.

The intricacy in *Cymbeline* of the interwoven patterns of motifs and verbal imagery is very much subtler than that of the plot, yet even in the most obvious terms of narrative design Shakespeare obviously seeks complexity.

   To examine more closely the detailed dramatic texture is to see how the sheer intricacy of the pattern is wrought, but there are confusing blanks and strange discrepancies of tone to be taken account of all the time. The clumsy and heavy-handed presentation of Cloten and his attendant lords in their first scene makes it difficult for an audience to attach any weight to the Lord's comment that Cloten's exertions have made him 'reek as sacrifice', and it is hard to believe that many will remember this remark (in context expressing both excessive flattery and disguised contempt) when much later in the Welsh wilderness Cloten's head is struck off and thrown into a creek taking it to the sea. Such an end might indeed recall the fate of Orpheus as described in Ovid's *Metamorphoses*, Book 11.

   Yet the young prince who disposes of Cloten's head in this way does so in a spirit discouraging any sort of archetypal resonance of his action. As Imogen enters the underworld, a spectator might well be reminded of Orpheus' fate, and begin to speculate on the latent analogy with Eurydice, too, though the analogy is so glancingly suggested that it will more probably strike some chord in the memory without becoming focused. The discrepancy between the crude humour of the style in which Cloten is consistently presented and the serious possibilities of his role is surely acute: there is something riddling about the gap between surface and depth, or 'outward' and 'inward' (in the repeated terms of the play's language). It is a riddle or (as some aver) it is a serious artistic fault. At any rate, it is a feature demanding further exploration before trying to decide the point.

Like Shakespeare's earlier romantic comedies *Cymbeline* makes much use of small hand-properties as signs: a diamond ring, a jewelled bracelet (a 'manacle of love' as Posthumus calls it), letters (Imogen keeps Posthumus' letters next her heart and only discards them when desperate), and a handkerchief. That the treatment of these tokens is by Shakespeare's own earlier standards bizarre may be shown by noticing that the series of letters becomes increasingly misleading to the recipients or exhibits the deception suffered by their author, until the arrival of the final one, which is indecipherably obscure at first, being sent by a god, and received in a dream, to be interpreted by an unreliable soothsayer. As for the handkerchief, we are told in Act I that Posthumus waved farewell from his ship with a handkerchief which he kissed. Hearing this Imogen exclaims 'Senseless linen' (she seems unaware of her own pun, for the 'sense' of the message is certainly clear to her though the kiss may be wasted on the linen). Yet the word 'handkerchief', associated with a newly married Shakespearean hero parted from his wife by a sea voyage, might strike a subdued ominous chord in the memory of a spectator who knew *Othello*. But the moment is fleeting. Much later, Pisanio is sent instructions by letter from Posthumus to kill Imogen, and exclaims

> O damn'd paper,
> Black as the ink that's on thee! Senseless bauble,
> Art thou a feodary for this act, and look'st
> So virgin-like without? (3.2.19–22)

The covert echo of *Othello* is in the association of black with damnation, staining on the inside the sheet which seemed virgin white before being unfolded.

There is an echo of part of Iachimo's temptation of Imogen (1.8.132–3) which is perhaps memorable enough to strike a chord in the spectator's memory: 'Should he make me / Live like Diana's priest, betwixt cold sheets': yet it is surely very unlikely that the repeated pun 'senseless bauble' will be noticed. It is almost as if such tiny links constitute a private code for Shakespeare himself, or are intended to represent the operation of the supernatural, however defined, or of the subconscious, ceaselessly transposing or displacing images in its dream-work.

It has been noticed that Shakespeare puns on the word 'trunk' with two of the most striking large properties used in the play, the jewel-chest in which Iachimo hides so as to gain access to Imogen's bedchamber, and the headless torso of Cloten wearing Posthumus' suit, laid beside the apparently dead, actually drugged, body of Imogen in the cave. Shakespeare makes a similar pun on 'suit':[19] Imogen rejects the courtship of Cloten, his love-suit (3.4.133), in preference for Posthumus, of whom she says to Cloten:

> His mean'st garment
> That ever hath but clipt his body, is dearer
> In my respect than all the hairs above thee (2.3.133–5)

Later, in Wales, Belarius tells how he stole the two princes from Cymbeline in anger at being banished, when treacherously denounced as a traitor:

> Then was I as a tree
> Whose boughs did bend with fruit; but in one night,
> A storm or robbery (call it what you will)
> Shook down my mellow hangings, nay, my leaves,
> And left me bare to weather. (3.3.60–4)

His trunk is stripped of its clothing. In the next scene, Imogen laments that Posthumus has been betrayed into believing her disloyal:

> Poor I am stale, a garment out of fashion,
> And, for I am richer than to hang by th'walls,

> I must be ripp'd. To pieces with me!　　　　　(3.4.51–3)

She chides the absent Posthumus for winning her heart so that she

> 　　　　　　　　put into contempt the suits
> 　　Of princely fellows　　　　　　　　　(89–90)

The pun is insistent later (4.1.17–18) when Cloten conceives the idea of ripping a rich suit now disliked. Cloten has got hold of a suit belonging to Posthumus and when he appears dressed in it he points out that it fits him exactly. Here we may suspect Shakespeare has combined the magic of fairy-tale with the superstitious power attributed to word-play. The suit 'fits' him because his love-suit was like Posthumus', addressed to Imogen, and because he is the double of Posthumus in not valuing Imogen at her true worth. He symbolises the discrepancy between the outward aspect of Posthumus (as Imogen saw him) and the 'stuff within' (1.1.23). Cloten's fantasy of beheading Posthumus, raping Imogen in his suit and then cutting his garments to pieces before his face (4.1.17–18) curiously parodies the ceremonial execution of an Elizabethan traitor; but a spectator at *Cymbeline* cannot readily grasp why Cloten would tear the garments rather than the body to pieces, unless it is recognised that there is a punning association between body–trunk–suit, one which Cloten repeats when he encounters his fatal opponent Guiderius: 'Thou villain base, / Know'st me not by my clothes?' (4.2.80–1). There is a distinctly naive and crude quality here which recalls popular romance comedy like *Mucedorus*, and there is an air of fairy-tale about the odd humour associated with Cloten.

　　The killing of Cloten has exactly the grotesque humour of the two episodes in *Mucedorus* when the hero saves the heroine's life, first by beheading a bear ('his carcase now lies headlesse') and presenting her with the severed head – a gift, she assures him, that 'contents' her more 'Then greatest bountie of a mightie prince' (1.3.19) – later on, by tricking the wild man Bremo into lending his club, with which Mucedorus promptly brains him, on which Amadine remarks, 'It glads my heart this tirants

death to see' (5.1.72). This callous tone is at odds with the fear
expressed moments before by the lady. In *Cymbeline* Guiderius
has the cheerful callousness of Jack the Giantkiller, and true to
the Mucedorus style Guiderius first takes Cloten's sword from
him, so Cloten is beheaded with his own sword.[20] The head,
once severed, is half-comic, not the best of the company's stage-
properties: Guiderius brandishes it to show it to be 'an empty
purse' (4.2.113).[21] Only much later in the play, when the
Romans come upon the headless trunk dressed in Posthumus'
suit beside the seemingly lifeless body of Imogen, is the verbal
and visual double motif of trunk–suit clear and complete, when
the Roman soldier exclaims, 'Soft ho, what trunk is here?'
(4.2.353). Yet the extraordinary change of mood and structure
of feeling at this point casts a retrospective light which is
unexpectedly sombre: the paradoxical form of this whole
trunk–suit motif leaves one uneasy.

There is a pattern announced at the very opening of the play
concerning the relationship between essence and substance,
spirit and body: the artfulness of the play's manner ironically
plays over a rich weave of verbal and theatrical images. The
critic who fails to take note of this play of irony can make the
image patterns seem to express an unquestioned design.
Nevertheless the Lord's commendation of Posthumus:

> I do not think
> So fair an outward, and such stuff within
> Endows a man but he   (1.1.22–4)

seems in a Jacobean context almost pure hyperbole – to assert
that a gentleman at court has an outward appearance according
with the mind's construction!

The outward–inward, essence–substance motif is developed
in imagery of hollow containers for something precious,
dangerous, mysterious – hinted at in the candle flame which
burns in Imogen's dark room, explicit in the box of poison-
potion the Queen gives Pisanio, humorously apparent in the
comment that Cloten's severed head is an 'empty purse,/ There
was no money in't', magnified in the jewel-chest concealing
Iachimo, varied in his likening of sleeping Imogen to a

monument lying in a chapel (2.1.33), visually alluded to in the mountain cave, which is at once a haven for the outlaws, their 'cell of ignorance' (3.3.33) and, for Imogen 'dead', like a tomb. The stagecraft associates this cave with the prison cell later in the play where Posthumus is shown lying asleep. The play's first scene also announces linked images which are developed verbally and in visual terms through the action: Posthumus and Imogen are likened to jewels (1.1.91, 1.4.153) and exchange actual jewels on parting in Act 1, Scene 1. Later Iachimo uses stealth to get into Imogen's bedchamber (in a jewel-chest), and so is able to slander her, so that Posthumus loses the wager and the jewel Imogen gave him. We hear how old Belarius robbed Cymbeline of his sons after he had been slanderously accused of treachery and falsely deprived of his place. The idea of robbery is announced again at the very beginning of the prison scene. Posthumus convicts himself of treason – though to Imogen, not to Rome; he is brought in, fettered and manacled, and the gaoler makes a black joke:

> You shall not now be stol'n, you have locks upon you (5.4.1)

This ironically recalls his first parting from Imogen when he gave her the jewel bracelet, saying

> It is a manacle of love, I'll place it
> Upon this fairest prisoner. (1.1.122–3)

If we find verbal and visual images, even whole narrative episodes, patterned so that they 'rhyme', as these instances show, nevertheless they are sown with a hand so liberal sometimes that they may easily be overlooked, turning up where no prepared context gives them recognisable importance, or so tiny, oblique or casual as to seem contingent, accidental. In Act 1 when Iachimo first meets Imogen he tells her in the midst of a flowery cascade of hyperboles that in Rome her Posthumus 'sits 'mongst men like a descended god': what likelihood is there that 'descended' will linger in the submerged memory of a spectator to be recalled when Jupiter descends in Act 5? Again, speaking of a farewell kiss, Imogen implies the metaphor of a jewel: she had it ready to give, 'set / Betwixt two charming words' (1.3.35). The audience is very unlikely to notice these as images belonging to a larger pattern; but intermittently, out of the corner of an eye, it might glimpse something. Surely this is what Shakespeare intends. He creates in *Cymbeline* characters whose speech as if unconsciously witnesses to a magical dimension, while not only in words but in their world, events apparently contingent and arbitrary have correspondences to one another. As the play unfolds the audience repeatedly can perceive patterns of which the characters are poignantly unconscious (though the intimations of benevolent destiny are also unreliable, being checked by the tricky and treacherous and shocking progress of the action). Only with the play's auspicious conclusion – and not before – can the characters themselves know their world to be shaped by an impalpable but benevolent power.

The world of *Cymbeline* has many suggestive analogies with that of *The Tempest*, especially if one understands this representation of a fabular world in terms of the nation's cultural history – as Shakespeare representing the savage mind of ancient Britain and its journey towards a modern consciousness.

As with *The Faerie Queene*, so in *Cymbeline* the spectator–reader is required to interpret shifting and ambivalent figures and events in a way that reflects the experience of the heroes within the narrative fictions, where surprises and tricks abound. The reader's alertness to changing verbal texture, to semantic instability, and to varying narrative point of view, is persistently quickened by the poem's and the play's own self-consciousness. This can be illustrated from the role of Iachimo.

Intent on winning his wager with Posthumus that he can seduce his pure wife Imogen, Iachimo contrives admittance to her presence, where he makes sensuous, seductive overtures; but only when he makes a direct and explicit advance – 'I dedicate myself to your sweet pleasure' – only here does Imogen stop him; and there is no outward sign in Imogen of conscious perturbation. The episode focuses on Iachimo and his initiative, Imogen seems unaffected; but a significant point is that, *for the audience*, the erotic words and emotions of Iachimo will have some influence on the way they look at Imogen, nevertheless.[22]

The wager scene earlier in 1.4 makes the audience conscious of jewels as metaphorically signifying chastity, sexual treasure. Iachimo's request to Imogen now, that she keep his chest of jewels overnight in her chamber, though seeming innocent to her, has for an audience an erotic meaning, and they know also that Iachimo is conscious of this meaning. When Imogen agrees, her language innocently touches on the danger as she vows to 'pawn mine honor for their safety'. Imogen is a victim of layers of irony visible to an alert audience.

Shakespeare presents Imogen in bed, reading. Beside her is a lit candle. The trunk of 'jewels' stands nearby. She puts the book down and goes to sleep.

The scene rests, silent and motionless. Then the trunk-lid opens and Iachimo rises erect. He approaches Imogen, bends to kiss her.

As a stage image, the figure rising erect from a trunk beside the sleeping woman has an obvious sexual symbolism, and the situation is bizarre enough to suggest dream rather than actuality – the dream of Imogen as well as the dream of Iachimo. It is important, however, to notice that Shakespeare, having made this initial effect with the silent stage image, then uses Iachimo to direct, and complicate, the spectator's viewing of the scene. Iachimo's commentary works elaborate imaginative metamorphoses on the woman and the chamber. Iachimo first thinks of Tarquin and Lucrece as he emerges from the trunk, but the sight of the sleeping Imogen at once begins to have an effect: as he gazes the idea of rape dissolves and the Lucrece story changes: now Tarquin instead of making ravishing strides 'did softly press the rushes'. This is a repetition of the effect Imogen had on Iachimo at their first meeting in 1.6. Shakespeare concentrates an audience's awareness on Iachimo's perception of Imogen in both scenes, on the strange power of her beauty, sensuous, erotic, and yet infused with purity, inspiring religious awe. Iachimo is always imbued with underlying menace – one thinks of Milton's Satan approaching Eve but in spite of himself struck, for a moment, 'stupidly good' by her innocence. Iachimo kisses Imogen without waking her, then describes her as she sleeps: ruby lipped, yet otherwise pure white as a lily: a Venus, but paradoxically chaste:

> How bravely thou becom'st thy bed! fresh lily,
> And whiter than the sheets! That I might touch!
> But kiss, one kiss! Rubies unparagon'd,
> How dearly they do 't! 'Tis her breathing that
> Perfumes the chamber thus. The flame o' th' taper
> Bows toward her, and would under-peep her lids,
> To see th' enclosed lights, now canopied   (2.2.15–21)

Iachimo's description of Imogen's body is too much in close-up for any spectator, but it arouses the imagination. The spectator is invited to share as voyeur the sensations of Iachimo: 'That I might touch! / But kiss, one kiss!' – 'On her left breast / A mole cinque-spotted'. Iachimo's rapture at Imogen's perfumed breath recalls Othello's – a moment before he kills Desdemona on her bed:

> When I have plucked thy rose,
> I cannot give it vital growth again;
> It needs must wither. I'll smell thee on the tree.
> (*He kisses her*).
> O balmy breath, that dost almost persuade
> Justice to break her sword! One more, one more.
> Be thus when thou art dead, and I will kill thee
> And love thee after   (*Othello* 5.2.13–19)

Here in *Cymbeline* the memorable visual stage image from *Othello* is 'quoted', transmitting a sense of tragic threat, but for the spectator who recognises the quotation the effect is confusing, indeed downright misleading – it is far too early in the action of *Cymbeline* for a tragic climax, only a substitute for the hero is on stage, he intends seduction or rape not murder, and in the event he even gives this up, overwhelmed by the heroine's purity:

> O sleep, thou ape of death, lie dull upon her,
> And be her sense but as a monument,
> Thus in a chapel lying!   (2.2.31–3)

But he removes the bracelet from her arm: the audience are thus invited to interpret his action as desecration and the bracelet as a holy relic. This will involve re-reading the body of Imogen as a sacred marble inset with rubies, which in Christian tradition symbolise chastity and martyrdom (Chaucer refers to 'This gemme of chastite ... And eek of martirdom the ruby bright'). According to one dramatic convention used elsewhere by Shakespeare, events presented on stage in the presence of a sleeping character can represent events in that character's subconscious. This poses a question of interpretation: the episode may be taken to represent Imogen's dream-struggle with Iachimo's temptation, as well as Iachimo's struggle with the temptation her body offers. The scene presents the spectators with a dream-Imogen, mediated by Iachimo, an Imogen who is erotically desirable and, at the same time, a saint or martyr in a candle-lit tomb. These suggestions are supported by allusions to Lucrece: 'Where like a virtuous monument she lies, / To be admir'd of lewd unhallowed eyes' (*Lucrece* 391–2) and to Juliet lying in a 'monument' (*Romeo and Juliet* 5.3.127). We learn from Iachimo that what Imogen had been reading before she fell asleep was the tale of Tereus; she stopped at the point of Philomel's rape. This Ovidian hint seems to be misleading, since Imogen is not hurt here by Iachimo: but, as the spectators will learn in due course, the tale is not yet over, either.

Iachimo returns to the trunk and the scene is exactly as it was before he emerged. It is as if nothing had happened, as if it had all been a dream (except for one difference, the bracelet now missing from Imogen's arm), only now the audience has been made aware of tragic possibilities; yet the plot does not seem to be turning out as the literary hints – especially the book Imogen is reading – seem to insist it will. The spectator is prompted to guess at the outcome yet teasingly confused and kept in suspense.

Iachimo's shape is always changing in accord with Shakespeare's larger dramatic purposes: Iachimo can be overcome, in Imogen's physical presence, by the harmony of her spiritual and sensuous beauty, yet he has no scruple later, in Rome, as he tempts Posthumus to believe her impure. At the Globe or Blackfriars the actual staging could not have matched (even had that been appropriate) Iachimo's retrospective, sumptuous description of Imogen's bedchamber (2.4.69 ff.), where Iachimo fills the scene with erotic and sensuous suggestion surrounding Imogen – there are 'winking Cupids' and the tapestry depicts Cleopatra at Cydnus with Antony. Should the audience, presented with these erotic images, and seeing how they might now, retrospectively, be associated with Imogen's bedtime reading of Ovid, interpret them as reflecting some impure sensuality in Imogen? The spectator must weigh this new alternative reading against the obvious motive Iachimo has to misrepresent Imogen; but then almost at once the audience's attention is switched to Posthumus, whose own sexuality is in violent crisis. Thus Shakespeare keeps altering the spectator's perspective, and Iachimo is an indispensable instrument to the dramatist when the audience is to be hoodwinked, tricked and surprised to the extent that occurs in *Cymbeline*. All this is generally reminiscent of Spenser, prompting one almost to wonder whether, in Iachimo's name, the echo of Archimago as well as Iago should be heard.[23]

W. B. Yeats says in his essay on Spenser of 1902 that Spenser employed allegorical nails to fasten his cloudy romance to a big barn door of common sense. In *Cymbeline* it is certainly clear that Shakespeare arranged three major scenes concerning an unconscious figure, spaced at significant points and with obvious visual, thematic and structural interconnections, two focused on Imogen (2.2, 4.2), one (5.4) focused on Posthumus. Although these linked scenes do develop major stages in the narrative with centripetal boldness, their allegorical mode is also troubled.

Shakespeare uses movement to focus on the unconscious figure at the scene's centre. This pattern is repeated in all three scenes – bedchamber, cave, prison. In the bedchamber scene there is specific allusion to Christian saints and their especially venerated tombs and chapels, whereas at the cave the surrogate father and the brothers perform a solemn rite and sing a dirge, scattering flowers on the apparently dead Imogen whose head is laid to the east, the opposite of Christian practice but according with Celtic rite. The scene with its images of human sacrifice and pre-Christian burial offers further, more remote, cultural perspectives. The prison scene makes a visual contrast with the cave scene by emphasising the symbols of the most advanced state of pagan civilised culture, just before Christ's birth; but Roman civilisation is represented in stern and hard images of authority: Roman costume, iron bars, locks, manacles. The choreography recalls the two earlier scenes as the sleeping Posthumus is circled by the ghosts of his family, expressing family pride and patriotism, protesting against injustice, and calling directly to Jupiter to restore the fortunes of hero and nation. The movement is from private inner life to national crisis, and it is conveyed in different dramatic styles.

In the bedchamber scene there is a strong suggestion of erotic fantasy in what the spectators see: by contrast, in the prison scene Shakespeare employs a consistently stiff, emblematic, public style for Posthumus' dream, like that in *Richard III* (5.3.117–80). There is no concern with private inner life here. Posthumus awakes aware of the dream-events the audience has been shown, and these are questions of national justice and national destiny. Nevertheless even here Shakespeare deliberately insists that the outward and visible is susceptible to various interpretations, different historical perspectives, even though the concern here is with British–Roman history itself. Jupiter makes his entrance explosively, throwing a thunderbolt (incidentally responding to the stoic Guiderius' 'Fear no more the lightning-flash' in the cave scene's dirge). The supreme classical god angrily denies that he is a tyrant and, though supreme, acknowledges that he is not above law (thus glancing at an issue in Jacobean theories of monarchy). Jupiter's gesture is sublime, it is miraculous, but it is also riddling in itself, and presented by Shakespeare in a riddling manner: Jupiter leaves on the sleeping hero's breast a 'tablet', a written message finely bound in rich covers: a rare book, but only speculatively to be interpreted.

Posthumus, entering a Roman prison, voices the metaphysical paradox 'welcome, bondage, for thou art a way, I think, to liberty?' As a Briton living just before the dawn of the Christian era, this is poignant (for an audience, who knows his intuition will be confirmed in the future life of Christ and recorded in another book, a history including myth, legend, national chronicle, fiction and prophecy: the Bible). Such allusions allow for the interpretation of *Cymbeline* in Christian terms. Edgar Wind, in his *Pagan Mysteries of the Renaissance*, remarks the Renaissance custom of veiling mystical matters with pagan imagery, presenting mysteries deliberately without removing all the veils, so that the viewer must figure out the concealed part for himself. I incline to believe that the play invites a Christian decoding, as the Jacobean age might have expected, but what is striking is how the perspective of paganism itself is given its own rights at the end of *Cymbeline*, and how the crises of the individual, the family and the nation can be understood in terms other than Christian. Through the play's insistent concern with multiple possibilities of interpretation, its diverse styles and kinds of history, the play makes us recognise its own narrative, multi-layered though it be, as itself a phase of history which forms only a part of a still unfinished matter of Britain.

CHAPTER 3

A speechless dialect: interpreting the human body in Shakespeare's plays

A silent and inert body may be alive, it may indeed be soundly sleeping, though it may also be unconscious, dreaming or dying. It may resemble in its beauty sculpted stone or it may be distorted and broken. A silent and inert body may be a dead thing, a corpse, the processes of corruption already at work within it, its human identity disappearing.

The silent and inert body is a sign both of renewal and extinction: it is as powerful as it is ambivalent, a focal image of Shakespeare's dramatic imagination. He returned to it repeatedly in many different forms, though it is particularly intriguing to notice that it is centrally significant in his early non-dramatic work – the narrative poem *The Rape of Lucrece*.

Drama is a performance art in which the set codes and patterns are expressed with the direct immediacy of the actors' live bodies: the instinctive life of the flesh becomes part of a premeditated symbolic language, yet that premeditated code is at the same time risked in the existential circumstances of live performance. Paradoxically, it is when the body is silent and inert in a play that its contrasting aspects – of corporeal presence, sign for a person in the fiction, and intermittent symbolic–sculptural image – may be most apparent, as in *Romeo and Juliet* when Juliet lies in the Capulet tomb, near Tybalt's body in its bloody shroud, or – a less obvious case – in *King Lear*, when the blind Gloucester lies ominously still, having leapt from an imaginary cliff, and his apprehensive son Edgar kneels to examine him.

Shakespeare exploits the ambivalent potential of the actor's silent and inert body in stage performance, read or misread either as living or dead, and if dead as monument or corpse; he is also much interested in representing the body as undergoing transformation. I wish to concentrate on instances where Shakespeare endows the human body on stage with a further significance beyond its biographical status in the dramatic fiction – suggesting visually symbolic images analogous to sculpture. Such effects may be made in any formal attitude – seated, as when King Lear is brought in unconscious in a chair, attended by his daughter Cordelia – or it may be upright, as when in *Coriolanus* (2.2) the hero shows himself to the people in the marketplace. Such effects can be brief and fleeting without sacrificing their power. So it is when Hamlet leaps from concealment to bring the funeral of Ophelia to a standstill, exposing to all eyes the fact of his presence, erect, and defiant, on his native ground: 'It is I, Hamlet the Dane'. In extreme contrast, Shakespeare is capable of using the device to grotesque effect, as when in *The Tempest* the disorientated Stephano comes upon the still body of a monster, strange, fearful, four-legged, fishy.

Even though they are non-verbal, these effects are necessary parts of Shakespeare's full theatrical language, integral rather than optional. The point needs emphasis since much debate among critics, designers and directors continues to focus on intermittently transmitted visual signs in Shakespeare.[1] Such visual signs depend for their effect upon an audience being alerted in advance so that a particular code may be recognised, and sometimes theatre directors, actors and visual designers are insensitive enough to interfere with such signals.

Given the deliberateness of Shakespeare's style, these features survive in intelligent productions, and it is in the theatre that their full importance is recognised. There is a difficulty in finding appropriate terminology to describe them. I would reserve the term 'icon' for images of religious significance and veneration. Common critical usage assigns a different meaning to iconography in the wake of the Warburg tradition[2] and where an episode's structure and wider application recall classical or medieval art I prefer to speak directly of sculpture, in order to keep in focus the three-dimensional art of com-

position the dramatist visibly practises. Shakespeare's dramaturgy sometimes calls for silence as well as stillness for these
effects, as if deliberately to signal the analogy with sculpture.

Renaissance emblems of the more recondite kind[3] seem
unlikely to be much used by a dramatist writing for popular
audiences, and since traditions of street pageantry, royal entry
arches, and Lord Mayor's shows[4] exhibit a wide, traditional, if
obvious, iconography, popularly classical and medieval, I
assume an equivalent conservative vocabulary to be the
iconography in the plays. Sculpture endows the body with
certain stereotyped attitudes expressive of codified meanings
recognised in a given culture. Shakespeare alludes to a pagan
classical and Christian sculptural code, but he also endows his
actors' bodies, at times, with fresh visual meanings derived from
the context.

This emphasis on the human body, at the moment its
significance becomes more than its biographical status in the
dramatic fiction, is apparent in Shakespeare's earliest tragedy,
Titus Andronicus, and I would like to explore it there by taking
account of actual modern theatrical presentation of several
episodes focusing on Lavinia and Titus. It is helpful to think not
only of the formal grouping of figures in sculpture-like attitudes,
but of the more fleeting occasions when a figure or several
figures are held in a 'freeze-frame' (to borrow a cinematic
term), where a sculptural significance is given by dramatic
context and physical attitude to a human figure on stage. The
modern theatre has represented *Titus Andronicus* in contrasting
ways, and this helps to bring out the fact that Shakespeare's
dramatic style makes effects by deliberate interplay of the
contradictory aspects of the body, stressing equally its frankly
direct physical spontaneity and balletic stylisation. Thus a style
of performance which suppresses either of these elements can be
shown, even in *Titus Andronicus*, to fail to transmit the play's
concerns.

In this book generally it can be said that appeal is made to an
'ideal' theatrical interpretation, and to general, again 'ideal',
audience response. In fact, experience of more than one

production of each play I discuss informs what I have said, but I have tried to restrict attention to effects practicable and plausible in Shakespeare's theatre. By attending to recent theatre practice, some check may be made on these speculations. Since the 1987/88 production of *Titus Andronicus* directed by Deborah Warner at the Swan Theatre, Stratford-upon-Avon, faced squarely the demands in Shakespeare's text that mutilation, bodily agony and violent death be simulated before our very eyes, there is the added advantage that this production affords a closer indication of the original's impact, performed as it was in a theatre whose size, disposition of audience in relation to actors, and staging resources, are close to Elizabethan conditions. The episodes in which the body, in moments of extreme experience, is presented in stillness for concentrated attention, are many; after mutilation, moreover, the body of Lavinia becomes a continuous visual image of violation and tragic suffering, her mutilation half-effacing her original identity.

As Eugene M. Waith notes in his edition of the play, (Oxford, 1984, pp. 56–7), a New York production by Gerald Freedman in 1967 avoided any suggestion of naturalistic action by using masks, ritual, and simple musical accompaniment on percussive instruments suggestive of 'our inherited primitive consciousness' played by on-stage musicians. The inspiration for the visual appearance of the production was Roman–Byzantine and feudal Japanese, mixed, creating impressions of an unknown people of a non-specific racial kind. The slaughter at the final banquet was accomplished in a style reminiscent of Japanese classical theatre, a Chorus enveloping each victim in a red cloth which unwound to reveal a black shroud beneath. Some reviewers felt there was too much theatrical artifice.

Peter Brook's production at Stratford-upon-Avon in 1955 had also borrowed stylistic details from Japanese tradition. Lavinia's rape and mutilation was presented by highly stylised means, the figure in a fixed attitude, 'right arm outstretched and head drooping away from it, left arm crooked with the wrist at the mouth'; from her wrists and mouth trailed scarlet silk ribbons representing blood. The sound of slowly plucked harp-strings was heard. It is an abstract image, and Brook furthermore cut the verbal description of Lavinia's wounds to make the image all the more abstract. Shakespeare had in mind a theatre which could simulate wounding with a degree of immediacy, and he certainly requires such simulation here. That might seem to be quite enough in itself, but Shakespeare adds a long description going into detail about the exact features of the mutilation, which intensifies in some ways, as it distances, the agony of Lavinia and the agony of Marcus as he puts it into words. Shakespeare actually doubles the stress that the audience has to face. Now the interesting thing about post-Elizabethan critical pronouncements about this episode is that they condemn it as visually excessive and rhetorically inappropriate without first-hand evidence of its effect when performed before live audiences in a theatre of the kind Shakespeare had in mind. Scholars are ready enough to document Elizabethan techniques of execution, torture and official mutilation; the weapons of the Elizabethan army are familiar, and a number of them had also been standard issue in the Roman army. The 1580s was a warlike epoch. Nevertheless, it is supposed that the 'horrors' of *Titus Andronicus* would have struck Elizabethan spectators as ludicrous, that Shakespeare hopelessly miscalculated, or that twentieth-century spectators and scholars can find no sympathetic response, only cauterised or disbelieving rejection, should actors simulate the physical woundings indicated by the text.

There is no doubt of Shakespeare's deliberateness here: for Lavinia is not only presented immediately after her rape with handless arms; she must appear in a number of subsequent scenes where she is required to perform actions emphasising her mutilation and implying further physical pain, when employing her handless stumps at a meal, writing with a large stick, or holding a pudding basin. It is impossible to present these actions without an element of the grotesque and absurd; yet each of them presents a graphic stage image expressing Lavinia's estrangement from normal communication with others. Moreover, this pitiable isolation is heroically overcome: great physical effort yields full communication of the essential

message, and achieves her revenge and cleansing. For Shakespeare the sheer physicality of her suffering is crucially
important, so he designs these memorable actions to commemorate it. Brook did not follow. He presumably used ribbons
and extreme stylisation of bodily attitude for his Lavinia because
he recognised the power of Noh drama's minimalist effects,
where intensely delicate and beautiful visual signs are found for
horrible events. A gesture that is elegant and beautiful means
something horrible and terrifying. In the contradiction, the
gap, between this elegant delicate gesture and its meaning,
Brook saw a way of getting at the extreme experience implicit in
Lavinia; in this extreme understatement something very atrocious is represented and in the gap the audience loses itself in
imagined pain.

Another production in 1967, by Douglas Seale at Baltimore
(referred to by Waith, p. 57), set the play in the Second World
War period and costumed it accordingly; interestingly enough,
reviewers observed that the cultural associations of modern
technology made the presentation of wounding highly confused
and unsuccessful. With modern weapons-technology goes modern medical science, first-aid in the field: so audiences were
provoked to ask how Lavinia could retain consciousness after
such a great loss of blood, why Marcus had not administered
first-aid or got her to hospital. The banal literalism of the
production obliterated the essentially mixed style Shakespeare
uses, in which immediate bodily experience is set against
formalised speech and ceremoniousness of physical and cultural
attitudes, and marked rhythmic shaping of events.

Deborah Warner's production of *Titus Andronicus* seen at the
Swan Theatre in Stratford-upon-Avon reinforced the play's
recently revived reputation for great excitement and deep
emotional response, and it gave imposing weight to ceremonious
patterns while showing the spectacular physical horror itself
naturalistically, with direct immediacy. If I were to find fault
with this production, it would certainly not be for presenting a
Lavinia whose violated body quivers and shudders uncontrollably as she crawls on stage after her rape, smeared by the earth
onto which she has been forced down, and uttering agonised

liquid sounds from a mouth bereft of its tongue. In the Swan
Theatre every spectator was inescapably close to this figure,
whose symptoms of nervous and muscular shock were registered
as clearly to the eye as was the compelling sight of her roughly
bandaged, muddy stumps of wrists. The figure was the more
appalling because the actress was a young and slight figure – it
might easily have been a boy-actor.

To present Lavinia at such close range, emitting such strong
animal signals, presents an audience with a direct first-hand
impression of her mutilated body, its sheer physicality intensified by the bestial mockery which her violators uttered to
accompany her entrance. Then Lavinia was left alone on stage.
The audience contemplated the still figure of agony. Shakespeare's stagecraft is deliberate here: after a moment, Marcus
enters: he in turn has to confront the figure of his mutilated
kinswoman. At first the shock overcomes him, as if it were an
hallucination. Then, as the spectacle's effect begins to sink in, he
registers his reactions in words. The audience now watch as
their own first reactions of pity and repulsion are replayed in
Marcus, expressed in his facial and bodily gestures; and then
they listen as Marcus tries to put his feeling into words, to
describe what the audience too can see. This sequence will soon
be repeated when Marcus brings Lavinia to Lucius and Titus.
Again the motionless figure of Lavinia will be presented, again
the audience must watch as in their turn Titus and Lucius face
the shock of seeing the figure, hitherto so familiar and dear to
them, now suddenly, frighteningly estranged by disfigurement.

Critics tend to assert that Marcus, in describing Lavinia here,
'anaesthetises' himself, translates the gruesome physical actuality before him into an ornate Ovidian rhetorical distance.
Yet the speech does deliberately focus on each raw wound of
Lavinia's body, making Marcus and hence the audience
recognise in detail the extent of Lavinia's mutilation. One must
ask, what is anaesthetising about being made to see how 'a
crimson river of warm blood, / Like to a bubbling fountain
stirr'd with wind' (2.4.22) rises and falls in Lavinia's mouth?
The speech does attempt verbal transformation through metaphor, countering the effect of repulsion, yet it does not flinch

from looking at the wound: it is an effort of will, and an effort of love, to overcome repulsion and fear, to recognise and identify sympathetically with the sufferer, but in so doing to dare to feel the agony. The speech transmits shock, but it also insists that Lavinia still has emotional meaning as Lavinia, for her former self is in mortal peril of obliteration. Marcus in his speech uses rhetorical means to release emotion that the initial shocking sight threatened to freeze. If Lavinia emits animal signals of shock, standing in an attitude distorted by agony, quivering all over, uttering low sounds, it is all the clearer how much danger exists that she may be lost at any moment, how desperate is the need for Marcus to touch and console her, if she can hear him. The Ovidian decoration commemorates a Lavinia who in one sense is no more. Marcus speaks to trace the transformation of the woman's body into an icon of pity. From this moment on it is impossible to know what degree of transformation she is undergoing. She is both a character struggling against agony to achieve cleansing, and a general symbol of grief and tragic agony, of archetypal significance.

Shakespeare follows this episode with the parallel scene in which Lavinia is brought before Titus and Lucius. Again the audience see the moment of recognition, match it against their own reaction and that of Marcus, contemplate directly for themselves the meanings of this silent, still figure of the violated woman as she stands, a monument of tragedy. Before her entrance the audience has just watched as Titus bowed himself down on the stone of Rome to plead for his sons' lives. The fixed attitude of supplication, the statue of humbled pride, of paternal passion, fails to arrest the ceremonious procession. It is a graphic visual event. Next Titus is confronted by another son's banishment. 'How happy art thou' (3.1.56), Titus responds to the news. It leaves him alone in Rome, now transformed into a wilderness of tigers. 'How happy art thou'. Then enter Marcus and Lavinia. Marcus' first words indicate that he positions Lavinia to stand alone, preparing to present her to view as an isolated, distinct figure for concentrated attention, centre stage. It is a gravely ceremonious ritual. In the production at the Swan, Titus was facing the opposite way, crouching; he heard

Marcus before turning round. A pause emphasised the grouping.

> MARCUS Titus, prepare thy aged eyes to weep,
>   Or if not so, thy noble heart to break.
>   I bring consuming sorrow to thine age.
> TITUS Will it consume me? Let me see it then.
> MARCUS This was thy daughter.
> TITUS Why, Marcus, so she is.
> LUCIUS Ay me, this object kills me!
> TITUS Faint-hearted boy, arise and look upon her.

> (3.1.59–66)

Titus responds, 'Will it consume me? Let me see it then'. If it
will kill him on the spot it is welcome. He has a kind of suddenly
swift wit utterly in contrast to the massiveness of the dramaturgy
at this point. A series of hammer blows beat upon him, and in
response he becomes unpredictably witty. Marcus says, 'This
was thy daughter' and Titus looks straight at her and he says,
'Why, Marcus, so she is'. He changes the tense from past to
present. It is a moment of simplicity and great power. Lavinia
expresses great reluctance at being approached by Marcus,
great reluctance at being brought now before her father. The
violated woman is polluted, a thing of shame. Titus instantly
responds to his daughter, whatever horrible disfigurement her
body bears; with intuitive quickness he responds to his
daughter's fear and abhorrence at her own body, and her fear
that defilement will estrange her from her kin. The father
instantly assures her, she is still his daughter, still herself. It is an
outpouring of love, astonishing from a man so beset, himself, by
catastrophe. Lucius, his son, has reacted by falling on his knees:
'Ay me, this object kills me!' Titus rebukes him. This is her, not
it: Lavinia, not an object; a human being, not an icon. We are
her kin, we must recognise her: 'Faint-hearted boy, arise and
look upon her.' It is done coarsely, but the sentiment is tender
and the perception subtle and the emotion pure. Titus in his
sympathetic response is kin to Marcus, who had sought in his
speech to restore Lavinia's selfhood, for her sake and for his own,
in recalling her skills in sewing and playing the lute and singing,
skills of which she has been robbed and whose loss must not be

allowed to destroy the person who exercised them, who could make

> those lily hands
> Tremble like aspen leaves upon a lute. (2.2.441)

The recollection brings added agony, but restores humanity and normal consciousness – exactly as the wearing-off of a painkilling drug brings back pain as the price for restored consciousness. In this way Marcus and Titus enter imaginatively into Lavinia's state of mind and body and so bring an audience to do so too. It is intrinsically through the body that Shakespeare focuses such experiences and mediates them.

As Titus absorbs the shock of Lavinia's mutilation it becomes intolerable for him still to have hands when his daughter's are lost: their stumps are an obsessive focus for him, as they already have been for the audience. To restore the bond with his daughter he will cut off his hands too, he says. In grief-stricken frenzy his mind fastens upon the significations of hands, as they pray, serve, supplicate, kill. He gazes in horrified alienation at his own hands, now seeming suddenly other, estranged – and an audience may recall seeing those hands deal death to one of Titus' own sons as well as mutely appeal for mercy when two other sons were led away. Titus seeks manically to dispel his horror at his own body and its awesome destructive power. The shock waves sweep over him like some unstoppable haemorrhage:

> My grief was at the height before thou cam'st
> And now like Nilus it disdaineth bounds. (3.1.70–1)

Later Titus uses his own tongue to speak for Lavinia, as a desperate and weird effort is made to discourse with her. All three men shed tears, too, and she can respond to this. Tears are a simple human communication, and though the men express only love and pity, Lavinia evolves a more varied code. Titus begins to read it:

> Look Marcus! ah, son Lucius, look on her!
> When I did name the brothers, then fresh tears
> Stood on her cheeks, as doth the honey-dew
> Upon a gath'red lily almost withered. (3.1.110–13)

It is, as Titus later says, a sign-system of tears, 'a sympathy of woe', in which the actor, denied his chief means of communication, hand-gesture and speech, contrives wordless eloquence of body. We watch the speechless body with special intentness.

Although the existential immediacy of Lavinia's 'lively body' awakes an instinctive response in the onlooker in these episodes, it is not only Lavinia's body which is significant here. In their physical reactions the men describe their own physical states; lamenting their loss of pleasure at Lavinia's beauty and musical voice, they pity themselves, their own cheeks stained by bitter tears. At the very end of the play Lucius bends to kiss the 'pale cold lips' (5.3.153) of dead Titus, drawing his uncle with him

> To shed obsequious tears upon his trunk. (5.3.152)

Lucius calls his son to view Titus' body, reviving it in memory as alive:

> Many a time he danc'd thee on his knee,
> Sung thee asleep, his loving breast thy pillow (5.3.162–3)

Attention is focused on the strangely still body of Titus, for so long the source of powerful energy and passionate speech and irrational action; the strangely tender domestic idea of Titus conjured up is not prepared for by anything in the play, yet seems no mere pious fiction fabricated for a child. This focus on the intense stillness of the dead body of Titus, and effort to restore to him human affections and domestic piety, comes after the savage and frantic carnage of the banquet scene. At the Swan performance Lavinia was killed by one quick twist of her neck accompanied by a sharp snapping sound. It was shocking, but the spectacle of her motionless body was compelling: finally it is free of agony, mercifully still. Precisely by denying Lavinia or Titus release, whether physical or mental, Shakespeare ensures that there is no full tragic crisis until the very end of the play, that the trajectory of their agony keeps its upward path relentlessly; although producers of the play in modern times have not risen to this challenge, considering such a trajectory unsustainable by actors and unendurable by spectators. The physical demands are held to be too great.

In the discussion that follows I shall be concerned, in the first section, with Shakespeare's exploration of the ambivalences of the body, read or misread either as living or dead and, if dead, as monument or corpse, sacred or abhorrent; then, in the second section, I shall discuss his presentation of the body in transformation and transfiguration, recalling more directly the Pygmalion myth which contains the fundamental antinomies; but I begin with a play in which both issues are equally important, *Romeo and Juliet*.

In *Romeo and Juliet* at the beginning of the play the audience only hear talk of Romeo's beloved: she is a name, Rosaline, a subject of idealising poetry. In contrast, the first young woman the audience actually see in the flesh appears directly when her name, Juliet, is spoken. She is then made the subject of the Nurse's comic story, told in her presence, which vividly recounts details of her infancy – of how she was weaned from the breast at the age of three, when she 'could have run and waddled all about' (1.3.37), of how she fell and got a bump on her brow as big as a young cockerel's stone. The next time she is on stage she is dancing with others at the Capulet feast. Romeo sees her for the first time, falls for her, and transforms her into a metaphysical conceit:

> It seems she hangs upon the cheek of night
> As a rich jewel in an Ethiop's ear. (1.5.44–5)

Here the quick, warm, dancing girl before his eyes is transformed into carved, anonymous stillness, precious stone. The same ambivalence plays upon their first kiss at the feast. The kiss is a stage image, a love-icon; at the same time it is a spontaneous physical event, an act in time. Its existential freshness transforms verbal quibbles on 'hands' and 'lips' and 'saints'. Yet Shakespeare has provided the audience in advance with a knowledge of Juliet not as a perfect erotic image but as a young girl at home with other women, amid talk of babies, toddlers, mild bawdy, and Susan (Susan and she 'were of an age') who died in childhood.

As the play's narrative develops, Shakespeare marks its progress with a series of visible images of Juliet, love-icons from poetry transferred to the stage and embodied; but they are rendered ambivalent in the process. Juliet appears at her window overlooking the dark orchard, after the feast, and Romeo seeing her from below turns Juliet into a Petrarchan conceit 'It is the east and Juliet is the sun!' (2.2.3) Yet Juliet is anxiously preoccupied at this very moment with what to do next in the real city of Verona where names cannot be wished away. In 4.3 the figure of Juliet being prepared as a bride poignantly evokes an image of ideal fulfilment, but the occasion (marriage to Paris) is in bitter contrast to the scene. There are two details, however, which constitute a cinematic 'flash-forward': the bridal figure has by her a vial of potion and a dagger. Juliet's speech draws the audience's attention to the uncertainty of the potion's effect. 'What if it be a poison' (4.3.24), she pointedly asks. 'I fear it is' (4.3.28), she says. The doubt is focused on the curtained bed which remains in view after Juliet drinks the potion and falls. Shakespeare keeps the audience in suspense during the ensuing scenes: the Nurse discovers Juliet: 'What, dress'd, and in your clothes, and down again?' (4.5.12). Her father examines the body:

> Out alas, she's cold,
> Her blood is settled, and her joints are stiff.   (4.5.25–6)

When Romeo enters the tomb in the final scene he inspects her still body with intense attention; he has been told she is dead:

> beauty's ensign yet
> Is crimson in thy lips and in thy cheeks,
> And death's pale flag is not advanced there.   (5.3.94–6)

Then Romeo recognises another body lying nearby:

> Tybalt, liest thou there in thy bloody sheet?   (5.3.97)

A trick of the mind chooses 'sheet' not 'shroud', associating the bodies with sleep; at the same time the putrefying corpse of Tybalt gruesomely asserts itself, and perhaps deflects attention from those signs in Juliet which show her to be indeed mortal, that is, alive, though suspended so close to death. The state is one to which Shakespeare returns, evidently fascinated by its strangeness and mystery, as well as by its effects on onlookers. Instinctive taboos surround the body at the point of death. Romeo does not live to learn that he is deceived by Juliet's body. Even the lover steeped in passionate physical adoration cannot know his beloved's body well enough. Its transformations mystify and deceive even him.[5]

Golding's translation of the Pygmalion story from Ovid's *Metamorphoses*, Book 10 tells how an artist, Pygmalion, uses his imagination and 'wondrous' art to make a life-size sculpture of a young woman out of ivory. Golding's vocabulary insists on the ambiguity of the life-like work of art. Its eyes are closed, as if asleep or dead, a 'counterfeited corpse', yet it is an artefact so life-like that the sculptor himself cannot resist touching it – imagining it to be flesh – or kissing it – imagining his kisses are returned, even though his senses still tell him that it remains ivory. Then, a greater wonder: Venus herself intervenes, and as Pygmalion kisses the statue, this time the ivory waxes soft, and 'He felt it very flesh indeed'.

At the close of *Romeo and Juliet* the Pygmalion motif is handled with a deceptiveness foreshadowing Shakespeare's most paradoxical late manner. When Romeo breaks into the tomb to gaze on the body of Juliet, he is struck by the contrast of her unsullied beauty to the bloody corpse of Tybalt, lying nearby. Fleshly beauty as perfect as sculpture lies beside gruesome putrefaction. Right up to the last moment, poignantly, Juliet's sheer life-like beauty fills him with wonder: 'Ah, dear Juliet, / Why art thou yet so fair?' He will not pause to consider his own question, being convinced that Juliet is dead – and the audience themselves, though they know more than he does, cannot be sure whether she is unconscious or actually dead.

As it will turn out, Juliet's sculptural stillness is an illusion (she is about to wake up), and it is only in Romeo's dying speech that her physical beauty is miraculously immune to mortal decay. Like Pygmalion kissing his statue, Romeo kisses Juliet, but here in order to join her in death. Like Pygmalion's statue too, but again ironically, Juliet does wake up directly after the kiss – but by pure coincidence, not because of it. She finds Romeo dead (poignantly, she finds his lips still warm). She stabs herself, exulting in the thought of how swiftly Romeo's hardened steel will rust in her heart:

> O happy dagger,
> This is thy sheath (*stabs herself*); there rust, and let me die.
>
> (5.3.169–70)

By one final paradoxical reversal, Juliet restores the Pygmalion myth while inverting it, dying 'with a restorative'.

The body always carries death within it, and in Shakespeare, where the body's pulse is so present to the dramatist's imagination, the possibility of its arrest must be so too. There is a certain feeling of awe associated with stillness, with inert and silent figures, in Shakespeare. It is partly that they aspire towards the ideal, the divine, beyond life. At the same time there is often a feeling of distaste, of recoil, since these still figures are associated with, insist on, our own death. Romeo's instinctive reaction against the corpse of Tybalt, or Falstaff's much stronger instinctive reaction against the corpse of Blunt, finds an answer in every spectator.

AMBIVALENT READINGS OF THE BODY IN SHAKESPEARE

Shakespeare locates key questions of interpretation in the image of the human body the audience see on stage. Certain characters' sheer physique is so extraordinary that their very bodies make a continuous implicit contribution on their own account, as powerful cultural signs, to the dramatic narrative: the deformed Richard Crookback, the corpulent Falstaff, the black Othello, provoke deep-seated irrational responses, activated and reinforced verbally: his visible body is a dominant fact of its owner's life, however much his other qualities promise choice or release. A silent visual code of this kind, even when deep ingrained, as with moral allegory's personifications, will be positively announced to an audience to ensure its recognition, to distinguish the body as sign in this new sign-system. Shakespeare is extremely conscious of this rule, and makes good farcical effect from burlesque of it in, for instance, *Richard III* 3.7, when Richard makes a seemingly unwilling appearance before the citizens of London. He appears aloft, between two bishops, apparently reading a prayer-book, as if impromptu, interrupted during his devotions; yet the stage image forms a clear emblem, a statue-group as if carved on some cathedral screen or facade, a stereotyped public ceremony. The audience, prepared with advance knowledge of Richard's cynical scheme, read the scene as deception, but the citizen audience in the play have no way of verifying their doubt, while Richard has his henchman impose a visual code by which they are required to read it:

> MAYOR See where his Grace stands, 'tween two clergymen!
> BUCKINGHAM Two props of virtue for a Christian prince,
> To stay him from the fall of vanity;
> And see, a book of prayer in his hand –
> True ornaments to know a holy man.   (3.7.94–8)

The attitude of prayer is found both in real life and in sculpture; in both cases the human body's attitude represents an experience inaccessibly inward, the body partly disembodied, in transformation. In John Webster's *The Duchess of Malfi* (1614), the Duchess, played by a boy-actor who presumably wore face-paint, contrasts herself to her effigy:

> What is't distracts you? This is flesh, and blood, sir,
> 'Tis not the figure cut in alabaster
> Kneels at my husband's tomb. Awake, awake, man
>   (1.2.369–71)

Shakespeare makes diverse dramatic effects from his knowledge that images of the body associated with veneration impose authority, often with superstitious awe: Hamlet himself for all his sharp-eyed scepticism is deceived in Act 3, Scene 3 by the spectacle of Claudius in the attitude of prayer. Only later does the audience learn that Claudius was not at that moment able to pray, the image of piety false. Like Shakespeare, Webster exploits the fact that sculptors at the time had to strive for life-like, recognisable tomb effigies. In Elizabethan England tomb effigies, and triumphal sculpture, were polychrome.

Webster's Duchess appeals to a concept of being that is

existential, but her assertion that she is warm and soft and breathing gains poignancy from her allusion to stone sculpture figures. In this play Webster develops an elaborate set of conceits on the theme of living figures resembling effigies and effigies mistaken for living figures. Webster thus shows a creative responsiveness to his contemporary, Shakespeare, in the use of this dramatic technique, though he has the heavier touch in handling it. Indeed what is remarkable about Shakespeare is that even his earliest explorations of this subject are so full of subtlety as well as power: a pressure of invention and intelligence is brought to bear upon it.

In battle against the French in 1 *Henry VI* (4.7), the English hero Talbot, dying, is given the dead body of his son, killed in action when they had become separated. Talbot speaks to the dead body, asks it to speak to him once more, intently gazing at his son's face:

> Poor boy, he smiles, methinks, as who should say,
> Had Death been French, then Death had died today.
>
> (4.7.27–8)

He takes his son in his arms and dies embracing him. The scene rests a moment, then the French enter. The Bastard advocates hewing the bodies in pieces, though he is restrained. The English knight Lucy is announced to a parley, enters and asks after Talbot, whose many noble titles he sonorously lists, without seeing the bodies. Joan la Pucelle interrupts:

> Stinking and fly-blown lies here at our feet.   (4.7.75–6)

The audience are presented with opposing significations of the father-and-son group. The context of family piety, simple courage and stoic acceptance of death endows the bodies with transforming meaning: the sweating, rugged Talbots become a monumental icon, a tomb-sculpture. But Pucelle enters to insist that from another perspective a corpse is a corpse, and in this case abhorrently so. The episode involves a transition from battle to truce, from unleashed instincts to ceremonious formalities, and has an uneasy and ambivalent quality. The death of Talbot which the audience witness establishes an atmosphere of gravity; but when the French enter from battle they inevitably bring with them an abrasive temper. They harshly interrupt the solemn scene. Joan, however, deliberately speaks to desecrate the body, offending deep taboos. Her insulting speech may be taken as evidence of her wickedness and of general French perfidy, yet from another point of view Joan, a shepherd's daughter, is here representative of the common people, seeing in the nobility's chivalric code an instrument of ideology which mockery can demystify. The Talbots seem at first a stage image evocative of generalised pity transcending national barriers, appealing to a common Christian culture. On the other hand the pressure of rival claims, French and English (and perhaps, for an audience around 1590, implicitly Catholic and Protestant), makes us see that the English, represented by Lucy, will seek to appropriate it to their propaganda in this moment of crisis for them. The French deny its iconic status, and their insistence on the mere carnality of the Talbot figures is no less an ideologically interested stance – whether seen in terms of their nationalist cause or of Joan's independent radicalism.

The situation of the erect figure gazing at the silent, inert body occurs in extraordinarily various contexts in Shakespeare. In *2 Henry IV*, Act 4, Scene 5, the mortally sick King lies asleep in bed with his son Prince Hal gazing at him. Prince Hal begins to speak a soliloquy (almost a sermon) prompted by the crown lying on the pillow, then his attention shifts to the head next to it. He suddenly thinks that the head seems unnaturally still, that the King has slept his last perturbed sleep:

> By his gates of breath
> There lies a downy feather which stirs not   (4.5.31–2)

Hal takes up the crown and performs a self-coronation:

> Lo where it sits,
> (*Putting it on his head*)
> Which God shall guard   (4.5.43–4)

The impression that this is a consciously staged ceremony (a private performance, as it were) is reinforced when he exits on a sententious rhyme – as if he were a player closing a scene. The body of the King lies alone on the stage a moment.

What happens next proves an embarrassment for Hal: the King's body stirs, he wakes, his first action is to reach for his crown.

> Where is the crown? Who took it from my pillow?   (4.5.57)

Shakespeare gives Hal's efforts at piety a rough ride, but an audience will savour its ironic fitness. Piety is, after all, not a commodity to be expected in the court of Hal's father: King Henry IV believes himself to have, in a sense, stolen the crown; his reign has been one long struggle to stop others stealing it from him, and now, just when the family seems to be acquiring the necessary sacredness, someone steals the crown from him. The audience will also recognise an irony the King cannot savour: what could be a more perfect confirmation to the King that his son and heir is a chip off the old block, than for Hal to rob him? The episode dares to activate taboos surrounding the body at the point of death, or just dead, precisely to give renewed vigour to the play's debate about sceptical, de-sacralising ideas – remembering that among the chief proponents of such views must be numbered not only Falstaff but the King himself. The audience observes Hal behaving in a way that would be culturally unforgivable from a public point of view but which is humanly understandable in private – and then there is the embarrassment that he gets caught – and having been exposed theatrically to the audience, he then becomes really exposed within the play. The episode is clearly designed to provoke questions: is the dying figure to be sympathised with, is Hal desecrating anything, is Hal to be sympathised with?

Earlier in *1 Henry IV* there is a short episode providing anticipation of this scene, in a low-comic key. Falstaff is discovered asleep behind the arras, 'and snorting like a horse', and Hal goes through his pockets – impossible to avoid a hint of the unsavoury in his action. Instead of gold all he finds is tavern reckonings. What is interesting is that the sleeping figure of Falstaff, thus subjected to search and ridicule, appears (as does the King in the later scene) in a strangely half-pitiful light:

otherwise so agile and witty an opponent, here he is transformed by sleep into a kind of innocence, surprisingly vulnerable. All the same, pity is misplaced – when he wakes up he is quite able to take care of himself, ready to exploit any situation to his own advantage, just like Hal's real father.

A third sequence, from the end of Part 1, shows Shakespeare intricately exploiting the moment of death to win various effects, each in its particular way disconcerting. The battle of Shrewsbury is raging. Two armed opponents confront one another. One says

> Know then, my name is Douglas,
> And I do haunt thee in the battle thus
> Because some tell me that thou art a king.　　(5.3.3–5)

His opponent confirms that he is indeed King Henry IV: 'They tell thee true.' They fight, the King is slain. Now Hotspur enters to see this chivalric tableau as Douglas proudly points to the dead body of the King. Hotspur bends to look and recognises the corpse as Blunt, not the King. Now the staged tableau of victory must be re-read according to Hotspur's matter-of-fact deflating explanation: 'The king hath many marching in his coats'.

They go, and the corpse of Blunt is left alone on stage.

A moment's pause ensues, then Falstaff wanders on, sees the corpse, and correctly identifies Blunt. 'I like not such grinning honour as Sir Walter hath. Give me life, which if I can save, so; if not, honour comes unlook'd for, and there's an end' (5.3.58–61). To Falstaff the corpse is simply a reminder of his own vulnerability: as carnival king he fears for his belly, lest it yield Percy a Gargantuan meal, carbonadoed. To be able to jest in such a fearful moment might seem an attractive quality, but Blunt's was a brave self-sacrifice, and Falstaff's mockery of the dead body is an offence: as Don Armado might say, not generous, not gentle, not humble.

Shakespeare reinforces the issue in the climactic episode of the battle, the single combat of Hal and Hotspur, a few moments later (5.4.59 ff.). While it is being fought Falstaff enters but is suddenly attacked by Douglas. He falls, and Douglas goes. An instant later Hotspur also falls, slain by Hal (a stage direction makes it clear that these two actions occur close together, with no words spoken: Shakespeare insists on the symmetry of the stage action). This leaves Hal standing alone above the bodies of Hotspur and Falstaff. Hal himself evidently sees the group in quasi-sculptural terms, with the emblematic subtitle 'Honour triumphs over Vice and Rebellion'. He emphasises the formality of the scene by making valedictory speeches to 'brave Percy' and to Falstaff, his 'old acquaintance', and resolves to have Falstaff's corpse 'embowelled'. Hal makes his exit on another rhyming couplet.

Again the stage is left clear except for bodies. Then, one of the two bodies stirs, gets up, and enunciates with orotund distaste the word 'embowelled'.

An audience may be happily surprised that Falstaff is thus raised from the dead, but such warm feelings will be short-lived. Falstaff, deciding to steal Hal's prize by claiming it was he who slew Hotspur, stabs the corpse and heaves it onto his back. Carnival bears off the desecrated corpse of Honour. The grim transformation is the last of a series that makes an audience *repeatedly* revise their sense of what is happening, even at the most basic level of whether a body is alive or dead. Shakespeare deceives the audience as a means to demonstrate the radical scepticism which informs his presentation of persons and events; the grotesque effects derived from breaking of taboos surrounding death show how determined is the offensive scepticism of these *Henry IV* plays. The dead body's meaning is shown to depend not on its sacredness but on variable context and interpretation. One may recall the cynical Casca's success in persuading Julius Caesar that his wife's disturbing dream of a statue spouting blood was not a bad omen at all, indeed quite the contrary:

> This dream is all amiss interpreted,
> It was a vision fair and fortunate.
> Your statue spouting blood in many pipes,
> In which so many smiling Romans bath'd,
> Signifies that from you great Rome shall suck
> Reviving blood.   (*Julius Caesar* 2.2.83–8)

In *Cymbeline* there are three major episodes (2.2, 4.2, 5.4) focused on an unconscious body: in the first two episodes the body is Imogen, in the third the sleeping figure is Posthumus. These three episodes are spaced at significant points to mark phases of the play's action. As I have already shown in chapter 2, there are obvious parallels between the episodes, in stage imagery and action, but what is important for the present discussion is the variety of puzzles confronting the spectator who tries to read the significance of the bodies.

The first of these scenes is of Imogen's bedchamber, Act 2, Scene 2. Imogen lies on the bed and has a bracelet on her arm. There is a table with a candle and a book on it. She dismisses her maid and draws attention to a book, but does not identify it.

She falls asleep. The scene rests a moment. Then Iachimo rises erect from the trunk.

He kisses her without waking her, then describes her. As I have already noted in chapter 2, at first his emphasis is on her erotic sensuousness, but this gives way to religious, devotional awe, and Iachimo resolves to give up his plan of seduction or rape, merely writing in a book a description of her body and the bedchamber. When in a later scene we hear Iachimo describe the bedchamber he asserts that it was decorated with pagan erotic scenes recalling Ovid and Plutarch – and North's Plutarch – of Cleopatra meeting 'her Roman' at Cydnus.

Here Shakespeare is clearly intent on keeping an audience in suspense by stressing the unstable variety of possible interpretations of the female body in literature and art both sacred and profane, in Biblical, classical Roman, medieval Catholic, and Renaissance cultural terms and, more directly, in Shakespeare's own previous plays and poems.

Turning now to Act 4, Scene 2 of *Cymbeline*, the audience is witness to a sequence of events combining ritual movement with physical stage-images of sacrifice and horror. First a severed head is brought in. A few moments later comes the stage direction '*Enter* ARVIRAGUS *with* IMOGEN (*as*) *dead, bearing her in his arms*', and soon thereafter the bloody, headless corpse of Cloten, dressed as Posthumus, laid beside his intended victim Imogen: Arviragus says she is dead. Having no evidence to the contrary, and the staged funeral rite to confirm it, an audience must believe Imogen to be dead. The figures might be seen as lovers, lying side by side as in the tomb in *Romeo and Juliet*; as it turns out Imogen is, like Juliet, only drugged by a potion which gives the illusion of death and the man is only a simulacrum of Imogen's husband, his symbolic double, Cloten.

The scene comes to rest in stillness: the mourners depart, leaving the two bodies lying. Then one of them, Imogen's, stirs and sits up.

When Imogen begins to speak the audience must make a complex re-reading of what they have seen: Imogen is evidently still dreaming – that she is still on her journey to Wales. While the audience watched an episode which seemed (since it occurred while she lay in their view, unconscious) to represent her death-journey in conventional symbolic terms as a kind of dream, Imogen was actually dreaming of the real journey just completed. Only when she wakes up does she see the stage situation with which the audience is already familiar. To Imogen lying next to it, this headless corpse in Posthumus' clothes must seem the realisation of her deepest nightmare, an atrocity. She falls unconscious again, provoking the question of whether this time her fate is the same as Juliet's, death.

The third scene in this sequence is Act 5, Scene 4. While Posthumus sleeps his presumed last night on earth, a procession of apparitions, preceded by music, make their entrance and circle round him as he lies sleeping. This choreography recalls that of the two earlier scenes, with pointed variations: in the bedchamber scene only Iachimo surveyed the sleeper, Imogen; in the cave-scene the surrogate father and two brothers perform a rite about the body of Imogen; here in the Roman prison the ghosts of both parents and two brothers, '*with wounds as they died in the wars*', make their appeal to Jupiter himself. Jupiter descends, throwing a thunderbolt and leaving a book on the sleeping Posthumus' breast.

The ghosts depart, leaving the single sleeping figure of Posthumus. The scene rests a moment. Then Posthumus wakes up, and finds the book.

The horrors of the cave-scene have been purged, so that it is the parallel to the first scene involving the sleeping Imogen which is apparent: she woke to find that the bracelet Posthumus gave her – the 'manacle of love' – had mysteriously disappeared; here Posthumus wakes to find a divine book miraculously lying on his breast. A messenger then enters with the command that his Roman prisoner's manacles be struck off! This is a witty, implicit allusion to that other manacle – Imogen's – which symbolises the Christian ideal of love, whose service is perfect freedom.

Shakespeare emphasises the very diverse possible states which may be represented by the inert and silent human body: from the most empty state of all – Cloten without a head and dressed as Posthumus – to the state of grace in which Posthumus himself experiences a divine vision. Imogen lying in the cave, still as death, turns out to be having a vivid and distressing dream. Imogen earlier, in her bedchamber, may in her dream be struggling with the temptation as well as the menace of Iachimo, whereas her silent and motionless, outward and visible, sleeping beauty converts him to wonder, as a sign of purity and virtue. It is characteristic of the deceitful manner of the play that Iachimo can so readily re-describe, reinterpret, the body of the sleeping Imogen in terms not of purity, which bespeaks mysterious, spiritual invulnerability, but of sensuous eroticism, the human body at its most physically sensitive – to pain as well as pleasure.

THE PYGMALION MOTIF

Rome, that city of statues, yields in *Coriolanus* a hero modelling himself on the gigantic proportions and attitudes of Rome's sculpted gods, her muscular idols. Rome glories in physical, bodily strength, skill and endurance, the nude male body aptly figured in the hardness of marble and bronze. The play opens with a confrontation between the many, plebeian, hungry, riotous, and the one, Menenius, patrician, big-bellied, authoritarian. Behind the corpulent figure of Menenius appears the image of lonely anger, the warrior–patrician Caius Martius (in Hobbes's formulation, force is shown behind fraud as the twin weapons of the class war). With one confronting the many Shakespeare presents an iconographic group which will be repeated with great variation of verbal and visual significance in the action to follow. Here it need only be noticed how the ironic implication of dismemberment, dynamically acted as Caius Martius scatters the mob in that first scene, proliferates in the play's language, insistently naming parts of the body rhetorically severed: the breast, the forehead, the razored chin, the bristled lips, the wounded shoulder, the head, knee, hand, foot.

When Cominius at the battle before Corioli learns that Caius Martius and his men are on the brink of a defeat, the ominous news seems confirmed by the appearance of a solitary figure, anonymous because so covered in blood. Even Cominius can only slowly recognise this image of violent death – or birth – as Caius Martius. Later Cominius recalls him in action: an automaton, a mechanical figure or statue:

> from face to foot
> He was a thing of blood, whose every motion
> Was timed with dying cries   (2.2.108–10)

Much later, Aufidius, declaring his love and embracing Coriolanus, thinks of his body as sculpted from material of adamantine hardness: it is a body, he declares, against which

> My grainèd ash an hundred times hath broke
> And scarr'd the moon with splinters.   (4.5.108–9)

Menenius likens Coriolanus sitting before Rome to a statue:

> I tell you, he does sit in gold, his eye
> Red as 'twould burn Rome.   (5.1.63–4)

Coriolanus seems sculpted from stone, so hard is his attitude:

> He sits in his state, as a thing made for Alexander.
>   (5.4.21–2)

The extraordinary body of Coriolanus is presented from various aspects: his own horror of being looked at is weirdly related to his mother's ruthless exposure of him when he was still a youth to the risks of hand-to-hand combat. For her the child's body was a surface to be inscribed with 'honour' spelt in wounds; once the text was long enough it would silently plead his case for the consulship. Shakespeare deliberately stages the ritual in which Coriolanus must stand in isolation, statue-like in the market place, wearing the ritual gown of humility, to show his wounds to the people and tell them his deeds (see 2.3.5–7).

This emphasis on the vulnerable, and the wounding, nature of the hero's body is made after a sustained visual exhibition of that body in action, entering alone the mortal gates of Corioli to emerge covered in blood, new-born, and new-baptised – but his mother's curious term for him as an infant, 'man-child', is significant here. She exults in calculating that after Corioli his body bears twenty-seven wounds. Since every gash, as he notes, is an enemy's grave, the body is a living monument to the dead, and to the mother's persistent power to shape him: 'Thou art my warrior,' she tells him, 'I holp to frame thee.'

Coriolanus, banished from Rome and bound to his rival Aufidius, seems finally free from his mother's power: indeed he is reported as saying he is 'a kind of nothing, titleless', until he forges a new name in the fire of burning Rome, his mother's city. Yet when his mother finally approaches he at once admits: 'I melt, and am not / Of stronger earth than others.' It is the motionless, kneeling, supplicating statue-group of wife, mother, and child, which brings this statue back to life, Pygmalion-like, but with the ironic effect of ensuring his death. The hard resolution of Coriolanus begins to soften and grow warm, in a tense moment of silent transformation, a bitter reworking of the Pygmalion theme. The mother having moulded the child into a thing whose motions shall be timed with dying cries, now determines that he must adopt a final attitude, fit for chronicle and monument. He is to soften only so that he may undergo final transformation through certain death. Coriolanus is quick enough to see that certainty, Roman enough not to flinch from it.

The strange paradox – its logic of sympathetic magic – that flesh making itself stony can turn stone into flesh, which Shakespeare presents in visual metaphoric terms in *Coriolanus*, may be glimpsed running through *The Winter's Tale*, associated

with other motifs already touched on.⁶ When, in the first court
scene, Leontes describes the attitude of Hermione and Polixenes
as they exit arm-in-arm, his manifestly disturbed state must
make an audience question his interpretation; by the time
Leontes puts Hermione on trial, any doubt of her innocence has
been erased in the audience. She stands motionless as an image
of slandered innocence. She appeals to the gods, they being
spectators whose sight is not diseased. Hermione sees herself as
a character in an old and obvious morality play, where the
characters and plot have emblematic clarity. Innocence aided
by Patience is certain to defeat False Accusation:

> if pow'rs divine
> Behold our human actions (as they do),
> I doubt not then but innocence shall make
> False accusation blush, and tyranny
> Tremble at patience   (3.2.28–32)

But Shakespeare is only just beginning to play tricks on the
play's spectators. Hermione falls unconscious at the news that
her son Mamillius is dead. Her body is carried out and a few
moments later news is brought that she is dead. When, at the
end of the play, Leontes, after sixteen years' grief and
repentance, is brought by Paulina to the chapel to see the statue
of Hermione, he will (like the audience) wonder at the sculptor's
art in counterfeiting: 'warm life, as now it coldly stands' – 'does
not the stone rebuke me/ For being more stone than it?' – 'The
fixure of her eye has motion in't' – 'Still methinks / There is an
air comes from her. What fine chisel / Could ever yet cut
breath?' – 'The ruddiness upon her lip is wet.' The transformation of the 'marble breasted tyrant' Leontes is mirrored in
the Galatea-like transformation of Hermione.

In *Antony and Cleopatra* the stagecraft offers similarities to
episodes just examined in *The Winter's Tale*, from the first scene,
where on-stage observers seek to influence the audience's
interpretation of a couple, Antony and Cleopatra, a couple said
to be (like Polixenes and Hermione) grossly infatuated:

> The triple pillar of the world transform'd
> Into a strumpet's fool.   (1.1.12–13)

From a Roman point of view it is accounted an image of a strumpet fawned on by a dotard, a degrading metamorphosis; in Antony's view it shows divinities, Venus and Mars. Cleopatra's moody behaviour at once reminds us that no single, fixed attitude can depict the relationship of Mars to Venus, since it is in essence mobile, unstable. A spectator cannot easily choose among these opposed interpretations.

I would draw attention to two features here: verbal descriptions of characters seen in terms of sculptural attitudes and monumental effect (in view of the deceptive and self-deceptive nature of the characters who do the describing, as well as of those who are so described, these accounts are not to be simply credited) and, secondly, the staging of figures explicitly or implicitly in sculptural terms. Shakespeare himself is very ready also to deceive the audience here, as if insisting on the complex relationship of honesty to treachery which marks all relations between people in the play.

When in due course Antony has left Egypt for Rome, Cleopatra becomes, paradoxically, constant: and she imagines him in heroic attitudes of monumental bronze or marble:

> Stands he or sits he?
> Or does he walk? Or is he on his horse?
> ...
> The demi-Atlas of this earth, the arm
> And burgonet of men. (1.5.20–1, 24–5)

It is not in fact a Roman view, for Caesar sees the physical, debased, animal Antony, one notoriously prone to changeability and diversions, to

> tumble on the bed of Ptolemy,
> To give a kingdom for a mirth, to sit
> And keep the turn of tippling with a slave,
> To reel the streets at noon, and stand the buffet
> With knaves that smell of sweat. (1.4.17–21)

The description is memorable, and is later to be twinned with a like one of Cleopatra: yet that, though reported by a Roman, Enobarbus, interprets the animal spirit delightedly:

> I saw her once
> Hop forty paces through the public street,
> And, having lost her breath, she spoke, and panted
>
> (2.2.238–40)

Enobarbus is intoxicated again as he recalls from memory his impressions of the meeting between Antony and Cleopatra at Cydnus. The monumental pose of Antony, enthroned in the market place, contrasts to that of Cleopatra, in which motion and rhythm lend fluidity to the visual effect: she lies in a Venus pose, a polychrome sculpture, a tapestry, a painting by Rubens,

> In her pavilion – cloth of gold, of tissue –
> O'erpicturing that Venus where we see
> The fancy outwork nature   (2.2.209–11)

yet these static images quicken, brought to life by the sensuous sound of flutes, the smell of perfume: the silken ropes swell at her women's touch. The effect 'o'erpictures', assaulting the other senses as painting and sculpture cannot. Enobarbus contrasts Octavia, resembling an uncoloured classical statue, 'of a holy, cold, and still conversation'.

Antony, receiving news of Cleopatra's death, (which the audience know to be false), prepares to fall on his sword: a Roman death. He utters final words echoing Romeo, and his last gesture is to Eros, his servant, who has just committed suicide:

> Come then, and Eros,
> Thy master dies thy scholar. To do thus
> I learned of thee. (*He falls on his sword*)   (4.14.101–3)

Antony falls. He lies still. Then – he speaks.

Incredibly, he has botched the suicide: 'How, not dead? Not dead?' When he is brought before Cleopatra's monument there is further absurdity, and physically agonising clumsiness. She is too scared to come down to him, and the women haul him up. Juliet had watched Romeo descend from her window after their wedding night and said

> Methinks I see thee now, thou art so low,
> As one dead in the bottom of a tomb.   (3.5.55–6)

Here it is exactly the reverse: Antony has to be hauled up to die, and he dies first.

Then Cleopatra falls. Iras confirms that this is the end: 'She's dead too, our sovereign' (4.15.72). And then Cleopatra revives, more like Rosalind than Juliet or Desdemona.

It is Shakespeare's claim for his own art, theatre, as an art of commemoration, like poetry, and visual memorial, like sculpture, that emerges in the conceitful allusions to 'playing', to 'extemporal' staging by the 'quick comedians' (quick because witty but also because alive). Shakespeare has already shown his audience Cleopatra's greatness 'boyed', and some of the postures she adopts in the play do suggest a whore. These allusive ironies serve to focus on the extraordinary doubleness of the final image. Cleopatra designs and arranges a tomb monument for herself, crowned and robed, her women lying at her feet. The circumstances of Antony's suicide emphasise pain, blood, humiliating disorder: Antony's sword-wound does not spare him physical agony, and the pain, as much as the absurdity, is stressed as he is ineptly hauled up. By contrast Cleopatra deliberately assumes an attitude of sculptural stillness while still breathing, and the moment of her transformation to death is imperceptible, even though she is the focus of concentrated attention directly before the spectators' eyes. Her final evocation of Antony had also sought to outgo sculpture, evoking him in a fluid sequence of 'dissolves', of protean transfigurations – only these appeal to all the senses, metamorphosing the bronze or marble attitudes of the Herculean hero.

Viewing Cleopatra dead, Caesar (after carefully making his police inspector's enquiries) commends the statue/sleeper as still seductively beautiful:

> she looks like sleep,
> As she would catch another Antony
> In her strong toil of grace. (5.2.340–2)

At the same time the forensic instincts of the Roman officers draw equal attention to Cleopatra's body as merely another dead body, a corpse betraying by minute signs the means of death: 'I do not see them bleed ...' – 'If they had swallowed poison 'twould appear/ By external swelling ...' – 'Here on her breast /There is a vent of blood ...' – 'This is an aspic's trail'.

Cleopatra like Juliet insists on the fierce processes of bodily decay after death:

> Rather on Nilus' mud
> Lay me stark nak'd and let the water-flies
> Blow me into abhorring!   (5.2.57–9)

Acceptance of bodily decomposition is inseparable from the frank delight in bodily ecstasy; yet through bodily ecstasy is the way to a true spiritual revelation. Or, in Donne's words,

> Love's mysteries in soules doe grow,
> But yet the body is his booke.   ('The Exstasie', 71–2)

The Pygmalion myth, so vividly narrated in Golding's Elizabethan English version of 1567, has potentialities which Shakespeare repeatedly explored: the metamorphosis of the sculpted figure into the living body suggested in turn the metamorphosis of life into sculpture, and the strange, ambiguous states of suspense between the two.

CHAPTER 4

Shakespeare's 'road of excess': 'Titus Andronicus', 'The Taming of the Shrew', 'King Lear'

Titus Andronicus and *The Taming of the Shrew* stand out among Shakespeare's early plays for their capacity to shock: both are intent on presenting the persecution of a deviant hero–victim, both press this persecution to extremes, and both concentrate on images of the hunt and of the feast: yet they are seldom compared, each being considered in certain ways isolated and apart from Shakespeare's main line of development. I believe that they are in important ways interrelated. Though one is set in Padua, in the civilisation of the Renaissance in Italy, and the other in ancient Rome, I consider that *The Taming of the Shrew* and *Titus Andronicus* have deeper affinities with *King Lear*'s archaic Britain than with those intervening Shakespearean comedies and tragedies with Mediterranean settings. The two plays are both concerned with extremes but they also share a special harsh quality, and it is this harshness which sets them apart; it permeates the play-world, it is apparent throughout, in the cultural rules as much as in manners and personal relationships; and it is kin to the harshness which is the key element, the special mark of injustice, which creates the bleak vision of *King Lear*.

The first phase in each drama presents a very intricate social, urban context. The Padua of *The Taming of the Shrew* with its marriage market, and its pressure on the family unit (of Baptista and his daughters Kate and Bianca) is itself at a critical point of change. In *Titus Andronicus* the state of Rome is seen at a moment of transition to a new – as yet unchosen – ruler, a moment foregrounding the Roman state's structural praxis: involving Titus, as an unwilling candidate for emperor, then his

79

daughter, Lavinia, whom he transfers as a bride from her promised husband to the ominous Saturninus. He in turn drops Lavinia in favour of the Gothic queen, Tamora; first as a strategy to dishonour Titus, second as an arbitrary defiance of custom and release of lust.

The second stage features a withdrawal to what we could call wilderness. In *The Taming of the Shrew* this is the carnivalesque marriage journey, a chaotic and harsh exposure of the body to the elements, as Grumio tells: 'how her horse fell, and she under her horse;... in how miry a place, how she was bemoiled, how he left her with the horse upon her ... how she waded through the dirt to pluck him off me' (4.1.54 ff.). Then the denial to Kate of sleep and food and proper clothes and even reason. In *Titus Andronicus* the corresponding phase of wilderness features the hunt, which, by a horrible transformation, turns into a persecution of Titus' sons and daughter Lavinia. Atrocity is unleashed by perverting the ritual of the hunt. Human beings become the quarry. Lavinia is hounded. Her hunters taste her blood, raping her and abusing her. Titus progressively realises that it is Rome itself, inverted by this anarchy, that is a 'wilderness of tigers'.

In the third and final stage the hounded exiled victims, having suffered mental disorientation (Kate as well as Titus), use cunning travesties of an established customary rite – the meal – to effect exact, vivid revenge, and thereby expose the hollowness that has corrupted cultural authority – in short, they point to shifts in the foundations.

But there is a process of persecution which amplifies as it reduces its victims, in all these plays. Persecution educates. It confronts the victims with energies and elements in the world they have neglected. Yet the process, once begun, energised by violence, cannot be predicted or clearly discerned. Once begun there is no knowing where the road ends, and this unpredict-ability is a source of great dramatic tension in actual per-formance, but it is unpredictable in a much more important sense – it is incalculable how much is learned by the characters subjected to this persecution.

'The wife lapped in Morel's skin' is one version of a folk-tale which forms an important source for the Petruchio–Kate story in *The Taming of the Shrew*. In this version violence and harshness seem unrelieved and humour absent: the husband decides to tame his shrewish wife, so he kills his mare, flays the skin and rubs salt into it; then he beats his wife until her skin is raw and wraps her in the mare's skin so that the salt stings her wounds. She then becomes obedient. Some modern critics consider source material like this was a stubborn obstacle for Shakespeare as he struggled to present the emergence of a 'humanized heroine against the background of depersonalized farce unassimilated from the play's fabliau sources'.[1]

While it is right to notice that Shakespeare reduces the crudity of his sources, it is at least as important to notice that he does choose such material in the first place – material which is atavistic, concentrates conflicting ideas and emotions, takes issues to extremes. Shakespeare's changes to his sources tend in general to involve a transfer of emphasis away from crude simplicity of emotion and idea, and therefore the major changes he makes tend to be in character and motive; Shakespeare does not follow his sources if they exploit undiscriminating sensationalism in action and spectacle; but though he is sparing in the presentation of extreme violence, he ensures an impact when he does present it which only Marlowe can sometimes rival. Is it really plausible that Shakespeare did not realise what would be involved in working with material related to the story of the wife wrapped in Morel's skin, or in choosing from the most fearful Ovidian tales of violence for *Titus Andronicus*? It seems more probable that he welcomed such stories precisely because they go beyond all bounds.

In *The Taming of the Shrew*, despite Shakespeare's changes, the source story's intrinsic violence still comes through, though more indirectly, especially in the language; but it seems clear that the play's imaginative interest, and theatrical appeal, is related to its concern with violence. There is no contradiction in observing that Shakespeare's treatment of source material repeatedly involves enhancing ideals, enriching and ennobling story and characters by endowing them with magnanimity, courage and love; only that the same concern to expand and deepen the story leads also to intensification of the destructive element. Shakespeare as an artist is too imaginative and inventive to accept customary ways of telling stories; in his imagination of human experience his strength is that he is too intelligent – he refuses, for artistic and philosophical reasons, the virtue of moderation. Even farce – the mode of drama which most confines and restricts a dramatist's technique and his scope in representing human experience, and most strictly predetermines audience reaction – even farce, in Shakespeare's hands, is disconcertingly susceptible to his reshaping power.

The language of theatre addresses the senses of sight and hearing, so that it seems an extreme strain on the medium, an outrageous risk, to concentrate a play, as Shakespeare does in *King Lear*, on the King's invisible and soundless, inner, mental experience – dream, delusion, hallucination, madness. However paradoxical the endeavour, Shakespeare could at least rely on the fact that such inner experiences do involve images, although they are images in which the material world is transformed, reshaped, by guilt and terror, forbidden desire or disgust. What appears from an outer perspective to be awry, may be correct from within, although at worst the mind's condition may become truly chaotic and the ability to distinguish fantasy from actuality will be lost.

In *King Lear* Shakespeare presents directly on stage images of the most extreme atrocity, of the most feared personal disasters; he presents a formidable case for the fragility of the guiding ideals of his society and culture: the play releases a seemingly boundless process of desecration and atrocity. The story is set in a pagan historical period, overlaid with religious and cultural ideas of Shakespeare's own time, with an effect of dialectical tension. It does invoke (anachronistically) Christian ideas and images, but it withholds affirmation of them – and it places a fierce emphasis on the material facts of life, and the body, in relation to the mind. The on-stage act of gouging out Gloucester's eyes is an almost unbearable event which the audience is forced to watch, and it marks the play's concern with mocking cruelty. If one considers the design of the play as a whole, however, this will be seen to take its place in a whole series of episodes of cruelty and mockery.

From the beginning Edmund, Goneril, and Regan show themselves expert at deception, a skill which confirms them in their cynical materialism. They strive to desacralise the whole hierarchy, founded on its paternal and marital system, by their sexually profligate behaviour and scorn for basic human values. Meanwhile Edmund exploits the sisters' sexuality as a version of power understood in Machiavellian terms; indeed he uses sexuality as just another power-system in the society, as if to take to its logical, final conclusion the view that family relationships, being an aspect of sexuality, are essentially nothing but power and appetite relationships. In the play's design all the intrigues involving Edmund have an exact pattern, as if his very success in scheming hides from him the fatal limitation of his philosophy, makes him deceive himself that the world works like a satiric comedy.[2]

Edmund's father Gloucester is his foolish victim, first of mockery, then deceit, then atrocity: Edmund looks on at his blinding; but the play's design involves Gloucester in being deceived by both sons: his loyal son Edgar will trick him too into mock suicide, though hence to piety and reconciliation. In Act 1 treacherous Edmund cloaks filial malevolence in seeming affection; in Act 4 loyal Edgar hides filial love beneath the guise of demonic treachery. Edgar, ironically, is brought to mock his father, just as the impious Edmund is made part of a pattern bringing Gloucester to a state of contrition. The pattern is exact, but though it seems to settle scores in terms of plot, its paradoxes are really unsettling. To the blind Gloucester his leap from the cliff to death is real; Edgar-as-Poor-Tom teaches the audience to see it as an inner, spiritual event of momentous change; yet as a physical action performed on stage its cruelty and absurdity remain apparent.

The contradictory reactions it provokes are part of Shakespeare's general scheme of disruption of audience expectations as the end of the play approaches. Some glimpses of the romance mode of the sources seem to promise a providential ending (the old play of *Leir* ended with the restoration of the king).³ The formal challenge and single combat, by means of which Edgar discredits Edmund and re-establishes himself, might seem to contradict Edmund's cruel nihilism, to augur the revival of chivalric ideals. And yet the atmosphere of Sidney's *Arcadia*, though hinted at here, seems somehow cut off from the world of *King Lear*. Edmund does recant as he lies dying – but again it is hard to suppress the question of how far this could be associated with his mortal weakness. It serves in any case as a false trail, misleading the audience to expect a happy ending which, in fact, is contradicted by the most shocking means, since it is by Edmund's and Goneril's command that Cordelia is killed. Yet even that is not the worst thing, nor is it the end.

In these episodes Shakespeare employs contradictory ways of presenting spiritual experience – as natural, yet also as remote or hieratic, as in pre-Shakespearean religious drama. The storm in Lear's mind wreaks grave destruction on his kingdom, much worse destruction than any bad weather can do, indeed the natural, wind-and-rain storm itself is a distinct phenomenon of the play-world which gives no sign of being what Lear takes it to be – and what a storm certainly is in *The Tragedy of Hoffman* or *The Revenger's Tragedy* – a sign of the intercession of divine wrath. Lear may appeal to Jove and claim divine status for himself, but the natural storm remains simply meteorological, and one that confirms the Fool's assertion, that the property of rain is to wet.

Lear himself at one point invites a surprisingly frank – almost medical – view of his derangement as physiologically interesting:

> When the mind's free,
> The body's delicate. This tempest in my mind
> Doth from my senses take all feeling else,
> Save what beats there   (3.4.11–14)

Shakespeare makes Lear consider the relative importance of physical suffering, and Lear seems to belittle it. Shakespeare then confronts Lear, who wants to be physically unfeeling, with the blinded Gloucester, visible testimony to atrocious reality, to the truth that the senses are so precious that they affect the spirit.

Lear undergoes extreme mental suffering, but also extreme physical suffering: when he falls unconscious it is impossible to know whether it is as much a spiritual turning point as it is a point of physical exhaustion. When Lear revives, he says he is 'bound upon a wheel of fire'. Is this a symptom of derangement, or half in dream? Could this be a mystical state? Is he somehow dragged back after passing from life to after-life, or does he speak metaphorically of his moral recognition? It is impossible to know, and surely that is the point. One can only question. Lear seems after this never quite certainly to recover normal consciousness, normal knowledge of Cordelia – or (so the play seems, urgently, to ask), is supranormal, childish–foolish knowledge the best, the fullest we can have?

This contrast and conflict between outer and inner ways of seeing, between outer and inner imperatives, is fundamental to the play; it is a concern which is apparent also in *The Taming of the Shrew* and *Titus Andronicus*, two plays which are illuminated when compared to the later *King Lear*, with which they have affinities and for which they provide an important storehouse of artistic and thematic ideas – indeed Shakespeare used them in a sense as sources. Nowadays, when *King Lear* is so much more familiar, either from reading or from stage performance, it is rather the other way round – we can see more in the less familiar dramas of *The Taming of the Shrew* and *Titus Andronicus* by approaching them through *King Lear* – by thinking of *King Lear* as, in a sense, a source for them.

In the middle of *The Taming of the Shrew* Petruchio's subjection of Kate to sensory deprivation reaches an extreme. The victim–heroine, denied any food since her wedding, now bedraggled, bruised, and muddy from falling off a horse, is at last permitted a seat at table. She is offered a meal, and then denied it. A scene later she is once again offered a meal by a servant, and again denied it. The food-fantasies of the starving-hungry woman are provoked, disappointed, provoked, disappointed. The servant plays upon her with skilful timing:

> KATE I prithee go and get me some repast –
> I care not what, so it be wholesome food.
> GRUMIO What say you to a neat's foot?
> KATE 'Tis passing good. I prithee let me have it.
> GRUMIO I fear it is too choleric a meat.
> How say you to a fat tripe finely broiled?
> KATE I like it well. Good Grumio, fetch it me.
> GRUMIO I cannot tell, I fear 'tis choleric.
> What say you to a piece of beef and mustard?
> KATE A dish that I do love to feed upon.
> GRUMIO Ay, but the mustard is too hot a little.
> KATE Why then, the beef, and let the mustard rest.
> GRUMIO Nay then, I will not. You shall have the mustard,
> Or else you get no beef of Grumio.   (4.3.15–28)

Here at last Kate thinks she can sense a breakthrough:

> KATE Then both, or one, or any thing thou wilt   (4.3.29)

But she underestimates Grumio. Just her submission is not going to be enough, and she has left herself wide open:

> GRUMIO Why then, the mustard without the beef.   (4.3.30)

Grumio's absurd reversal of the basic position – that Kate must not have choleric food – is one part of the joke: the other is her not anticipating such a reversal. She suffers, the comedy does not pity her: the audience enjoy an obvious comic routine, a game-fantasy. But Kate does perceive – and alerts the audience to the fact – that a word can make the mind trigger actual physical appetites, and emotions, far beyond the bounds of mere physical actions, and this opens the way to the full force of this drama, discovering the area of deep affinity between comedy and tragedy:

> KATE That feed'st me with the very name of meat.   (4.3.32)

In an approximately equivalent position in *Titus Andronicus* the persecuted Titus and his family gather for a meal. In the preceding action Titus has stabbed one son to death and cut off his own left hand in a futile attempt to save two other sons. His ravished daughter now confronts him: her tongue has been torn out and her two hands lopped off. Titus begins to speak but is so overwhelmed by these mutilations that his thought can make no progress. He obsessively repeats the word 'hands' as he tries to grasp what it means that they have no hands. The emphasis on the repetition of the mere word 'hands' draws attention to the state of extreme distress. Titus suddenly finds horrifying alienation and terror in the simplest and most familiar elements of the world – indeed in the parts of his own body which seemed inseparable from his identity, his hands. Then even the word 'hands' suddenly seems fearful:

> TITUS What violent hands can she lay on her life?
> Ah, wherefore dost thou urge the name of hands,
> To bid Aeneas tell the tale twice o'er
> How Troy was burnt and he made miserable?
> Oh, handle not the theme, to talk of hands,
> Lest we remember still that we have none.
> Fie, fie, how franticly I square my talk,
> As if we should forget we had no hands,
> If Marcus did not name the word of hands! (3.2.25–33)

Here Titus' madness emerges; meanwhile Lavinia, having no tongue or hands with which to communicate, weeps. Suddenly Marcus stabs at his plate. He then explains he was killing a fly, a fly as black as Aaron. This is so absurd it may force laughter from an audience, but then they may wonder, is Marcus cracking under the strain, too? Or is this childish fantasy calculated to soothe his mad father, or on the contrary to provoke Titus to a crisis and hence cure him? Or is this an oblique way of putting the idea of revenge in his mind? It is impossible to be sure. Titus first reacts with bizarre concern for the insect: was not this a displaced act of murder, a blow that would kill a man directed at an innocent fly, scarcely visible? (Perhaps, we may think, actually hallucinatory.) When Marcus says the fly is Aaron, Titus stabs and stabs at the plate.

The violence is true violence, but expended absurdly, and so with an effect of farce. Furthermore, at this moment Titus' state of mind is unfathomable: and then an audience will have to accommodate itself to the later revelation that it is in this, of all moments, that Titus engenders his idea of revenge, so exact in plan and execution, an act of justice and yet at the same time fantastically atrocious.

The ritual of the meal is vital, structurally and thematically, to both *The Taming of the Shrew* and *Titus Andronicus*. The spoiled and denied meal is, as we see here, a key moment marking a crucial stage in the action of each play; whereas each play concludes in a memorable feast. It is only the most obvious of many significant structural and thematic parallels between the two plays.

The Taming of the Shrew begins with an Induction which constitutes a small play in itself: it serves, albeit obliquely, to introduce some major concerns of the main play that follows, but in particular it registers the impression of harshness – indeed the Induction might well begin with a crash of breaking glass and voices raised in anger, even before the drunken figure of Sly the tinker is thrust into the audience's view as the Hostess kicks him out of her ale-house. After an abusive exchange with her, Sly falls asleep and a Lord and his servants enter from hunting, warmly discussing their sport. The contrast between these vigorous men, bound together by shared enjoyment as well as fealty, and the dead-drunk tinker Sly, is emblematic. They discuss the performance of the hounds, bringing a tang of country air with vivid directness: Merriman, the poor cur, is embossed, but 'Silver made it good / At the hedge corner, in the coldest fault'. Physical well-being is as manifest as the sense of their close communal life in a familiar place.

The spectacle of Sly, subject to the Lord's practical joke and treated to all manner of luxuries, serves to emphasise by contrast his fixed harshness and coarse nature. At the very beginning, when the Hostess ejects Sly as a 'rogue', he defies her, insisting on his name though ridiculously boasting of his lineage – 'Look in the Chronicles'. When he revives from the ensuing drunken stupor, it is to be greeted as a lord, but he insists on his dignity in other terms:

I am Christophero Sly – call not me 'honour' nor 'lordship'. I ne'er drank sack in my life, and if you give me any conserves, give me conserves of beef. Ne'er ask me what raiment I'll wear, for I have no more doublets than backs, no more stockings than legs, nor no more shoes than feet – nay, sometime more feet than shoes, or such shoes as my toes look through the overleather. ... Am not I Christopher Sly, old Sly's son of Burton-heath, by birth a pedlar, by education a cardmaker, by transmutation a bear-herd, and now by present profession a tinker? Ask Marian Hacket, the fat ale-wife of Wincot, if she know me not. If she say I am not fourteen pence on the score for sheer ale, score me up for the lying'st knave in Christendom.

(Induction 2. 5–10,15–20)

Here is a harsh existence, a material world of discomfort; the masterless man has no reciprocal bonds with a lord to secure him; Sly's successive employments tell a graphic story of the other side of country life, vagrancy and poverty. He is no doubt one of the rogues who deserve to suffer – it seems as if Marion Hacket would confirm this in no uncertain terms – nevertheless this assertion of defiant nonconformity, and of bleak material hardship, is direct enough to prompt a shiver in anyone. These issues are presented in the tradition of carnival, to be sure, but carnival implies a degree of ambivalence. It does not encourage a sense of immunity in anyone, be they high or low.[4]

Such humour is essentially violent. A similar ambivalence is generated by the rebel leader Jack Cade in Shakespeare's *2 Henry VI*, who boastfully announces his own blazon, but is mocked as he does it by Dick the butcher and Smith the weaver:

CADE We John Cade, so termed of our supposed father –
DICK (*Aside*) Or rather of stealing a cade of herrings

(4.2.26–7 ff.)

At first sight this might be supposed simple enough, but the implications of this topsy-turvy version of society are aggressive – a caricature of the class system based on birth, and possession of wealth; it suggests that the law is only displacing violence to concentrate it on the unprivileged – in the form of denial and oppression. Sly's boastful blazon of his name, ancestry, and social position is, like Cade's, not random. It accurately mirrors the gentleman's code, and exactly inverts it. It serves in advance as a direct parody of those the audience will soon be hearing from the rich young men in Padua, especially Petruchio (2.1.47 ff.).

In Sly significant concerns of the play are first voiced: the emphasis on respectable birth, possession of wealth and social rank as well as the comedy of lost and mistaken identity and of instinctive appetite denied. Yet above all Sly's contribution to the play is to set a tone of harshness which never really evaporates.

A hunt celebrates violence while also sanctioning and culturally transforming it. Hunting is felt to be a celebration of bodily well-being as well as a test of strength and skill. The instincts which drive hunter and hunted in the wild result in highly complex patterns of behaviour; human society devises rituals of the hunt in closely similar ways.[5] Elizabethan society in general, and Renaissance monarchs in particular, took hunting very seriously as embodying in its rituals a cultural myth, and an affirmation of the prevailing hierarchy. Men transcend the animal kingdom, symbolically, by making the hunt a ritual. The metaphoric status of the actions in a hunt is all the more strong when the actual violence is fully recognised. The frenzy of hounds, the terror of the quarry, the bloody wounding and dismemberment, the awakened and satisfied appetites, bring together the antinomies – of nature as energy, multiplying, creating, destroying, mutating forms, and nature as goddess of wisdom and a hierarchical realm.

The wild hawk is trained, civilised into hunting with the hunter in mutual cooperation: rather than remaining itself wild, it will hunt and kill at the command of its master. Extreme violence is cultivated, made unnatural, and only released according to rules inculcated in the creature by a process of denial and reward. When Petruchio, in 4.1.188 ff., tells the audience that he plans to tame the wild Kate as if she were a hawk, the implied denial of her humanity in itself offends cultural law, and in addition this particular metaphor is equivocal about whether it implies that hunting is necessity or sport. Petruchio does seem at times to treat society as wilderness, to stress harsh and anti-social impulses. Denial of nourishment, and rest, and self-will, are the means by which Petruchio trains Kate (as he would a hawk), but Kate is a human being, not a hawk, and the suffering she experiences is demonstrably more complex and serious than Petruchio's breezy analogy with animal-training allows for. The experience to which Kate is subjected – until she gives in only near the end of the play – seems designed to go (possibly) beyond a joke, in terms of the violence generated in both Kate and Petruchio, certainly so in terms of their discovery of the possibilities of cruelty. Here, above all, Shakespeare's treatment of the folk-tale material keeps in touch with its violence.

Petruchio accepts the challenge of Kate before he has met her, because of her money: this is a sour basis for a love comedy, and it is important that it be taken seriously, whatever the interpretation of the play one prefers. Indeed, acknowledging this harsh beginning can only make for a more affirmative conclusion, if affirmation is what one seeks. It seems important to grasp that the harshness is of the essence, whatever the interpretation of the ending.

In *Titus Andronicus* the hunt is a central metaphor, but is also part of the action – hunting horns and the cry of hounds are heard as Act 2, Scene 2 begins, and the characters must be dressed and accoutred as befits this most splendid and noble kind of royal hunt, of the panther and the hart. Tamora rejects the hunt as an alien cultural rite; she inverts this ritual honouring the emperor by using the hunt as a decoy and cuckolding him on the first day of their marriage. Her two sons follow Aaron's plan, and like pitiless hounds 'single' the 'dainty doe' Lavinia and 'pluck her to ground'. These insults to Rome are deliberately intensified by timing them to coincide with the emperor's hunt: it is a brutal onslaught on the whole culture – custom, hierarchy, law, and morality.

The crucial episode is focused on a pit, dug as a trap for human quarry – Bassianus is murdered and thrust down into it. No less significantly, the pit is given metaphoric sexual significance, as a grotesque vagina–grave, a 'blood-drinking pit', the 'very fatal place'; it soon traps Lavinia's two brothers;

they recognise the irony in calling it a 'swallowing womb'. Its associations with sexual nausea, guilt, and fear, are stressed in Tamora's description of it as beset by hissing snakes and swelling toads. It becomes a displaced image of Lavinia's rape, a hole

> Whose mouth is covered with rude-growing briers,
> Upon whose leaves are drops of new-shed blood
> As fresh as morning dew distill'd on flowers   (2.3.199–201)

This metaphor comes as the climax to a sequence of stiffly elaborate rhetorical exchanges in which characters give figurative interpretations of the landscape of the hunt.

Tamora, as alien and infidel, does not see the wide landscape Titus sees as he looks forward to the hunt; instead her perspective is enclosing, erotic. She focuses on particulars, not only the expected melodious birds but the snake, 'rolled up in the cheerful sun'. In her version the hunt is heard not seen, and then it is only heard as a rapid diminuendo of sounds; and these soon remote echoes serve to recall Dido's cave.[6] This is a wish-fulfilling fantasy which Aaron cannot mistake, but he can and does reject it: he wants to see something different, transforming her description into vigorous images of erotic cruelty; he turns Tamora's snake into a phallic nightmare vision as he meta-morphoses himself into Gorgon:

> My fleece of woolly hair that now uncurls,
> Even as an adder when she doth unroll   (2.3.34–5)

These pointed literary allusions are only the most graphic signs of the highly elaborate rhetorical artifice with which the descriptions are composed, and this rhetorical artifice itself is part of a much more important issue in the play: we are made to recognise that, beyond the personal will and design of each speaker, the shaping power of a whole culture is expressing itself through these compositions. It is obvious that this cultural system is extremely rigid. A particular culture develops a system of rules, selecting and excluding elements from the natural world's multiplicity and its play of boundless energy and instincts; when an extremely rigid system breaks, the disruption will be proportionately violent.

The climax of this episode of violence is marked by ironic literary allusions to hunting. Bassianus mockingly pretends to mistake Tamora for the chaste goddess Diana, and Tamora threatens him with Actaeon's fate, killed by his own hounds; then, fatefully, a moment later her two sons appear. Acting as Aaron advised, like hounds, not men, they first kill Bassianus and then strike down the 'dainty doe' Lavinia, but, worse than any wild animals, they leave her still alive. When Marcus discovers the mutilated Lavinia he delivers a speech, intense in its effort to feel, though numbed with extreme shock. He seeks through rhetoric to overcome the speechless horror which severs Lavinia from him:

> Sorrow concealed, like an oven stopp'd,
> Doth burn the heart to cinders where it is.
> Fair Philomela, why, she but lost her tongue,
> And in a tedious sampler sew'd her mind;
> But, lovely niece, that mean is cut from thee.
> A craftier Tereus, cousin, hast thou met,
> And he hath cut those pretty fingers off
> That could have better sew'd than Philomel.
> O, had the monster seen those lily hands
> Tremble like aspen leaves upon a lute,
> And make the silken strings delight to kiss them,
> He would not then have touch'd them for his life!
>
> (2.4.36–47)

The speech summons up her physically exquisite delicacy, and as it does so intensifies understanding of how agonising Lavinia's suffering must be. This literary allusion to Ovid's tale of Philomel, far from helping to measure the present situation, only brings Marcus and his audience to feel that Lavinia's plight exceeds all comprehensible or imaginable precedent: it brings out the fearful power of language to confront the mind with things beyond human toleration.

The hunt has its formal phases: rousing the game, the chase, the kill, the feast.[7] The exuberant brutality of the sport is licensed by strict cultural rules; if these rules are infringed, the result, instantly, is abhorrent atrocity. In *Titus Andronicus* it is atrociously perverted by Aaron and Tamora, but they provoke

Titus who answers by catching the game (Tamora's sons), hanging it, butchering it, and serving it at the feast.

Misapplying the rules of the hunt, to shocking effect, happens in *The Taming of the Shrew* too. At first, in the Induction, hunting is presented as requiring skill and discipline – obedience to rules – a cooperative exercise which results in vigour, good humour, and physical well-being. The hunt is presented as colourful and earthily attractive – a first positive statement of a most important motif in the play – and the element of persecution, as directed at Sly, seems to do little harm to him, though it is callous. Later, however, when Kate is persecuted, it does become offensive. By contrast, in *Titus Andronicus* the hunt looks fierce from the first and its rules are broken as soon as it begins: persecution is directed at human beings, in deadly earnest, designed to maim and kill, and it actually does this; yet at certain points, even though this is a tragedy, events become so extreme that they seem surreal, detached from any recognisable, credible cause. Violence is manifestly itself, yet when it goes beyond all bounds it seems to acquire the configuration of its opposite, fantasy, and this produces an effect like farce. The resultant laughter in an audience, in its scorn for the defeated notion of hope, is a kind of relief similar to that of the victim, Titus himself, in his agony:

MARCUS Why dost thou laugh? It fits not with this hour.
TITUS Why, I have not another tear to shed. (3.1.265–6)

What distinguishes comedy from tragedy is not that violence is present in the tragedy but absent from the comedy: on the contrary, violence is a central feature of both. Rather it is that while a negative principle is confronted at the beginning of a comedy, it is finally transcended through irony and evasion, whereas tragedy overrules the self-protective instinct and acknowledges an extreme of anxiety, guilt, despair, resulting in destruction and the hero's death.[8] In *The Taming of the Shrew* violence is expressed at the outset, but it is then detached from a normal system of cause and effect. Fantasy supported by trickery creates a situation in which violence becomes abstract, and can be reacted to by spectators as a pleasure, licensed by awareness that the usual destructive consequences are miraculously absent; yet their laughter is also in part quickened by a latent guilty awareness of what violence normally entails. Taboos are broken and yet not broken.

In each play, *Titus Andronicus* and *The Taming of the Shrew*, opposed views are presented of cultural rules – as sacred, and as brutally arbitrary. Both plays depict the alternation between ceremony and riot. At first it seems simply a disintegrating process, but it is really dialectical. Both plays juxtapose high civilisation to the primitive – a yoking together to most violent effect. Take, first, high civilisation. In *Titus Andronicus*, as Terence Spencer notes,[9] 'The play does not assume a political situation known to Roman history; it is, rather, a summary of Roman politics. It is not so much that any particular set of political institutions is assumed in *Titus Andronicus*, but rather that it includes all the political institutions that Rome ever had. The author seems anxious, not to get it all right but to get it all in'; still, Spencer admits, 'The claim that it was a "noble Roman history" was a just one'. Spencer notes how Rome seems at times a free commonweal with patrician and plebeian institutions; Titus is a devoted adherent rather of the hereditary monarchical principle in a commonwealth that only partly takes account of this. Saturninus embarks on despotic rule, passing through Byzantine intrigue until overthrown by popular acclaim. Then follows the election of Lucius 'to order well the state'.

Shakespeare's purpose is to give a concentrated sense of ancient Rome as a high-wrought culture but one where rigid public values prevail; the limits of this civilisation are emphatic and clear, its austere military code standing for general repression of the private need *pro bono publico*: marble or bronze hardness yoked to all too fluid blood, tears and sweat. Rome's codes underpin a belief in law, the sacredness of which, from the opening scene of *Titus Andronicus*, is stressed and radically called into question, set over against a rival system of sacrifice. The comic rite is one of sacrifice like the tragic – the drama imposes a more atavistic pattern than history does. The coincidence of these two systems of law and of sacrifice is a major source of conflict and turbulence. The challenge to the sacred rule of law is graphically signalled by the transfer of the action from within the city to the country; there the highly codified ritual of the royal hunt is barbarously perverted.

In *The Taming of the Shrew*, after the Induction, with its carnival sketch of Elizabethan Cotswold life, the Italian comedy is emphatically located in Padua. 'Padua was famous throughout Europe as a university city, the centre of Aristotelianism', as Brian Morris notes:[10] 'Tranio advocates a wide syllabus – philosophy, logic, rhetoric, music, poetry and mathematics'. But the brisk bargaining and matchmaking which ensues after the entry of Bianca reminds us that Padua is also a society of merchants and adventurers. In *The Taming of the Shrew* the tough bargaining system of the merchants which underpins the wealth and civilisation of the Italian Renaissance city extends to marriage, here emphatically an institution not a private, spiritual experience. Kate is unjustly, in her view, trapped and deformed by this archaic custom, humiliating her the more because she is the eldest sister. It is possible to ignore this social context and to read the play as dominantly concerned with personality and psychology. I believe this to be wrong, since Shakespeare shows a strong interest in depicting this background and in emphasising its influence on everyone. Petruchio, certainly, lays exaggerated emphasis on treating Kate as a piece of property: he declares to everyone at the wedding:

> She is my goods, my chattels; she is my house,
> My household stuff, my field, my barn,
> My horse, my ox, my ass, my anything   (3.2.219–21)

Of course this is also ironic mockery – to their faces – of the Paduan merchants and the calculating greedy wooers of Bianca: but that is no help or comfort at this moment to Kate. In revenge, then, Kate will deny Petruchio all that belongs to a true marriage.

The Italian cities named in the play, Pisa, Padua, Florence, Verona, Venice, Genoa, Mantua, Bergamo, are famous for sophisticated high culture, but, at the same time, they name a mercantile system and insist on the harsh facts of the market and its rooting in frank bodily life, in the restricted imperatives of survival, in getting and spending. Stress falls at once on these physical imperatives (underlying the codes of a commercial culture) whenever the artistic or ethical codes appear in the play. The ancient Rome of *Titus Andronicus* and the Renaissance Italian city of *The Taming of the Shrew* are depicted as complex and tight-knit in their social identity: this close-knit structure is something thrown into high relief by the incursion of the hero in each play newly arriving in the society, in each play laden with esteem which is yet in a form capable of generating unease and instability when too frankly and candidly named – as Titus displays his sons, killed fighting Rome's wars, or demonstrates battlefield authority but in the middle of the city: by putting a son summarily to death; or, as Petruchio beats his servants, and frankly accounts for his social value, now he has buried his father:

> Antonio my father is deceased
> And I have thrust myself into this maze,
> Happily to wive and thrive as best I may.
> Crowns in my purse I have, and goods at home,
> And so am come abroad to see the world.
> ...
> I come to wive it wealthily in Padua;
> If wealthily, then happily in Padua   (1.2.51–5, 72–3)

All the heroes, Petruchio, Titus, and Lear, are outspoken and hence potentially dangerous members of their respective civilisations. They thus reveal the systems devised to contain and regulate violence – a working definition of civilisation[11] – or they are, as exceptional persons, deeply influenced by the obscure shifts in belief before others have become aware of them; or simply, they are beyond integration. Through the exceptional person is acted out a conflict which conformist citizens consider it shockingly offensive to admit. The conformist obeys unspoken taboos, holds them unspeakable: in Hamlet's words, 'all which, sir, though I most powerfully and potently believe, yet I hold it not honesty to have it thus set down'

(*Hamlet* 2.2.196–8), an observation which prompts Polonius to note 'though this be madness, yet there is method in't'.

In the Rome of *Titus Andronicus* naked military power is identified as the raw expression of one aspect of the society; it immediately brings havoc when the taboo separating or excluding it from the seat of political, civic power is broken. In the Padua of *The Taming of the Shrew* brutality accompanies the entrance of both hero and heroine – Petruchio enters beating his servant (it is not merely high spirits) while Kate (second entrance) drives her sister Bianca on stage, having tied her hands together and then, in a fresh burst of rage, strikes her and chases her off again. The social rules privilege the master and the elder sister; in return the rules restrain them from releasing the implicit violence underpinning a hierarchy. In both plays the rigid social hierarchy is demonstrated in the working social structures.

Shakespeare begins *King Lear*, as he did *Titus Andronicus*, with the breaking of basic cultural codes, starting with the imminent unkinging of Lear himself. His unforced abdication contradicts the deepest principles of monarchy in the England of Shakespeare's time, where the king is sacred. Lear's scheme of dividing the kingdom inverts the recent (1603) unifying of England, Wales and Scotland under King James I – perhaps pointedly, in a play to be performed before King James. Dividing the kingdom also contradicts a well-known Biblical text: 'Every kingdom divided against itself is brought to desolation' (Matt. 12. 25). In terms of the family and its intimate kinship bonds, Lear perverts the transfer of inheritance from father to children into a commercial transaction, a public auction and a scene of gross vanity. Even though he abdicates, moreover, he still insists on retaining 'the name and all th'additions to a king', which contradicts his act; although he has his will read and enacted as if he had died, he is still very much alive. He brings in a map to display the divisions already decided, but yet he insists that where he will draw the divisions depends upon how well his daughters speak. He will be no king and still a king. He has and he has not decided how much to give his daughters. He acknowledges his coming death, and yet the business of the will implies that he is trying to evade death by trickery. These profound and obscure drives in him produce distortions so strong that the bonds of the family and the state, which are centred on him, are broken.

Lear is evidently entering, himself, a second childhood, of old age, but in this second childhood there is no innocence. Lear is aware of his waning bodily strength, of imminent impotence and death; in struggling to accept this his temper becomes ungovernable, but he also takes refuge in escapist fantasies of a second childhood, as when he speaks of spending retirement in Cordelia's 'kind nursery'. A child's weakness is positive in being full of future promise, and in being innocent. Lear pretends to himself that his old age will really be like this: converting an old man's 'crawl' to the happy progress of a baby. The first scene of *King Lear* is designed to emphasise the contradictions and to identify a whole network of cultural ceremonies, laws and taboos which are abruptly and catastrophically broken, so releasing a tidal wave of anarchy.

The tragedy, *Titus Andronicus*, like the comedy, *The Taming of the Shrew*, begins by presenting an issue of social and moral justice. Tamora, Queen of the Goths, appeals for mercy for her son. Shakespeare seems to have emphatically placed this issue before Titus and the audience (in Q1, lines 35–8 suggest he hesitated whether to leave it as an already accomplished fact).[12] Coming immediately after the Andronici tomb is opened, the appeal to Titus by his sons to 'hew the limbs' and 'sacrifice' the 'flesh' of Tamora's son is uncomfortably close to revenge, and so Tamora, powerless now, but in her own tribe supreme, challenges the religious rite from her cultural perspective: 'O cruel irreligious piety'. Yet on the other hand she is also impelled by a mother's instincts. The audience is forced to consider whether the religious rite, which requires that the noblest prisoner taken in battle be hewn in pieces as sacrifice, seems archaic here in Rome – even a Gothic queen finds it incredible. This killing unlocks the brutality prevailing for the rest of the play, which nevertheless is stiffly constructed, formally massive, its language ornately rhetorical.

In *King Lear*, the abdication involves grave disruption of

custom, law and kinship. Lear precipitates a constitutional, not merely a political, change – one that arbitrarily breaks powerful taboos. He puts his kingdom on the verge of disintegration and sets his daughters against one another. Demanding that his daughters each tell, in public, how much they love him, is an offensive attempt to improvise a ceremonial act of succession; it denies dignity to the successors, and the king himself breaks the decorum of the occasion, causing the ceremony to break up in angry disorder. The public ceremonial is confused with an intimate family rite, the line dividing private from public is broken. One can go further: the bond between child and father is different from that between subject and monarch, but even in terms of the family bond there is a threat, since Lear demands expressions of devotion to himself which are excessive, given that his two elder daughters have husbands and the youngest is on the point of marriage: in short, Lear demands obedience of a kind which would only be proper if his daughters were still children – the implicit confusion between infantile love and sexual love threatens further deep taboos.

If Lear, Titus, and Petruchio are exceptional, larger than life, they are also exemplary cultural constructs, each embodies ideals in his society. They are matched with females, Goneril and Cordelia, Tamora, and Kate, who are exceptional in their readiness to break convention, but who are shown in a serious sense to act justifiably – to be violent because law and custom oppress them. Tamora plausibly compares her situation as mother to that of Titus as father; what he claims as sacrifice she answers is mere revenge. Kate's wrongs at the hands of a neglectful father, a sly younger sister, and an unsympathetic community, are the worse for their indirectness. Kate and Tamora are subject to brutality concealing itself as reason and law, and they respond with more brutality. This is not of course the whole story. Tamora exploits the instability following the election of Saturninus – she seeks to reign, though as a queen of Goths might reign (remember Aaron); Kate, forced to be married to 'a mad-brain rudesby full of spleen' – Petruchio – resolves to maintain her violent aggression to him, though using the public status of a married woman to assert her own sense of worth. We see from her rage, when Petruchio does not seem to be coming to the wedding, how it is public shame, not private loss, that makes her anxious. Petruchio, she cries,

> Yet never means to wed where he hath wooed.
> Now must the world point at poor Katherine
> And say, 'Lo, there is mad Petruchio's wife,
> If it would please him come and marry her!' (3.2.17–20)

Eventually Kate seems to accept subjection to Petruchio, even to the point of becoming isolated from ordinary, non-alienated, non-ironic communication with other people. This danger of becoming cut off – as in madness – is represented exceptionally clearly, though farcically, in the sun/moon episode, where Kate replays on someone else the disorientation-techniques Petruchio played on her. When they meet an old man, Vincentio, she obeys Petruchio's nonsensical and contradictory orders, bewildering and disorientating her victim, addressing him as 'young blushing virgin'. Gratified by her obedience, Petruchio then demands a kiss, and she kisses Petruchio, in the public street. The act is wordless – all the better, one may say, or all the more equivocal – but she calls him 'love'.

It is in the exceptional – and in a sense marginal – person that a culture's values come into question, have less than absolute sway. The actions of *Titus Andronicus* and *The Taming of the Shrew* are dramatisations of cultural systems under pressure, and this may explain why the main issue that unites the plays is persecution. The action is focused on the rite – if it is indeed a rite, here – or the process, of persecution. Going with it, I would note the emphasis on the human body, depicted as ungovernably strong and energetic, and then, in deprivation or mutilation, as so weakened that it becomes the worst of all threats, a threat to the mind.

Persecution implies cutting an individual off from membership of society, dismembering him or her. It is carried out by rituals of exclusion and shame. The tragedies present this in terms of beheading, cutting off hands, cutting out the tongue, rape, blinding, banishment and madness. The comic action of

The Taming of the Shrew works through public humiliation, broken ceremonies of wedding and feasting, abuse, physical exhaustion and deprivation, and in the tailor scene (4.2.60 ff.) even a fantasy mutilation, where the gown's sleeves are said to be snipped and nipped and cut and slished and slashed, the gown itself said to be cut to pieces, the tailor dismissed as a rag, a remnant. Kate complains Petruchio is making a puppet of her. Finally, as the last stage of persecution, comes mental disorientation.

Yet through persecution and madness the victim–hero achieves a new ability, founded on his or her exceptional – or marginal – quality, and both plays end in an act of revenge subverting a socially conserving ceremony, a feast. Although this conclusion offers a formal and rhetorical completion to the action, it does not provide an intellectual or a moral conclusion, and its cultural function is, to say the least, equivocal. It seems in each case to open up the question of justice itself, not absorb it into the fabric of the culture.

Titus was wont to speak of Rome, of duty, of piety, and virtue. He spent twenty years in the name of Rome dealing mutilation and sudden death. All this killing and mutilation seemed sanctioned and lawful, conducted according to the rites of war. This code, infringed by enacting it in the wrong context of the centre of the city of Rome, produces obscene atrocity in proliferating forms. This drives Titus in upon himself as he is publicly exiled and stripped of honours and his daughter and sons are mutilated and he himself chops off his own right hand. The element of violence, the wild and brutal, expressed itself in him and through him all along, but it was encoded as sacred. The warrior was unswervingly pious. The contradictions are unleashed in the city, at the moment he enters it, in transition from warrior to citizen: the cultural zones blur, so signals are confused, but they also witness to far deeper shifts and stresses in the structure. Titus is extreme, and astonishingly exceptional, not least in his stupidity: it is through such figures that painful changes are manifested in a culture.

I find it helpful to notice here René Girard's account[13] of the two cultural systems, the modern, based on law, the primitive, based on sacrifice, but each centrally concerned with the regulation of violence, sensed as something exterior to man, and hence part of all the outside forces that threaten man, forces collectively known as the sacred. Violence, says Girard, is the heart and secret soul of the sacred. The function of ritual is to purify violence, to trick it into spending itself on victims whose death-sacrifice will provoke no reprisals. In society under law, also, the authority of law is transcendent, its supremacy renders it immune from reprisal and the proliferation of reciprocal revenge. Law concerns itself with the communal, though it operates by exacting revenge on guilty individuals. But law can exist only in conjunction with a firmly established political power – and once this is discernible, its sacredness is lost, or imperilled – and a view of the inner workings of the system is a sign of its disintegration, awakening the spectre of reciprocal reprisal: the sacred then no longer contains or regulates violence.

We might see these plays as designed to present issues and open up normally repressed questions rather than to resolve and conclude judgements. If dialectic is the key to the treatment of subject-matter, the central concern might not be the characters' fulfilment and narrative's closure. These plays might be understood as dynamic and explorative, concerned with re-actions to restricting social laws; these produce distortion, or deformation, and the plays show deformation as just that.

In retribution for the crimes committed against his family and himself, the justice Titus wants is one which will justify the world itself. And in demanding that justice, by shooting arrows at the gods, he devises a paltry theatrical show, where what seems needed is another category of discourse. The arrows are absurd, but they certainly expose the puniness of human efforts, in his world, to regulate and order violence, where now neither religion nor law nor culture have authority. If the reaction of Titus is to be considered beyond the extreme, excessive, mad, by his fellows, the audience can recognise that it has a certain lucidity and, so far from being excessive, it might even seem to fall short. Then, however, Titus returns to Rome, that is, he emerges from his isolation in his house, emerges from shameful obscurity where he and his family have been cast – and he does it by announcing a grand feast for the Emperor Saturninus and Empress Tamora.

The meal, in symbolic terms, is the central communal rite, expressive of integration, secure ease, self-affirmation, and it celebrates the body's appetites as integral to humanity. It is through precisely that rite that Titus expresses his revulsion against the state of Rome. Rome denies and breaks ordering principles, eviscerates meaning from its customs – as Titus believes – so he provides a meal which will annihilate the desire to eat. As Petruchio puts it, in describing his treatment of Kate, he kills the guests in their own humour.

The action of *King Lear* rapidly precipitates the patriarchal absolute ruler from his state. Bare-headed, half-naked, drenched by the storm, Lear confronts Poor Tom, a naked beggar, and the two constitute a kind of double image of 'unaccommodated man'. Poor Tom at once attracts Lear's attention as though part of Lear's inner phantasmagoria. Yet it is consistent with the ironic and paradoxical cast of the play that the stark image of man in his nakedness should be in fact Edgar, the true (though banished) heir of the Duke of Gloucester. In this world of treachery and deceit nakedness is itself a disguise. A further irony is that Lear is fooled by the disguise so well that he actually sees a truth in it, whereas he has seemingly been blind to vice and injustice for years. Lear begins to grasp what the capering, gibbering image of the poor naked wretch means in human terms: though it takes an image of man-as-beast to do it.

There is a parallel with Shakespeare's method in previous plays: in *Titus Andronicus* the hero is confronted by a series of progressively appalling encounters: with his own two sons being led, bound, to execution; with their severed heads and his own severed hand, brought by Aaron; then with his mutilated daughter Lavinia. These encounters force him to recognise his own folly and violence as well as his loss of power. Similarly in *The Taming of the Shrew*, Petruchio acts out, with harsh exaggeration, a grotesque version of Kate, confronting Kate with a mirror image, a spouse who looks awful, is unkind and repels affection, who has bad manners, a vile temper, refuses to provide meals, rejects affection, and will not even go to bed. Worse still, having given up her original, unmarried, identity, yet refusing a new one as a wife, Petruchio shows her that she risks losing all identity.

While Lear learns something about himself in the image of Poor Tom, for his part Edgar as he begins to play Poor Tom considers his own true identity to be lost: 'Edgar I nothing am.' Stripped of family name and social rank he becomes anonymous, wild: yet the negative state has its strange fortitude. Edgar survives. (In an ironic parallel, Edgar's bastard brother Edmund insists that his lack of identity – his illegitimacy – has its strength, although for Edmund it is a fixed condition he was born with. Though Edmund illegally acquires a name when ennobled in his father's stead, he still remains alien, secret and deadly, 'simply the thing' he is. Even his change of heart at the point of death comes too late to save Cordelia.)

The encounter between Lear and Edgar-as-Poor-Tom seems to present a simple emblem, like that of the Dance of Death: that king and beggar are interchangeable when both are naked, which makes privilege appear arbitrary and precarious. Yet Lear is guilty of injustice, and Poor Tom confesses to sins and crimes, though Edgar himself is innocent. Subject to extreme pressure, as here, the social system becomes ungovernably violent, rather than being revealed as inherently violent. The apocalyptic typology[14] might be susceptible of interpretation as politically revolutionary; but it is clear that starving or shivering or raving are shown to be natural, have causes and therefore can be alleviated, they are not simple signs of just punishment. Lear is right, no doubt, to say that filial ingratitude and human injustice do great damage: these wound Lear to the heart, and rightly so. Yet the play shows how equivocal, how inadequate, it is to use the word 'unnatural' about Goneril or Regan.

King Lear's first scene is designed to emphasise the contradictions and to bring out the infringement of cultural laws and taboos. There is a complex of folk-tale motifs at the core of the narrative, concerned with parent–child relations, and the confrontation with death. Above this Shakespeare constructs an allegorical pattern signalled by the use of morality-play conventions; and above this the characterisation and dialogue is cast in contrasting styles, of exaggerated stiffness in an outmoded convention and a more rapid, supple, and detailed style of naturalism. Lear himself employs a clumsily stiff public manner and demands that others use it too, but Shakespeare has already attuned the audience to a more naturalistic and direct speech in the prose exchange between Gloucester, Kent, and Edmund.

The contrast ensures that the public manner of Lear seems repressive, arthritic, archaic. His daughters Goneril and Regan seem pliant but manipulate him with hyperbole exaggerated to the point of covert mockery (their artificiality of conceit betraying quite explicitly the fact that they are not telling the truth); this further undermines, as it calls attention to, his rhetoric of authority. The scene ends in more prose between Goneril and Regan, its speed and direct bareness revealing how they read events in terms of closely observed psychology, a bleak analysis of power-play. Their speech in private is all terse, forceful, practical.

The play of *Titus Andronicus*, like *The Taming of the Shrew*, makes rhetoric, in all its forms, palpably part of the experience, and yet faintly archaic. The artifice might be seen as consonant with the rigid cultural sanctions governing the society in each play; the rapidity with which, in *King Lear*, chaos and atavistic desire break out is accelerated by the fatal weakness of formal rhetoric, and this is a marked feature even in the first scene of the play. The concern with these issues in *Titus Andronicus* and *The Taming of the Shrew* is clear, however different the tone. While Shakespeare in *King Lear* uses parody to subvert the stiffened emblematic medieval dramatic mode, and limits the physical cruelty in the Dover cliff episode, he revives, indeed intensifies, the spiritual dimension of drama. If the outworn conventions no longer carry conviction in their own terms, the dead metaphors can be revived; physical suffering is shown to be a sign for the other: so tears may scald. The pain of injustice and ingratitude, though abstract, is a true agony. The spiritual is rediscovered within the individual and particular mind.

In madness a certain freedom is discovered, a release of energy in breaking taboos – in Yeats's phrase, 'gaiety transfiguring all that dread'. In Edgar's mockery and self-mockery as Poor Tom, and in Lear's capricious vigour and weird jests when fantastically crowned with wild flowers – 'I will die bravely, like a bridegroom' (4.6.189) – there is something strangely free and spontaneous. In his role as Poor Tom, Edgar cries out 'the foul fiend bites my back' – role-play which uncannily extends Lear's own hallucinations. Lear's madness is marked by a coming and going of hallucination so that he cannot tell physical actuality from phantasmagoria. This concern with the ambiguous and shifting borders between actual and imagined is something Shakespeare explores with the full resources of the language of his theatre, new and old.

The Fool, on first seeing Poor Tom, calls him a 'spirit', and his appearance, wild and naked, resembles medieval depictions of the demonic, so exacerbating Lear's confusion of the actual and the hallucinatory. It is also consistent with medieval ways of imagining the demonic that harsh comedy, farce, and satire, 'eldritch'[15] humour – should be a principal dramatic mode through which its terror is expressed. Poor Tom insists on the pain of persecution, as one

whom the foul fiend hath led through fire and through ford and whirlpool, o'er bog and quagmire; that has laid knives under his pillow and halters in his pew   (3.4.45–8)

and on the terror of sudden attacks by the fiend:

Tom's a-cold! Bless thee from whirlwinds, star-blasting, and taking. Do poor Tom some charity, whom the foul fiend vexes. There could I have him now, and there, and there again!   (3.4.51–4)

In such 'matter and impertinency mixed' there are constant abrupt shifts from full and reasonable consciousness to disconnected nonsense and mere animal yelps of pain. There emerges a fragmentary biography of Poor Tom,

A servingman, proud in heart and mind ... False of heart, light of ear, bloody of hand; hog in sloth, fox in stealth, wolf in greediness, dog in

madness, lion in prey. Let not the creaking of shoes nor the rustlings
of silks betray thy poor heart to women   (3.4.74, 79–83)

Such an outcast deserves his fate as a criminal vagrant, recalling
Christopher Sly in *The Taming of the Shrew*; but if his suffering
recalls Sly's, it also gives a glimpse of a much harsher
contemporary historical actuality:

Poor Tom, that eats the swimming frog, the toad, the tadpole, the
wall-newt ... swallows the old rat and the ditch-dog, drinks the green
mantle of the standing pool; who is whipped from tithing to tithing,
and stock-punished and imprisoned.   (3.4.112–17)

There is also an invisible demon who interrupts him to cruelly
comic effect: 'Beware my follower. Peace, Smolkin; peace, thou
fiend.'

The effect of Edgar's role-play as Poor Tom here is not to
draw attention to Edgar himself, behind the persona, rather it
is to reflect Lear, the overwhelming centre of attention, and
Lear's own obsessions with lust, and deceit, and the terror of
guilt – Edgar's improvised role seems accidentally to confront
Lear with a mirror, just at the moment when Lear's own worst
private obsessions and unconfessed terrors overmaster his grip
on ordinary consciousness. His reactions to Edgar-as-Poor-Tom
are unmistakably deranged. Poor Tom's violent language and
his weird performance as a soul in hell create the maximum of
derangement and panic in the old man.

In Act 4 Edgar-as-Poor-Tom leads his blind father to the
imaginary cliff-top whence Gloucester leaps in would-be
suicide, another event involving Edgar in subjecting a feeble old
man to extreme and incalculable risk. This time Edgar's
performance as Poor Tom involves a high degree of self-
consciousness, and making the audience privy to his risky
scheme. Shakespeare also wishes to make varied metaphorical
use of the idea of theatre being delusion as much as representation. Edgar points out to the audience how he is
deceiving his blind father. The style of theatre alluded to in this
'Dover cliff' episode is one dating back to pre-Shakespearean
drama and it is naively 'presentational'[16]: that is to say, where
acts of theatre are undisguised, there are directly expository

speeches, explicitly announced motives, and a frankly acknowledged audience who are required to 'piece out' with their
imagination the bare stage's 'imperfections'.

Edgar, in an aside, forewarns the audience that what they are
watching is fake: he is only playing a trick on Gloucester,
though trying to make him suppose that walking on the flat is
instead a very difficult climb is so absurd that even Gloucester
finds it hard to credit:

> GLOUCESTER When shall we come to t' top of that same hill?
> EDGAR You do climb up it now. Look how we labour!
> GLOUCESTER Methinks the ground is even.
> EDGAR   Horrible steep.
>   Hark, do you hear the sea?
> GLOUCESTER   No, truly.
> EDGAR Why, then your other senses grow imperfect
>   By your eyes' anguish.
> GLOUCESTER   So may it be indeed.   (4.6.1–6)

The verbal description Edgar then makes of the view down
the cliff is in fact consistent with the conventions of this
'presentational' mode, but Shakespeare himself plays a trick on
the audience: even though forewarned, the hearer finds it
almost impossible to resist the powerful imaginative reality of
the scene: these words make us blind to the fact that there is
nothing but two figures on a flat wooden platform to look at:

>   How fearful
>   And dizzy 'tis to cast one's eyes so low!
>   The crows and choughs that wing the midway air
>   Show scarce so gross as beetles. Halfway down
>   Hangs one that gathers samphire, dreadful trade!
>   (4.6.11–15)

Gloucester 'leaps', and lies ominously still.

This is a moment of real anxiety: perhaps, says Edgar, he is
actually dead? Was his imagination all too strong?

>   And yet I know not how conceit may rob
>   The treasury of life when life itself
>   Yields to the theft....
>   Thus might he pass indeed   (4.6.42–4,47)

Then Gloucester revives. We see it is a mock-suicide, and in a certain sense it is a mock of Gloucester, but beyond that it is disconcerting to the audience, who may recognise in their own absorbed involvement in this thrilling and strange piece of theatre, the disconcerting truth of the imagination's power to deceive. Trickery at this dark level – by the son of his father – carries grave moral risk: such cruel trickery, involving the deepest taboos, was traditionally the perquisite of the medieval stage devil, and Shakespeare is accustomed to invoke the association of cruel trickery with the medieval stage devil, for instance in his Aaron, or Richard Crookback, or Iago[17], as well as Launcelot Gobbo in *The Merchant of Venice* (2.2) who tricks and mocks his blind father. (That episode has to be very brief and quick-paced, otherwise its true violence and darkness might flood uncontrollably.) Shakespeare's method is complex here. Through Edgar he uses parody to subvert the stiffened emblematic medieval dramatic mode, thereby withholding its full power to convince an audience, but inferring, also, a question about the demonology it was meant to represent. While Shakespeare limits the physical cruelty imposed on Gloucester in the 'Dover cliff' episode, he revives and indeed intensifies the suffering in the mind. To the dazed, half-conscious Gloucester, who having fallen might think himself in the next world, the description of the supposed fiend which stood beside him as he fell must be terrifying – though an audience is made to recognise it from a detached, external point of view, as a piece of eldritch humour, if not of ironic scepticism – black and cruel, all the same. After Gloucester's mock-suicide Lear meets him, and Gloucester must again suffer cruel mockery, mockery which his intense vulnerability seems somehow to invite. Perhaps it is the fear prompted by the idea of blindness which arouses compulsive aggression in those who still have eyes. Lear and Edgar-as-Poor-Tom keep telling Gloucester to look, to read, to use his eyes: 'do but look up' – 'O thou side-piercing sight' – 'I remember thy eyes well enough' – 'read thou that challenge' – 'you see how this world goes'. The mad king seems to know this is cruel and obscurely enjoys it: one recalls Titus repeating the word 'hand'.

Shakespeare's presentation of Cordelia also raises awkward questions about 'goodness' when associated with complex motives in difficult personalities such as these. At the play's beginning Cordelia fights her father: his demand that she say how much she loves him is made in a way that seems to deny the expression of real affection. In order to protect what he seems so ready to destroy, she will resist at all costs, and answers 'Nothing'; but as the subsequent action shows, she will sacrifice all, even her own life, for her father. Lear's self-discovery is half-precipitated by Cordelia's first denial – 'Nothing' – and then Cordelia's self-discovery results from Lear's; both, it should be noticed, exalt the father–daughter bond over the husband–wife bond, and the attendant destruction is extreme.

Both father and daughter at first find only in violent conflict and extreme crisis a means of self-expression. The polarisation of opposite states marks each of them: child–father, choice–forsaken, king–beggar, disinherited–queen, wrath–grief, tears–smiles. In a scene (4.3) omitted from the Folio version, she is explicitly described in religious terms, is almost metamorphosed from woman to saint: 'she shook / The holy water from her heavenly eyes' in pity for Lear's suffering. Cordelia succeeds in achieving reconciliation with her father – he sees her, as he awakes, as 'a soul in bliss', but nothing seems to prepare him for her death. It is worse in the Quarto version,[18] even though only the Quarto version has the scene, 4.3, which asserts Cordelia's symbolic religious significance. In the Quarto version not even the frailty of Lear's sanity can shield him from a sense of actual, inconsolable loss:

> And my poor fool is hanged. No, no life?
> Why should a dog, a horse, a rat have life,
> And thou no breath at all? O, thou wilt come no more,
> Never, never, never.
> Pray you, undo this button. Thank you sir.
> O, O, O, O.

The story of *King Lear* is set in pre-Christian times. It is significant that Lear not only appeals to archaic deities such as

Jupiter but that he even imagines himself to be a god (Tamburlaine-like), commanding the thunder to do his bidding and to smite his enemies with lightning. The play does not show direct divine intervention. When Albany learns that a servant attacked Cornwall for blinding Gloucester, he declares this to be a sign of divine intervention: 'This shows you are above, / You justicers.' The episode is one the audience have already seen, but it seems rather to show the revival of a human sense of justice: one servant explains the principle behind his courageous act: 'I'll never care what wickedness I do, / If this man come to good.' The great gods above to whom Lear appeals send no brands from heaven. The play presents human behaviour. It is highly sceptical; it stresses the almost inexhaustible human capacities for self-deception and superstition. Discourse concerning divinity is placed in a paradoxical relationship to events in the play; at times one may recall the radical irony with which religious interpretations of events are presented by Marlowe in *Tamburlaine*. While in *King Lear* Christian ideas and images do have great power, as a whole the play withholds a Christian affirmation. Lear's journey into the wilderness is also a journey back into the cultural past and the buried layers of the self. It is a reversion to an extremely archaic state before civilisation has begun, like the ancient Britain described in Spenser's *The Faerie Queene*,[19] a place guarded by forbidding white cliffs, its hinterland the abode of giants. Such a country is discovered by Lear in hallucination, buried within himself: it is an internal territory – not, as in *Tamburlaine*, spread geographically across central Asia, instead it reaches inwards into the mind.

Titus Andronicus is Shakespeare's first sustained response to Marlowe's *Tamburlaine*, and comparison of the two is instructive. The challenges which confront Titus are in a sense the reverse of those that Tamburlaine faces, since *Titus Andronicus* as a play is concerned with the refusal of the hero to rule, not with the acquisition of power. The soldierly virtue of fortitude is shown in the defensive posture of Titus as he withstands atrocity and injustice, not as with Tamburlaine in the offensive expansion of cruelty and dominion. Titus suffers progressively appalling injustice while Tamburlaine perpetrates it. Titus is so besieged that he goes mad, yet in this seeming defeat his colossal fortitude holds out deep within, a retaliatory force husbanded for future use. The change from Roman self-discipline to the madman's wildness enables him to regain the initiative – and in genuinely inventive, almost unthinkable, shocking ways. Tamburlaine, by contrast, progresses from triumph to triumph, claiming he holds the Fates bound fast in iron chains and with his hand turns Fortune's wheel about (1.2.173–4).

The emblematic shows in *Tamburlaine* are devised by the hero and reach a crescendo of barbaric, grandiose violence, from the chariot drawn by conquered kings, to the hanging of the Governor of Babylon on the walls of his own city, and the burning of the Koran. The play concludes with a fierce funeral pyre with Tamburlaine's corpse: Marlowe's design is characteristically equivocal, however, for while this spectacle might be understood as symbolising the hero's assumption into the sublime element of fire itself, the narrative shows Tamburlaine as simply mortal: he sickens and he dies, a human being. Heroic energies simply run down and peter out. By contrast, if in *Titus Andronicus* Rome becomes 'a wilderness of tigers' then Titus himself becomes the most fierce of all the tigers, unpredictable as Fortune herself.

Shakespeare, like Marlowe, devises a sequence of shockingly violent and emblematic stage images to plot the progress of the action in his play, but to different effect. Tamburlaine's shows are of self-glorification and they display martial triumph and atrocity on a progressively vast scale. In *Titus Andronicus*, in contrast, the scope of the action and its focus shrink progressively. The play begins with Titus returning home in triumph after a foreign campaign. He is offered but declines the supreme power, loses the initiative, and after disastrous tactical blunders is humiliated and must withdraw from the public world. Finally, within the walls of his own house, driven mad, he stands at bay and plans an amazing revenge, at his own family table. The heroic scene is shrunk to the confines of the domestic, but only to explode with immeasurable violence.

Titus, in the depths of misfortune, is visited by Tamora, his mortal enemy, and her two sons: they are costumed as Revenge,

Rape, and Murder. This highly Marlovian emblematic show fails to impress Titus, however. He not only sees through it but instantly and brilliantly out-performs Tamora in deceit: if he is mad, then they will expect him to take her sons for what they say they are, Rape and Murder. And being Rape and Murder, obviously they deserve to be put to death. Accordingly, he cuts their throats. The emblematic shows Titus devises are at once fantastic and actual, wild and exact. He slaughters the sons of Tamora like game and after being butchered they are served in a pie to their own mother by Titus in the costume of a cook. He exactly mirrors her attacks upon him as royal huntress and as Revenge.

This spectacular inverted ceremony, this precise paradox of the barbaric–civilised, is exactly the one explored in *King Lear*. Titus parodies the meaning of the feast but, given the atrociousness of the guests who have themselves broken every kind of law, it is fitting and hospitable. In a Rome given over to anarchy Titus must improvise a mock-ritual to re-invent justice – one which in his view involves execution and sacrifice, though which from another view looks like murder. An audience is aware of a double perspective: apprised of Titus' suffering and his predicament they may rule the killing just; aware of his moral guilt and heroic strangeness, and of his continuing madness, they may simultaneously feel his actions to be beyond the bounds of the tolerable, atrocious.

Lear's capacities as a disruptive force are certainly propelled by an exceptional, indeed gigantic, idea of himself. Here is the link with Tamburlaine. This idea of himself undergoes dilation and contraction of the most violent kinds, but his capacities are of a heroic scale and ensure that he endures, so exploring immeasurable extents of inner and outer experience. Pride exalted to a giant scale – 'come not between the dragon and his wrath' – is crushed by the storm, whatever god-like pretensions he may claim. A poor animal, then, even the little dogs dare to bark at him. Lear moves out from the confines of the court to wander in a wilderness, returning at last in body, though only intermittently or partially in mind, to a prison and to the court.

The fact that the outcast Lear meets no actual beggars or

madmen and that the outcast Gloucester meets only his son in disguise, is significant in showing how firmly Shakespeare has concentrated on the paradoxical expanding-by-diminishing movement of the tragedy. It is inexorably inward, the direct opposite and inverse of *Tamburlaine*. Unlike *Tamburlaine*, this movement inward produces a sudden sense of limitless expanding space – 'Thou art a soul in bliss, but I am bound / Upon a wheel of fire'. Lear, unlike Tamburlaine, knows fear: fear of the dark half of his world drives Lear to immerse in the deep destructive element. The career of Titus moves rapidly towards madness, and in madness he sees certain truths he could not see when sane. This is an important link with Lear. That Tamburlaine and Titus and Lear all dare go forward to meet what their imagination suggests to them, however appalling or forbidden or self-destructive it might be, is a profoundly important shared quality – it is in this that their heroism ultimately consists. By developing Marlowe's scheme in *Tamburlaine*, Shakespeare in *Titus Andronicus* joins a crisis in the public world to a crisis in the family.

In *Titus Andronicus*, Shakespeare presents an epic history of a state, but this is linked to the history of a family. In *King Lear*, the history of Britain is inseparably bound to the history of Lear and his family. They are themselves the national royal family, Lear is hero–king–father, the instigator of political and family chaos and the heroic victim, his daughters his key enemies and, in Cordelia, the key to restoration. The epic scale of *Tamburlaine* lives anew in the great speech and turbulent inner world of Lear in his madness. In *Titus Andronicus*, as in *King Lear*, there is a culture which, in its harsh simple imperatives, locates a nation's constitution in archaic terms of kinship. This is rent and broken, which exposes its working: it is an anatomy as well as a tragic process.

Titus learns slowly; but he is transformed in striking ways. He is taught by Tamora's tortures to be double, ironic, witty, instead of slow, orderly, and pious. He learns from the image of the suffering Lavinia that his earlier idea of himself was as absurdly discrepant from reality as was his fixed – or petrified

– idea of Rome. But the violence that Titus demonstrates also makes his demand for knowledge and justice fiercer.

Petruchio teaches Kate with physical and emotional hardship; he makes her shamefully admit her weakness of will when subjected to her body's distress, he confronts her with an inverted image of her own violence – but how does her daemon change in response? The word shrew, etymologically, originally meant devil. Her real – or not – change may be silent and inward, it is a choice in interpretation, but her social change, her appearance, speech and attitude in conformity to Petruchio's requirements, is verbal and visible.

Emrys Jones in his study *The Origins of Shakespeare*[20] argues that the major source of *Titus Andronicus* is the *Hecuba* of Euripides, one of the most famous of Euripides' plays in the Renaissance. In this play, first of all Hecuba's daughter is sacrificed despite Hecuba's protests and in the face of her pleas for mercy. Still in a state of extreme grief, Hecuba is preparing to wash her daughter's body when she learns that a corpse is floating nearby in the sea. She recognises it as her remaining son, Polydorus. He had been sent for safety to the Thracian king Polynestor, and with him was sent gold to sustain him. She realises that Polynestor has murdered her son for the gold. Meditating on revenge, she invites Polynestor to her tent, saying that something attractive awaits him. He arrives with his two sons and they are invited in. Hecuba's women then help to kill the sons and Polynestor's eyes are gouged out with brooches. In his blindness he prophesies that Hecuba will be metamorphosed into a howling, glaring dog. What is striking about this is not only the structural and thematic affinity with *Titus Andronicus*, but also that in its concern with the mutilation of blindness it is an anticipation of *King Lear*. It is as if, in the complex of motifs in the story of Hecuba, we see at once the generation of *Titus Andronicus* and the germination of *King Lear*.

CHAPTER 5

Always topical: 'Measure for Measure'

Measure for Measure (1604) stages, clearly, certain contentious issues which the interval between Queen Elizabeth I's death and the arrival of the new King James must have brought to mind. In this play the Duke in a sense abdicates, so that both he and his subjects have a chance to experience society without a sovereign. They are involved in witnessing majesty, defamiliarised, precariously as much as sensationally achieving restoration. *Measure for Measure*'s readiness to imagine a form of abdication, and in terms more down to earth than the sublime and apocalyptic, has provoked surprising reactions in recent generations of British directors. Thus however much energy Peter Brook may have found in the play's 'rough' element, in his admirable and influential production in 1950 he endowed his Duke with great 'holiness' (these terms are from his book *The Empty Space*, Harmondsworth, 1972). Furthermore, Brook made substantial cuts to protect the Duke from his author's irreverence. Brook presumably did so as part of his scheme to stress the play's contrasts of 'rough' and 'holy', although stage productions generally in the 1940s and 1950s protected the Duke. The national trauma of Edward VIII's 1936 abdication, followed by George VI's admired performance during the 1939–45 Second World War, which re-established the monarchy's prestige, was no doubt an influence (whether unconscious or conscious) in presenting the Duke: thus Anthony Quayle, in 1956, gave his Duke a large crucifix to carry about, to make him above criticism. Early in *Measure for Measure*'s stage history, in the Restoration theatre, began the radical adaptation (and massive cutting of its low-life) in order to suppress its

provocativeness. Even in the twentieth century its outspokenness on sex, class, and monarchy has been selectively or generally
muted; but when these aspects were all simultaneously exaggerated, as by Keith Hack in his Royal Shakespeare Company
production in 1974, it may be significant that he succeeded in
offending virtually everybody.[1] The stage history reveals how
rarely directors or audiences are ready to appreciate the
extraordinary catholicity of Shakespeare's scheme for this play,
involving a wide range of competing interests, social, religious,
and emotional, and weaving a dialectic from them. His
questioning presentation of the sacred institutions of the
monarchy and the Church was then – and still is now –
troubling.

The need for the Church to use special rituals and special
costume was violently disputed in the sixteenth century, and
extreme Puritan hostility to stage plays had similar grounds.
The Duke in *Measure for Measure* achieves his political aims,
greatly strengthening his personal authority, but in doing so by
setting up Angelo he shows, as King Lear puts it, that 'a dog's
obeyed in office': he exposes both monarchy and Church to the
risk of desacralisation. His cunning does draw with the subtlest
and finest 'spider's strings / Most ponderous and substantial
things' (3.2.237–8), and he does exercise great power; yet he
makes plots like those of a stage play because he depends on his
audience's (his people's) readiness to be intrigued. Shakespeare
pinpoints his limitations: at the critical moment his powers of
manipulation fail, leaving him and everybody else at the mercy
of accident, or destiny. When sacred authority becomes
inseparable from the arts of theatre, monarchy risks becoming
indistinguishable from role-play. The Duke's concern about this
at the beginning is well-founded when he says

> I love the people,
> But do not like to stage me to their eyes   (1.1.67–8)

Nevertheless he knows he has no alternative, and he succeeds in
making himself an expert showman, though he finds it a high-
risk business. What is striking is how uninhibited Shakespeare
is, especially in gaining comic effects from the Duke's risk-

taking. While in its past stage history the play has from time to time provoked the reaction that if it were new it would be banned for its outspoken treatment of sexual matters, most recently, since the 1930s, it seems to have been the frankness with which it depicts political and religious issues that has been the trouble.

Several stories, each substantial enough to make a play, are combined in *Measure for Measure*; the result is, even by Shakespearean standards, so charged with material and energy that stage interpretations tend to baulk at the full challenge, and content themselves with only a selective interpretation. It is an instance of Shakespearean excess. The play interrelates three stories with ancient folk-tale origins: the disguised ruler, the corrupt magistrate and infamous bargain, and the substituted bedmate. In Cinthio[2], whose novella served as a major source for Shakespeare, precisely because the heroine is young and untried at the beginning her sudden power of emotion surprises everyone, even herself. Cinthio seems most interested in the bizarre twists of the story, the extreme violence and shock, for their exposure of the secrets of human motivation. The Deputy condemns a young man to death for rape, even though he pleads he loves the victim. His sister comes to plead for him, young, untried, but beautiful, eloquent. The Deputy tells her she must satisfy his lust to save her brother's life. For her to agree to sleep with the Deputy is an act of undoubted courage as well as an expression of love for her brother, though other emotions (which Cinthio leaves to the reader to speculate about) could be imagined to play a part. She accordingly sleeps with the Deputy, but her brother is nevertheless killed. Stricken with grief she travels to Rome and personally convinces the emperor of the Deputy's guilt. Then, at the very moment of the Deputy's downfall she has an extraordinary change of heart: she discovers not only that she forgives him but that she loves him, and pleads to marry him. Cinthio's version of the tale has an emphatically secular and naturalistic setting and a modern, psychological interest, yet it is also recognisably of its time in dealing with one of the most difficult injunctions of Christianity, love thine enemy.

WHAT TRUMPETS: JACOBEAN 'MEASURE FOR MEASURE'

A version of the novella in an English dramatisation by George Whetstone, *Promos and Cassandra*, was published in 1578. This ostensibly sets the action abroad but offers many added episodes of low-life intrigue actually depicting Elizabethan London and providing topical comment on social problems there. In what follows I want to argue that Whetstone's play is indeed of interest; I would emphasise, however, that it is of interest, not because through *Promos and Cassandra* we can infer the style in which *Measure for Measure* was staged in 1604, but because *Promos and Cassandra* may serve to refresh our sense of how much potential for stage spectacle is implicit in *Measure for Measure*, a text which in the First Folio has only the most terse stage directions, and even in some necessary places none at all.

Whetstone's play is usually considered dismissively as a play only in name. There is no record of its ever having been performed. Nevertheless, it appears to be a practicable script for performance in its time, and even twenty-five or so years later, in 1604, it seems to have offered Shakespeare a practical model for the dramatic adaptation of a foreign novella to Elizabethan stage conditions, its visualisation of the story in stage terms. Whetstone's stagecraft has attracted little attention because the play was apparently not performed; because it was dedicated to Fleetwood, the Recorder of London, who was hostile to theatres; because in the preface Whetstone supports Sidney's strictures on English comedy's 'grose Indecorum'; because Whetstone sounds bookish when describing his play: 'for the rarenesse, (and the needful knowledge) of the necessary matter contained therein (to make the actions appeare more lively), I devided the whole history into two Commedies: for that, Decorum used, it would not be convayde in one.'[3]

Whetstone says in the preface that having written it he had laid it aside and just happened to find it again 'amonge other unregarded papers' when clearing up before going on an exciting voyage with Sir Humphrey Gilbert, so perhaps he had no one but himself to blame that only Shakespeare found it interesting. Yet, if one considers the position of Shakespeare, confronted with the task of making a play for the Globe stage out of Cinthio's long narrative, it seems almost inevitable that he would have looked particularly at Whetstone's version for its adaptation of the story to Elizabethan stage conditions. Admittedly, Whetstone is no genius, but Shakespeare repeatedly shows his imaginative power in his selective borrowing from others. He had known Whetstone's play for a number of years before 1604 (there is an allusion to it in *Love's Labour's Lost* of 1594), and a further reason for recalling it in *Measure for Measure*, apart from the suitability of its concern with the law, the Church, and the monarch, might have been that Whetstone's formula combined this conflict-of-conscience drama with comic low-life sub-plots in ways which very much interested Shakespeare, as is evident not only from his *King Henry IV* of 1598 but also from the comedies *Much Ado About Nothing* (*c.* 1599) and *Twelfth Night* (*c.* 1601). Perhaps because the comic low-life scenes in these three Shakespeare plays are so memorable, and may be seen as precedents for the low-life episodes in *Measure for Measure*, scholars have seen little or no need to look further, and have paid virtually no attention to *Promos and Cassandra* in terms of its stagecraft.

Whetstone's play may be recognised as an early Elizabethan hybrid form, a romance in which the shadow of allegorical morality persists; its low comic episodes utilise conventions of the moral Interlude. An exemplary didactic design underlies them; the characters embody moral abstractions or exemplify social issues, and they have recognisable contemporary dress and a familiar local context. Shakespeare himself found much vitality in this dramatic heritage in his *King Henry IV*,[4] with its patterning of Prince Hal's career on the prodigal son story and its widespread use of formal, structural, and stylistic elements recalling the moral plays; thus in Part 2 Prince Hal's role shifts 'from that of Lusty Juventus to that of Good Government,' and Falstaff, the 'reverend Vice' of Part 1, becomes Old Mortality.[5]

The stage conventions of morality drama shared with public and official ceremonies in Elizabethan England certain sign systems, in costume and symbolic action. Some of these costumes and ceremonies survive to the present day, though no longer expressive in the same direct political and cultural terms. Every tourist brochure about England features royal, ecclesiastical, and civic robes, the gowns of scholars, the badged coats of those in liveries, heraldry on shields and flags, ceremonial weapons such as swords, pikes, and staffs. In Elizabethan society, and in Elizabethan drama, these carry serious meaning, signal different kinds of authority, of political affiliation, of religious conviction. They display social rank; they exemplify the public systems; they are typical; they were also topical. In Whetstone's play, as I shall show, the carefully specific and practicable stage directions make use of these conventional signs as a continuous expressive means of relating the story to current conditions.

A satiric comedy, *Eastward Ho*, performed within a year of *Measure for Measure* (though at a different playhouse by a different company), is of interest for the detailed stage directions, the absence of which is so tantalising in Shakespeare's play. *Eastward Ho* uses as its basic plot the common Interlude theme of the prodigal son, here handled in the debate form which contrasts the industrious and the idle apprentices. The play treats this subject as material for parody, through which the hypocrisy, pride, and avarice of Jacobean citizens are mocked, and it ends with a speech ironically invoking the didactic pieties of the old Interlude style:

> Now London, looke about,
> And in this morrall, see thy Glasse runne out.   (5.5)[6]

In devising this rumbustious parody the dramatists were clearly sure of their audience's familiarity with the morality tradition, and indeed the detailed stage directions in *Eastward Ho* indicate a type of stagecraft, and scale of performance, which Whetstone would have found familiar:

Enter Maister Touch-stone and Quick-silver at severall dores, Quick-silver with his hat, pumps, shortsword and dagger, and a Racket trussed up under his cloake. At the middle dore, Enter Golding discovering a Gold-smith's shoppe, and walking short turns before it. (1.1)

Here the stage directions ascribe typical, not uniquely personal, identity to characters; the characters are personified moral abstractions, though given locally familiar and topical guise. This concrete, practical detail makes a largely formulaic action engaging and lively in its truthfulness to the specific. Indeed the attention to detail is somewhat surprising, as with these directions for a goldsmith's shop on stage.[7] One might well have expected that its existence would have been left to the Elizabethan audience's supposedly 'trained' imagination. If such affinities are demonstrable between the staging of *Eastward Ho* in 1605 and that visualised (though it seems not realised) in *Promos and Cassandra* of 1578, there do seem to be grounds for thinking that *Measure for Measure* could have been staged in a similar way even though it is certainly true that the play can be powerfully impressive when performed with the simplest staging.

Whatever the reader's impression of slack and turgid prolixity in its longer speeches (this is my own impression), *Promos and Cassandra* is not much longer than *Measure for Measure*; and it is an over-hasty reaction to assume it was never intended to be performed simply because there is no record of its having been staged. A variety of features of *Promos and Cassandra* show the author's attention to staging and acting. Whetstone's authorial directions, like those of other dramatists, might well have had to be modified during rehearsal or changed if the number of actors was unexpectedly small, but they do not seem outlandish or otherwise unlike authorial stage directions generally in texts of the period. They are particularly interesting when they mark action not otherwise to be inferred from the dialogue or narrative, as a number of instances illustrate. Before addressing Promos in Part 1, 3.2, Cassandra has the stage directions *'Speakes to her selfe'* and then *'Shee kneeling speaks to* Promos', and later in the scene speeches are marked *'to hir self'* and *'To himself'*. In Part 1, 2.7, as the prisoners are led, singing piously, to execution, there is the direction, 'The *Preacher* whispering some one or other of the Prisoners styll in the eare.' These are simple enough ideas, but they suggest a more than merely literary approach. Much more importantly, Whetstone offers a strongly visualised treatment of his story, and Shakespeare's own response to Whetstone is in interesting ways visual.

Whetstone devises a number of strong visual emphases for being arrested and suffering legal punishment, which reach their sombre climax when at the end of Part 2 Promos is led in procession to execution, watched by Cassandra clad in mourning. In Part 1, 2.6, there is a comic–macabre scene: 'The *Hangman*, with a greate many ropes abought his necke', is directed to enter and he says: 'Here is nyne and twenty sutes of apparell for my share.' 'Here is' does not require that the suits be visible to the audience, though this would add interest to the scene. The hangman then examines some of the ropes round his neck: 'how are my knots, I fayth syr slippery'. Shakespeare recalls this episode in *Measure for Measure*, and though the executioner there has an axe, several references are made to ropes and hanging, and he shares with Pompey (who is the source for the comic element) a jest about the suits of those executed (4.2). Again in *Promos and Cassandra*, Part 1, 3.6, Whetstone has an episode which Shakespeare may have remembered. The courtesan Lamia is brought in by officers, under arrest; she complains they are spoiling her 'brave' gown and she is roughly told she will have to get used to the prisoner's garb of blue. This staging of a more or less gentle roughing-up by arresting officers may be recalled in the scene where Pompey is shown being taken to prison (*Measure for Measure*, 3.2), and Lamia's sexual bribe to the justice is parallel to Pompey's in his trial by the Provost (2.1). The situation encapsulated in Whetstone's stage image is transposed by Shakespeare's imagination, but it seems likely that Shakespeare was struck by the repeated visual demonstration in Whetstone of arrests, prison, and people fettered.

The most spectacular episode is in Part 1, 2.7, where the stage direction is 'Six prisoners bounde with cordes, Two *Hacksters*, one *Woman*, one lyke a *Giptian*, the rest poore *Roges*, a *Preacher*, with other Offycers.' These types, chosen as visually telling examples of current social problems, then make their public professions of repentance, though interruptions are made by a '*scoffing catchpole*' and a '*churlish officer*'. They exit singing a pious lament in chorus. Shakespeare seems to have remembered this episode when writing Pompey's speech at the beginning of Act

4, Scene 3 of *Measure for Measure*. The strongly visual and physical quality of Pompey's caricatures of the inmates of the prison might tempt a modern producer to present on-stage actors of Dizie, Deepvow, Copperspur – not forgetting Wild Halfcan. If this is done, it is an unconscious salute to Whetstone's stagecraft, though we cannot be certain that this is what Shakespeare required, or what was actually done with the scene by the King's Men in 1604. Shakespeare's writing ensures a strong effect no matter which staging is chosen, but it is striking how vigorously his imagination seems to have responded, especially to the stage images Whetstone devised when translating his source, a novella, into dramatic form: for instance in Part 1, 4.4, the gaoler brings Cassandra (the prototype of Isabella in Shakespeare) '*a dead mans head in a charger*', and Cassandra's lines give implicit stage directions:

> let mee kis thy lippes, yet ere I fall to mone.
> O would that I could wast to teares, to wash this bloddy face.

As the scene ends she takes the head with her, vowing to see it buried.

Whetstone selects strong stage images in his translation of a novella into a play: Promos led, disgraced, toward execution and watched by a black-gowned Cassandra; the King receiving the city's sword of justice and its keys, and being greeted by a consort of music; an official receiving petitions one by one from citizens; a poor man kneeling before the King in the street; a courtesan in her fine gown brazenly tempting the judge trying her; Cassandra kissing the bloody, severed head she believes is her brother's; the hangman and his ropes. These images left their impression on Shakespeare, and his imagination worked on them powerfully. Some appear in his play in equivalent terms; one, the severed head, appears as a physical object brought on stage in the middle of the play and also feeds the imaginative concern with the ambiguities of love and cruelty. It is striking that these ambiguities are played out in the erotic darkness at the moated grange, in a scene which Shakespeare withholds altogether from his audience. It must be imagined.

The stage history of *Measure for Measure* shows that the play can be interpreted as primarily concerned with the personal experiences of the chief characters, but it can also be given a more public and political emphasis. How far does Shakespeare's design invite this, and what considerations might have seemed important when staging the play for the first time, whether at the Globe or before King James in 1604?

Whetstone calls for strong emphasis on citizens, prisoners, and ceremony. The certainty that Shakespeare read *Promos and Cassandra* suggests that he must at least have considered the idea of a crowded city and the city's familiarity with public ceremonies. For an acting company the achievement of this effect would be partly a question of the number of actors available. Shakespeare's writing and design in this respect are characteristically flexible; presumably calculatedly so, because of the likelihood of different kinds of occasion, of playing place, and of cast size, which would require different kinds of adaptation. Consideration of the example of *Promos and Cassandra* serves therefore to alert us to just one possible type and scale of interpretation in Elizabethan terms. Spectacle and crowds present the events in the largest terms of political dialectic; these are implicit in Shakespeare's text, but would have an explicit topical impact if presented in Whetstone's style, which might spell trouble.

Shakespeare displays no consistent pattern in his use of *Promos and Cassandra*; one cannot say, in any given case of a parallel episode, that Shakespeare required the staging to correspond to Whetstone's. However, it is certainly interesting that the King's Men could have presented a similarly detailed interpretation, and thence could have much enhanced the play's direct topical application. That such a staging, either at the Globe or at court before King James, could even have been contemplated might seem unlikely; that it would have been provocative seems certain; but precisely because he worked on Whetstone's play, Shakespeare must equally certainly have weighed the question. Perhaps, then, we should do the same.

The first scene of *Measure for Measure* is usually interpreted today as requiring a minimum of ceremony, and is usually acted as a hurried, even clandestine, episode with only the speakers present. The corresponding scene which begins *Promos and Cassandra* goes like this: 'Promos, Mayor, Shirife, Sworde bearer: One with a bunche of keyes: Phallax, *Promos man*'. Promos begins by addressing the Mayor and his companions and commands that the letters patent be read out: 'Phallax *readeth the Kinges Letters Patents, which must be fayre written in parchment, with some great counterfeat seale.*' Curiously, the actual words on the parchment are not given (and this is also true of the 'commission' which the Duke hands Angelo in Shakespeare); still, Whetstone's directions suggest what such a property document was like. The sword of justice is presented by the Mayor, distinguished presumably by his chain of office, and the keys of the city by the Sheriff; both of them, as stage directions later indicate, wear scarlet robes. The ceremony establishes a civic presence and a chain of command in the city government. Stage ceremony imitates real-life ceremony in London. In Part 2, 1.9, when the King is to make a formal royal entry to the city, the reception committee enters in advance to take up their positions: '*Promos, Maior,* three *Aldermen,* in red Gownes, with a Sworde bearer, awayghtes the *Kinges* comming.' Promos makes his 'briefe Oration,' then 'The *King* delyuers the Sworde, to one of his Counsell' and replies. Then 'The *Maior* presentes the *King*, with a fayre Purse.' The King thanks him but returns the gift, and everyone says 'Lord preserue your Majesty.' Then comes the entertainment:

Five or sixe, the one halfe men, the other women, neare vnto the Musick, singing on some stage, erected from the ground: During the first parte of the song, the King faineth to talke sadlie with some of his Counsell.

Then the King's usher commands 'Forewards my Lordes,' and they all go out 'leysurablie' as the song is sung to its end. Whetstone intends that the monarch be shown as not aloof but ready to listen to others; later this impression will be reinforced by his response to petitioners. Here it should be noticed that in Part 2, 1.4, Whetstone has a scene in which preparations are being made for the royal entry. Stages are ordered to be erected, the first of which is possibly to be erected there and then on stage, judging by the dialogue:

> Dispatch Dowson, vp with the frame quickly.
> So space your roomes, as the nyne worthyes may
> Be so instauld, as best may please the eye.

He orders another stage 'at saynt *Annes* crosse' for the waits (musicians) and says the Four Virtues are to stand at 'Iesus gate'. He goes off to see the 'Consort of Musick' (referred to in the stage direction from 1.9, quoted above) well placed. This little scene seems designed to create a sense of civic life as well as excitement in preparing for the big scene to come. After such a build-up, some spectacle seems guaranteed the audience, and the music seems a practical way of adding effect economically. Reference to the Nine Worthies does not require their presence, but suggests possible decoration of the stage façade. Glynne Wickham comments that he does not think Whetstone intended this royal entry as burlesque nor that his audience regarded it as such.[8] I certainly agree with him. The question of how far we might imagine the King's Men staging the beginning of Act 5 of *Measure for Measure* must remain speculative; what is clear is that Whetstone's version indicates the practicability of spectacle for an Elizabethan stage, and reinforces the assumption that audiences would appreciate as much of it as could be provided. Whetstone clearly has English ceremony in mind.

While there are few indications of staging in *Measure for Measure*, the text at 4.5 has the Duke ordering 'trumpets to the gate', and this presumably implies their presence and their at least sounding a flourish at the opening of the fifth act. On being welcomed the Duke places Angelo and Escalus on either hand, saying 'And good supporters are you,' thus punningly alluding to the heraldic figures which support either side of an armorial shield. The idea seems to be suggested by their central and emblematic place in the ceremony. The remark would have little point if ceremony were lacking.

The Folio text of *Measure for Measure* has only the barest stage directions for the beginning of Act 5: '*Enter* DUKE, VARRIUS, LORDS, ANGELO, ESCALUS, LUCIO, CITIZENS *at several doors.*' The

Duke's first speech there indicates that this is indeed the moment he meets the reception committee. The play was certainly performed at court on St Stephen's Day in December 1604. It was very probably performed at the Globe before then. The real royal entry to the City of London on 15 March 1604 had been a most lavish and memorable affair, with the construction of seven triumphal arches along the route through the City taking six weeks (three were begun the previous March but because of the plague were left unfinished for months). Dekker says eighty joiners, sixty carpenters, twenty-four carvers, seven chief painters, over seventy labourers, and numerous other artificers were employed.[9] The first arch, at Fenchurch, had at the top 'moddells of all the notable Houses, Turrets, and Steeples, within the Citie'; the gate through which the king passed was twelve feet wide by eighteen feet high; the arch bore the name Londinium, and featured live figures personifying 'The Brittayne Monarchy, Diuine Wisdome, The Genius of the City, The Counsell of the City, and Thamesis the Riuer.' The Genius was performed by the actor Edward Alleyn, who delivered a speech, and Thamesis by a boy-actor, who also spoke, and the City Waits provided music. Dekker implies that the king was somewhat keen to press on, and he was in a grand procession, 'richly mounted on a white Iennet, vnder a rich Canopy, sustained by eight Barons of the Cinqueports'. The route was lined with double rails from St Mark's Lane to the conduit in Fleet Street, and the livery companies spread on these rails their 'Streamers, Ensignes, and Bannerets' in front of their seats. The glass windows of the houses on the route were taken out so that everyone could get a good view. At Cheapside Cross the official address was read by the Recorder of London and gold cups were presented to the king, queen, and prince.

Here, then, was a remarkable piece of street theatre which Shakespeare, wearing the livery of a groom of the king's chamber, had witnessed as an official member of the royal procession. Most modern scholars agree that the façade of a triumphal arch, with its upper level and wide central opening often flanked by openings on either side, could correspond to the façade of the tiring-house in the Globe Theatre, and it certainly seems plausible to suppose that what carpenters could erect in a street would not be beyond imitation in a theatre.

When the Duke returns to his city at the beginning of Act 5 of *Measure for Measure*, the Folio stage direction has the common formula '*At several doors*', which could mean 'at two opposite doors'. Possibly the Duke is to enter with his group after Angelo, Escalus, Lucio, and the citizens have taken up their positions to receive him. The 'Trumpets' (that is, trumpeters) might be stationed 'above' at a gallery, and the façade might have been decorated in the manner familiar from the recent real royal entry to London. It might, however, be objected that this sort of large spectacle would distract an audience from the real business of the scene, and this begins, it will be recalled, with Friar Peter nerving Isabella up to

> Speak loud, and kneel before him.   (5.1.19)

Isabella then cries out,

> Justice, oh royal Duke! Vail your regard
> Upon a wronged – I would fain have said a maid.

The heraldic group of Duke, Angelo, and Escalus must unfreeze, turn aside to attend to her. She is insistent:

> justice, justice, justice, justice!   (5.1.25)

The more formal that opening ceremony is, the more festive the music or trumpeters' flourish, the louder and more assertive must be Isabella's show-stopping interruption. But then might the emphasis on speaking loud actually gain in point if made in a context of trumpets, cheering, and colourful pageantry? Is it a trace of implicit stage direction? It could also be significant that Shakespeare has transposed and reshaped some rather feeble episodes concerning petitioners from later in *Promos and Cassandra*, Part 2. In 2.5 and 2.6 poor petitioners submit complaints to an official who is seen, according to the stage direction, 'with divers papers in his hand,' and in 3.3, the King receives these petitions and administers justice. A stage direction then reads, 'As the King is going out, a Poore man shall kneele in his waye.' In *Measure for Measure*, by contrast, the Duke seems shockingly biased against the petitioners Isabella and Mariana who kneel in his way.

The more formal and dignified his authority in the ceremonial entry, the more striking could Isabella's appeal be, and the more shocking his hostile bias against her. At the same time, any suggested allusion to James I in this Duke might run a certain risk, and the more visually topical the staging the greater the risk. It needs to be stressed that a highly spectacular and ceremonious staging of this episode would not be in danger of distracting from the dramatic force of what follows, indeed quite the contrary is true; and such staging potential in Shakespeare's text is made clearer by reference to Whetstone's.

Right from the start Shakespeare's handling of the narrative is, by contrast with Whetstone, compressed and rapid, with the effect that intense pressure is placed on the inexperienced characters. No sooner is Angelo invested with the ducal robes than Claudio and Juliet are seen being taken to prison, Claudio already condemned to death for getting Juliet with child. Isabella, his sister, is called from the nunnery in this emergency: young, inexperienced, but quick to emotion, she encounters an equal instability in Angelo: it is the insecurity underlying his rigidity which makes his loss of self-control so violent. In contrast to Cinthio and Whetstone, Shakespeare stresses his characters' personal inexperience in contrast to their sophisticated moral standpoints based on the intellect rather than working knowledge; he greatly concentrates the pressure on them by simplifying and accelerating the build-up to the crisis in Angelo's second interview with Isabella. The effect is to insist on vulnerability, especially in those with real strengths: the Duke's wisdom, like Angelo's intelligence and Isabella's emotional power, is shown liable to lapses.

In Act 1, Scene 2 the young and socially respectable couple Claudio and Juliet appear as innocent victims of Angelo's excessive severity, while the more obvious malefactors such as Pompey and Mistress Overdone remain (for the moment) at large. Yet it soon transpires that, as Claudio and then Juliet confess, they did knowingly break the law and admit guilt (their protest is at the extreme punishment). The apparently clear-cut contrast between the young and pregnant Juliet and the old, worn-out bawd ('Overdone by the last', as the old joke has it) conceals some disconcerting similarities. Angelo, serious and modest, seems at first impression to be diametrically opposite to the scurrilous Lucio, but it transpires later that each of them has callously deserted a woman. It is Angelo who turns out to be the greater sinner and also capable of judging himself unworthy of mercy. Escalus seems a shrewd and seasoned magistrate at the trial of Pompey and Froth (2.1), in contrast to the impatient and inexperienced Angelo, and this contrast deepens as the action proceeds. When the Duke returns in his own person at the end of the play, he places Angelo on one side and Escalus on the other as if equal supporters of justice. He knows of Angelo's villainy, so the audience will understand this as deliberate irony, implying that a truer simile would be to liken them to bad and good angels, to extremity and temperance, to tyranny and justice. Yet encouraging the audience to make such a judgement is part of Shakespeare's manipulative and deceptive technique here, for when Escalus takes over the interrogation of the Duke-as-Friar later in this same scene, Escalus too dispenses flagrant injustice when he is taken in completely by the plausible Lucio's lies.

The play's dialectical structure is based on a series of one-to-one encounters, generating debate in a range of social and rhetorical styles concerning major public issues; Shakespeare's debt to Whetstone is clear and important here, though his art of characterisation adds a whole dimension to the debate: replacing the rigid stereotypes with complex, deceptive, mobile personalities, showing what men do, not what they ought to do. In effect, Shakespeare finds Whetstone invaluable because *Promos and Cassandra*, with its abstract moral debate and estates-morality stereotypes condenses into practicable theatrical expression the influential, actual, Puritan attitudes to social problems of sixteenth-century London.

Shakespeare's direct experience of the City authorities in his years as an actor–playwright could have led him to take particular, ironic note of Whetstone's dedicating his play *Promos and Cassandra* to William Fleetwood, because his duties as Recorder of the City of London, which involved him in trying to clean up the underworld, gave Fleetwood a jaundiced Puritanical attitude to the theatres, which he believed to be a significant source of civil disorder.

Shakespeare's playhouse the Globe was situated on Bankside, a liberty in Southwark lying outside the ancient City of London's borders, but incorporated in it since the 1550s, and Bankside had traditionally based its livelihood on entertainment, mostly in the form of taverns and brothels – the 'stews' which Shakespeare's audiences would have observed on their way to and from the Globe Theatre. Shakespeare, unlike Whetstone, owed his livelihood to the theatre and was a sharer in the Chamberlain's Men, the most commercially successful acting company of the time. Shakespeare would therefore have been very aware of the frequent legal measures enacted by the City council and aimed at restraining the 'abuses' by the players, such as that in 1600 when the Privy Council bowed to pressure and decreed that certain playhouses should be pulled down. Shakespeare's company successfully evaded such measures, but the experience may be reflected in parodic terms in the Overdone–Pompey sub-plot in *Measure for Measure*.

Shakespeare's technique here may be compared to that of the playwright Henry Chettle who, in his 1592 pamphlet, *Kind-Hartes Dreame*, uses parody in defence of the professional theatre and against official charges that it encouraged idlers and unthrifts. Chettle brings back to life the recently dead actor Tarlton to play the ironically conceived part of a brothel-keeper. All the familiar official arguments to attack the theatres are put in the mouth of this character, who laments the decline in his own thrifty business as a result of the rival attraction of the theatres. He pretends to virtuous outrage at the amount of money young people spend on 'that unprofitable recreation of Stage playing'; public-spiritedly he deplores the loss of business to shops which are not sited near the theatres, and the loss of trade for the bowling alleys which now stand empty in the afternoons; but worst of all is the fact that even his own whores have no customers: 'its pitie Players should hinder their takings a peny' (sig. E3). In short, the theatres encourage sinful idleness and should be forbidden – 'Out upon them,' the tavern-cum-brothel-keeper cries, 'they spoile our trade.'[10]

In *Measure for Measure* (1.2) Shakespeare presents a tavern-owner, Mistress Overdone, whose complaints sound like an old and oft-repeated litany: 'Thus, what with the war, what with the sweat, what with the gallows, and what with poverty, I am custom-shrunk'. In fact these allusions were also contemporary realities:[11] the Duke of Holstein was in London recruiting for the war in Hungary in 1604; the royal entry to the City of London in 1603 had to be deferred until March 1604 because of an outbreak of plague; and Elizabethan extreme Puritans had for years been advocating (noisily, but in vain) the death penalty for sexual offenders. Then (1.2.78–80) her tapster Pompey tells her about 'the proclamation' that all the 'houses' in the suburbs are to be pulled down. There had been a recent proclamation, that of 16 September 1603, calling for houses in the suburbs to be pulled down, but that had been an anti-plague measure. In Pompey's version an equivocation may be heard on 'house' – as 'dwelling-house', as 'hot-house' (bawdy-house) and as 'playhouse'. Pompey and Mistress Overdone are ironic spokesmen for Shakespeare to choose for the enter-tainment industry, and we notice Pompey's comment (1.2.83) that friends in high places can be useful – the new law does not apply to the City's own 'houses', because 'a wise burgher put in for them'.

There have been editors ready to ascribe this scene of the play to another hand, Middleton's; the coarse prose of Lucio, the Gentlemen, Mistress Overdone and Pompey is felt to be too shockingly discrepant from the dignified surface of the opening scene's verse. Yet the function of the second scene is to expose, by contrast, what the first scene conceals or represses. The underworld scenes with their informal language, slang, in-decency, and abuse, represent from one point of view crime, disease, and sin in need of reformation; but these scenes are no less integral to the play in its concern with the irrepressible energies of life. The energies of life in this case are rampant, disrupting what is good. Yet if laxity will not do, repression, so it seems, judging by Angelo or Claudio, will not do either, since it is deforming.

For Whetstone the problem of disease and disorder is a matter of lax morals and neglect of the holy scriptures. Shakespeare's insistence on the positive aspects of instinct and appetite, even when embodied in such apparently unsavoury persons as Pompey and Mistress Overdone, corresponds to his depiction of corrupting processes close to the heart of extreme piety, self-denial, and the attempt at impersonal justice, not only in Angelo but in Isabella and the Duke. This is represented also in the language of the play, and it is represented further in the large-scale design of the plot, interrelating while opposing main plot to sub-plots.

Building on Whetstone's model, Shakespeare greatly develops the local and topical setting of the story, presenting a detailed and more unflinching impression of London and Bankside. The City as a whole and the political establishment are subjected to a penetrating and, by implication, critical analysis, so much so indeed that an otherwise unmistakable London has to be called 'Vienna' and the religious debate must be removed from the English Protestant context at the time of James I's accession, to a far-away state that is emphatically Catholic. As further confirmation of this we may note that in *Measure for Measure* Shakespeare more than once echoes phrases from the extremist Puritan propaganda of Philip Stubbes's *The Anatomy of Abuses* (1581).[12] Extreme Puritans demanded rigorous reform of ecclesiastical law – the ecclesiastical courts of the Church of England were, they maintained, unable to enforce moral discipline and their sanctions were too easily evaded. Extreme Puritan pressure-groups demanded wider authority for scripture as a basis for law (and for a mercifully short period, in the Commonwealth Act of 10 May 1650, spiritual misdemeanours were reclassified as secular crimes: incest and adultery carried sentence of death without benefit of clergy and fornication was punished by three months in gaol, while brothel-keepers were to be whipped, pilloried, branded, and gaoled for three years; a second offence meant death).

When James I ascended the throne of England in 1603 religious issues were political issues, since the monarch's claim to absolutism offered to infringe the Church of England Bishops' ecclesiastical power. The continuing operation of ecclesiastical law in Church courts, for example in the matter of marriage and slander, both important issues in *Measure for Measure*, are examples of such ecclesiastical power, under pressure when James came to the throne.

Since extremists constituted significant pressure-groups in both Protestantism and Catholicism at the time, and since obsessive anxiety about sexuality has a venerable place in the history of the Church, it is perhaps unwise to identify Shakespeare as an opponent only of Puritan extremists: what does seem certain is that his changes to Whetstone are designed to focus on the dangers of absolute dedication to rigorous principle, especially because of its temptations to those preoccupied with doctrine, whether of government of the self, of secular society, or the Church. The Duke makes this the main point of emphasis in the play's opening scene. This might have been meant to appeal to James I, the author of *The Trew Law* and *Basilikon Doron*,[13] although it might also have been intended as an oblique disputation with him.

ROLE-PLAY AND SIGN-SYSTEMS

It is striking that in this play, the first Shakespeare wrote for performance at court before the new king, James I, he should have presented a ruler in effect going through a version of abdication, the subsequent story graphically exposing the power structure and class system of the state and bringing into sharp focus central Jacobean constitutional questions. It may indeed be because Shakespeare found the material so engrossing that he returned to it soon afterwards in *King Lear*, another anatomy of the state which begins with the abdication of the ruler. In *Measure for Measure* the Duke's choice of deputy licenses an exploration of his own city and a searching, difficult, and finally dangerous confrontation with lawlessness and violence, especially sexual violence. The Duke, like King Lear, concludes that in effect he has 'taken too little care of this'. The play presents an anatomy of the system from top to bottom; the state and its law are seen from a ducal perspective but also from that of the citizens, whether criminal or law-abiding. The presentation of two aspects of a ruler (in the Duke and Deputy) also permits an analysis of the qualities of character and personality and the laws of power.

The Duke is forced to adopt the exotic scheme of the bed-trick to save Isabella from Angelo. The bed-trick scheme brings the Duke uncomfortably close to looking like a bawd. This might be supposed a difficulty Shakespeare inherited from the Italian sources he was using, but, on the contrary, it is Shakespeare's own addition to the story: Isabella's counterpart in Shakespeare's sources agrees to sleep with the Deputy. Evidently Shakespeare is relishing the surprising, bizarre, and disconcerting qualities of the tragicomic mode, but this is less important than the fact that, in making Isabella refuse the corrupt Deputy's demand that she give herself to him, Shakespeare is radically changing the characterisation of the heroine, and he does this in order to redirect the chief emphasis of the play away from Isabella's personal love story, and towards the larger public questions of justice, good government, and the question of the Duke.

Shakespeare invents a character not in his sources, Lucio, who offers a running commentary of criticism of the Duke as secretly sexually perverse and politically corrupt. Lucio thus serves to voice a questioning view of received Renaissance wisdom, that it is part of the art of a ruler to use secrecy and to be known to use secrecy. Shakespeare shows Lucio to be malevolent and untrustworthy in his dealings with other characters, but also to be acute and intelligent; what he says must therefore be treated with scepticism, but although he exaggerates and distorts, Shakespeare evidently invented him to subject the Duke to questioning.

I would like to examine the deceptive grammar and vocabulary of the Duke's first full speech, relating this to the stagecraft and its emphasis on costume and role-play. There is the larger issue of lying and self-deception (or self-betrayal), and true and false interpretation of appearances, which, in this play, Shakespeare makes problematic for the audience as well as for the characters. There is a link generally in the play between lying and disguising (both deliberate) and self-delusion and seeming (in varying degrees of unconsciousness): a complex interrelation between language and appearance. The question of doubleness, of folded meaning, is presented right away in the language and visually reinforced in the stage properties, the letters and the ducal robes transferred to Angelo by the Duke as he 'removes' himself:

> Of government the properties to unfold
> Would seem in me t'affect speech and discourse,
> Since I am put to know that your own science
> Exceeds, in that, the lists of all advice
> My strength can give you. Then no more remains
> But that, to your sufficiency, as your worth is able,
> And let them work. The nature of our people,
> Our city's institutions, and the terms
> For common justice, y'are as pregnant in
> As art and practice hath enriched any
> That we remember.   (1.1.3–13)

The Duke's first line here, while giving prominence to the important nouns 'government' and 'properties', withholds closer definition of them, makes the listener note the possible association between 'properties' and 'unfold' in a theatrical sense ('property' meaning any portable article of costume or accessory used in acting a play), which slightly destabilises the metaphoric sense 'qualities' or 'characteristics'. The Duke equivocates on the outward displaying of authority, its emblems and robes of office, but also their function of enfolding, of making hidden and secret, the character of the ruler and his power and humanity. The word order is very unusual, delaying the main verb and thus creating suspense as to the outcome of the sentence. The repeated delaying of the grammatical structure by such syntactic means calls close attention to the way the Duke speaks, the sense in which he is using the words must be guessed at, and variable possibilities come to the listener's mind – some of them disconcerting. The words tell –

'properties' – 'unfold' – 'seem' – 'affect'; then a little later, the delayed verb 'enriched' is surprising:

> y'are as pregnant in
> As art and practice hath enriched any (1.1.11–12)

It is easy to misconnect these to make 'art' and 'practice' suggest manipulation in a bad sense, especially when the result is the practiser being 'enriched', and this half-submerged suggestion will be particularly picked up in 2.2.150 by Isabella's words to Angelo, 'Hark how I'll bribe you', a mere figure of speech, as Isabella intends it, but ironically one which excites Angelo as it unwittingly names what he desires. The Duke's oblique manner does not control and restrict the semantic function of his words. Meanwhile the listener, in the confusion of the syntax, fastens on the individual words and on what he can see on stage in his effort to comprehend. The result is that the listener in his search for meaning is alerted to a number of mischievous or scandalous possibilities, and this is a necessary preparation of the audience for what is to come. The Duke then explains he has chosen Angelo as his deputy:

> we have with special soul
> Elected him our absence to supply,
> Lent him our terror, dressed him with our love,
> And given his deputation all the organs
> Of our own power. (1.1.17–21)

The Duke chooses Angelo to 'dress' with his love and the emblems of his power, and we see him do this on stage. He then tells Angelo to his face, with a seemingly generous tone but to somewhat daunting effect, that he can 'unfold' his history, he can read him like a book:

> There is a kind of character in thy life
> That to th'observer doth thy history
> Fully unfold (1.1.27–9)

This psychological interest is well beyond Whetstone's dramatic resources; it immensely enriches the intellectual quality of the play's argument. 'Character' means handwriting, the expression of one's individuality (so it is that banks trust a signature as a guarantee of identity). But 'character' also means cipher, encoded secret writing, as well as the modern sense, personality. Deciphering becomes unfolding, making the obscure, the secret and doubled, clear and open. Angelo, says the Duke, should be a script unfolded to be read in public, and he begins this *unfolding* by the physical action of *enfolding* Angelo in the ducal robes. As he announces this, he alludes with deceptive straightforwardness to the Sermon on the Mount:

> Heaven doth with us as we with torches do,
> Not light them for themselves: for if our virtues
> Did not go forth of us, 'twere all alike
> As if we had them not. (1.1.32–5)

This might at first, indeed, seem clear: 'Let your light so shine before men' (says the text, Matthew 5) 'that they may see your good works and glorify your father which is in heaven.' Yet Angelo is dulled rather than ignited by the appointment:

> Let there be some more test made of my metal
> Before so noble and so great a figure
> Be stamped upon it. (1.1.48–50)

He offers an alternative metaphor – not of a light shrouded in the folds of a cloak, but of metal, not yet assayed as pure gold, being stamped with the ruler's image to become a coin of the realm. He questions whether he might be counterfeit.

When the Duke tells Angelo 'Mortality and mercy... Live in thy tongue and heart' (1.1.44–5), we might suppose 'mortality' means 'the death sentence', in direct opposition to mercy; but 'mortality' is also 'the condition of being alive', while the Christian concept of life, embracing death as the redeemable punishment for original sin, is mercifulness. The word 'mortality', then, is itself a paradox.

This issue, this antithesis, is brought into play in the most intimately inescapable way in the two scenes featuring the encounters between Isabella and Angelo, when she comes to sue for her condemned brother's life. Both Angelo and Isabella are committed consciously and explicitly to an extremely fierce and austere excluding principle. Their whole rule of life, their grammar of life, so to speak, as they see it, is based on excluding and suppressing or repressing what they believe imperfect in themselves. Clearly they are to some extent doubles of one another and when they meet the effect is that everything which each has sought to repress and exclude in the name of virtue erupts in grotesque form. Isabella's challenge to Angelo has ironic effect: it penetrates the judge's robes to arouse the man beneath:

> Go to your bosom,
> Knock there, and ask your heart what it doth know
> That's like my brother's fault.   (2.2.140–2)

It suddenly makes both of them aware of their close and heated physical proximity to each other: it strikes, unwittingly, at Angelo's guilt for his past treatment of Mariana and, to an Angelo now caught in desire for Isabella, it tantalisingly puts into words directly what he does desire, so that now he himself can confess his guilty desire to himself.

The release of the repressed (in the comic low-life episodes as in the relationship of Angelo and Isabella) might be interpreted as, in a sense, a healthy thing, a movement towards stability, whereas at the play's beginning the act of imposing order on a word, a person or a system creates manifest deformation, provokes both conscious and unconscious rebellion. The play makes an association between authority and deformation (and damage), which induces a division between tongue and heart. Seen in politic terms of a ruler's guile, such dividing of tongue from heart is defensible – Machiavelli regards it as essential to any ruler's survival, and so it is to the Duke in *Measure for Measure* – but in Angelo it is the personal consequences that are explored, and self-division erupts within him to produce first suffering and then despair; indeed an audience may feel compassion as well as repulsion for him at the end of Act 2, Scene 2:

> What dost thou or what art thou, Angelo?
> Dost thou desire her foully for those things
> That make her good?   (2.2.177–9)

THE SACRED

Shakespeare twice tempts his audience to take the worse view of the Duke. At the very beginning when he seems irresponsible in abandoning his dukedom, he tells Angelo:

> nature never lends
> The smallest scruple of her excellence
> But, like a thrifty goddess, she determines
> Herself the glory of a creditor,
> Both thanks and use.   (1.1.36–40)

Later we see he really means to be a creditor, lending excellence to Angelo in order to get back great thanks and also profit for himself. Shakespeare extracts excellent ironic comedy from the Duke's failure to foresee how speculatively risky an investment Angelo will prove, but here the Duke declares a Machiavellian motive to improve his position in power uneasily associated with a social (and personally therapeutic) process of cleaning up the city, and with the spiritual issue, the state of certain souls. The sacred is entwined with its opposite. The Duke forces Angelo to act, at the outset, and through Angelo – by lighting the torch Angelo – the darkness of that enfolded heart and of the whole body politic is to be illuminated. Even the Duke's own explanation seems to try, and fail, to conceal uneasiness:

> I have on Angelo imposed the office,
> Who may in th' ambush of my name strike home,
> And yet my nature never in the fight
> To do in slander.   (1.3.41–4)

The Duke-as-Friar smoothly deceives Isabella, too, in preparation for the Duke's return in Act 5, Scene 1, but he then abruptly rejects her appeal for justice and sends her off to prison. This episode has several deliberate echoes of a bitter episode of tyranny in Jonson's *Sejanus*. Certainly this tension contributes to the sense of wonder at the joyful climax, as the mode of Jacobean tragicomedy decrees; it is also true that for a while Isabella does suffer as if indeed the victim of sadistic tyranny. At another level, the episode displays how susceptible to perversion is the political system of absolutism in 'Vienna'.

Keyed to the moral debate of black against white, the visual prominence given to the robes of judge, nun and friar seems deliberately designed to show how powerful is their authority as sacred in the culture, but equally how it is vital for the men and women wearing those robes to preserve the spirit of the law they represent. Through the play's language of theatre Shakespeare spells out a thesis: the robes confer no immunity, and nobody is above the law. 'Oh 'tis the cunning livery of hell', cries Isabella at Angelo's deceit,

> The damned'st body to invest and cover
> In prenzie guards. (3.1.95–6)

She visualises his naked soul black as the devil, disguised in the dress of virtue, while he tells her she must yield him her virtue, 'put on the destined livery' of a woman, strip her black nun's gown and reveal her white nakedness.

With the official robes of Elizabethan public life (even gallants and whores, like city officers, liveried servants, prisoners, judges, and nuns and friars, are signalled by their dress) go badges and heraldry. Angelo, wearing the robes of Justice while wickedly betraying the office, confesses that though we 'write "Good Angel" on the devil's horn, / 'Tis not the devil's crest' (2.4.16–17). Earlier the Duke refers to himself as of saintly sexual virtue: 'Believe not that the dribbling dart of love / Can pierce a complete bosom' (1.3.2–3), he boasts to a Friar. This immobile image of the saint, the chill icon immune to the prompture of the blood, is applied in turn by Claudio to the hypocrite Angelo, this 'outward-sainted deputy' (3.1.88) – a Deputy, it is to be remembered, whom the audience hear confessing his inability to make a prayer.

Thus verbal images keep an audience aware of Shakespeare's stage metaphors, in which the human body in its varied clothing is the central image. Nashe[14] had mocked extreme Puritans who enquire into 'every corner of the Commonwealth, correcting that sinne in others, wherwith they are corrupted themselves'. Nashe turns their obsessive attacks on sensual pleasure, on gaudy clothes, and the theatre, against them: 'the cloake of zeale, should be unto an hypocrite in steed of a coate of Maile:

a pretense of puritie'; such extreme Puritans, says Nashe, are
ham actors: 'It is not the writhing of the face, the heaving uppe
of the eyes to heaven, that shall keepe these men, from having
their portion in hell. Might they be saved by their booke, they
have the Bible alwaies in their bosome, and so had the Pharisies
the Lawe embroidered in their garments'. Shakespeare is not
concerned merely with the satiric aim of exposing hypocrisy,
but to explore repression and its destructive effect on the human
psyche, that of the tyrant no less than the victim. The subjection
of human personality – even of strong personalities like Isabella's – to rigid social roles in the society of 'Vienna' is one of
the play's most striking emphases, reinforced by the manifest
power of costume, whether it be the judge's robe, the prisoner's
blue garb or the nun's habit.

A second group of images both verbal and theatrically visual
concern the head, the emblem of the ruler stamped on coins, an
image also conveying a sexual connotation of the father's image
imposed on the metal in the matrix, or bed, where a coin is
struck or a child conceived. Printing off coins, children, and
words are all acts licensed by law; forgery, like slander and
begetting bastards, is at the centre of the play's action, which is
focused precisely on heads, on fathering, counterfeiting, beheading. The play's climax is a big public scene, a royal entry,
a civic pageant which thus becomes a trial, a legal ceremony,
ending in attacks on a religious Father whose hood is ripped off
to reveal the head of the Duke. The action thus ends with the
putting of heads back on to bodies (Mariana, Claudio) and the
putting of the Duke's head back on the body politic, making
both bodies human, giving both their restored identity. In terms
of the metaphor of clothing, the city is unfolded as an allegory
of the unfolding of the Deputy Angelo's 'secret history', and
vice versa. The play's climax is the multiple stripping of actual,
visual disguises and unveiling of true identities, and this is
accomplished in a series of *coups de théâtre*: the Friar's hood is
ripped off by Lucio to reveal the Duke, then Lucio and Angelo
are stripped of their respective disguises, a mysterious veiled
woman is revealed as Mariana, and finally a muffled fellow is
discovered to be Claudio, alive.

The exposures force certain characters to confront personal sin as well as political crimes. From the play's beginning – indeed from its very title, which is taken from Matthew 7 – religious ideas are prominent. The Duke's role as Friar, and Isabella's passionate commitment to life as a nun, give emphasis to the enclosed world of the devout. The Church is also seen in a political as well as a social context, when the Duke-as-Friar claims that the Holy See of Rome confers on him immunity from arrest.

The Catholic robes of friar and nun keep an audience visually conscious of the powerful sign-system of religious garments. At first sight the secular realm of government, subject as it normally is to short-term political measures, to expediency, might be thought of as set in contrast to the religious realm, which is supposedly devoted to eternal salvation and damnation, the laying-up of treasures in heaven spiritually. Yet in *Measure for Measure* the Duke-as-Friar learns rapidly to use the religious network in society, an independent system, and he uses it to effect urgent practical subversion of state power. The Church's code of confidentiality, its deputising of impersonal authority, empowers the Duke-as-Friar to learn secrets, to make secrets, and to exploit secrets. It is not a large step to recall the political potential of dissident Catholic priests in the actual British society of the time. Of these the well-known Father Garnet of Gunpowder Plot (which would be discovered one year after *Measure for Measure*'s first performance) is only the most obvious instance.

The trial scene is structurally and verbally reminiscent of Jonson's classical tragedy *Sejanus*, performed by Shakespeare's company the previous year. Shakespeare's most striking change is from pagan to Christian Catholic robes, the sacred immunity of which is violated in the climax as the Friar's hood is ripped off and the Duke is revealed beneath – a friar, representing a medieval order of holy authority, is turned into a politic prince of a modern nation state. Is this an exposure of the fading power of Rome? Or a tactful comment on how State and Church work hand in glove? And hence a gloss on King James being head of both the Church and the State in Britain? Or is this visual event a tacit comment on the covert truth that Church and State are competing power systems, both using ceremonial robes and secrecy to clothe their devious methods of rule? The visual stage image poses a question, while seeming to make a conformist statement, when it shows two meanings doubled in one person.

That is to say stagecraft, stage imagery, and dramatic narrative reinforce the verbal doubles and deceptions with physical doubles, visual deceit. Codes are broken, face values questioned, ciphers exposed; through the language of theatre are enacted painful and exuberant unfoldings of private lives, of public slanders and of capital treasons. All may end well, the 'measure' devised by the Duke to extirpate vice being answered by the 'measures' of Angelo to satisfy extreme severity, then unbridled lust and murder, yet ending in the harmonious 'measure' of a comedy's dance-like completion. The plot nevertheless makes an audience recognise the limitations of prescriptive, inflexible systems of government and self-government; the sequence of crises in the plot bring into focus varieties of individual human intransigence, from the unassimilable stubbornness of a Pompey or of a Barnardine to the very different intransigence of Juliet's private decision to give herself in love to Claudio, and 'take the shame with joy', or Isabella's youthfully intense aspiration to holiness. The power of these two women characters is in their direct impulsiveness; and here Shakespeare went beyond Whetstone, and touched the quick of Cinthio's story.

CURRENT TOPICALITY:
MODERN 'MEASURE FOR MEASURE'

A key characteristic of Shakespeare the dramatist is the structural resilience of both his individual scenic episodes and overall designs, so that his plays survive as narrative and go on generating graphic stage action when subjected to many different kinds of cutting, adaptation, and interpretation. The richness of his material, also, allows for very various emphases while still ensuring that an audience has something substantial to get to grips with. The stage history of *Measure for Measure* in the present century displays its special quality of inviting adaptation in response to topical contexts, including many which could not have been originally envisaged.[15] A key source for this topical adaptability, which makes the play a perennial focus of contention in the theatre as well as the academy, is its relation to the morality tradition.

In *Measure for Measure* the contrast between the contemporary London atmosphere and the Catholic regime (visually stressed by the religious robes of nuns and friars which are prominent), helps focus attention specifically on the ruler's relation to religion, and hence on the political aspect of religion in Britain as well as in Europe at the time. This seems to be a deliberate allusion to Jacobean realities, not simply a conventional motif deriving from sources in novella and folk-tale.

The story of the Duke abandoning his position of ruler and then living in his State, disguised as a friar and learning to exploit the alternative system of the Church, seems designed to explore the differences and the similarities of these two institutions. When James VI of Scotland became James I of England he was emphatically keen to exercise his rights as head of the Church as well as of the State. It was believed that the structure of authority in Church and State ought to be similar, and that the one ought to support the other and to be actively concerned in its affairs: bishops claimed the right to advise the king, and vice versa. In that moment of change to a new reign much was at stake for factions within the Church as well as for James I.[16]

Shakespeare's further changes to his sources make the Duke not a remote emperor but the long-standing ruler of the city, thereby insisting on the shock of his impotence once he is bereft of his former authority. Furthermore, his restoration to his dukedom affirms his right on the basis of his personal qualities: there is no reference to inherited right as such. His hidden power is revealed to the audience as craft, and nerve, and also fortune: and – strikingly – without the aid of a friar and the authority of Catholic robes he could never have succeeded.

Because *Measure for Measure* is based on traditional folk-tales which encode certain key cultural issues, and yet represents them in terms of up-to-date social and psychological complexity – because, that is to say, even in 1604 it was detached, as well as engaged, in its presentation of Jacobean culture – it is always being rediscovered as topical, and as being too outspokenly so – as can be seen if we apply it to recent British history, the 1980s decade. The action of *Measure for Measure* critically exposes the practical systems of power, but also its mystique, in the State. Thatcherism in the early 1980s proclaimed itself to be a force for radical change, and whereas this is usually a routine politician's cliché, this time the policy began to be put into practice and, like a barium meal, illuminated fundamental, quasi-instinctive processes in British public life.

Yet rather than depict the severe Deputy in the play with allusion to the draconian rule of the 'Iron Lady' Mrs Thatcher, professional productions (subconsciously, even perhaps consciously, sensing a new hardness in the atmosphere) chose consistently the much less politically direct issue of feminism.

For all the major differences between the religious and political situation under James I and that in the 1980s, what is striking is how easily, in fact, ironic parallels could have been brought out between the play and the British situation in the 1980s, and this is so, precisely, because Shakespeare's play, in its allegorical mode, invites an audience to think about the central institutions in the State and the nature of their authority.

In Jacobean England the two most important institutions were the monarchy and the Church, both of them invested with sacredness as well as direct, legally endorsed executive power. These two institutions were obviously no longer important in executive terms in 1980s Britain: indeed in the period since 1945 as a whole, their importance in the culture has usually been dismissed as residual. Recent history, however, suggests that such a verdict is an over-anticipation, and that the sacred itself remains a source of real power in British culture. The power of the sacred is one of the central issues in *Measure for Measure*, but, contrary to what might be expected from the remote and supposedly more superstitious culture of the Jacobean age, in the play the sacred is treated to a disconcerting extent as a cultural construct, and one shown to need active maintenance: this is implied in the ironic analogy between the ruler, the priest, and the actor, combined as they are in the Duke. It may illustrate the way in which *Measure for Measure* is itself radical in its exposure of the structures of authority, both legal and sacred, to read the most recent past in British history in the same spirit.

The present British royal family offer an instructive example of the sacred, if we accept as a working hypothesis that the sacred is culturally derived, and may be usefully discussed in terms of cultural anthropology. The monarchy and the Church both claim to be above party politics: this transcendence preserves the taboos surrounding these institutions, insisting on the sacred, unquestionable element inherent in them. At the same time, as mediators of divine will and divine wisdom, both monarchy and Church claim power in the State; the monarch opens parliament and bishops sit in the House of Lords. Elizabeth II, like Elizabeth I and James I, is simultaneously the head of the Church of England and the head of State. The parliamentary government (so-called Westminster democracy) today is still formally known as her majesty's government and the 'premier' actually carries the title 'her majesty's prime minister'. What is striking about *Measure for Measure* is its candour – given that these are highly sensitive issues in 1604 – in exploring these two institutions, the monarchy and the Church, as institutions, that is to say, as cultural structures which are shown to depend on maintenance, whose authority is vulnerable to cultural and political change and is shown to operate by periodic adjustment and modification of the sacred codes.

For the subjects of Queen Elizabeth II the status of the monarch became politically interesting during the 1980s, and in the same period the Church of England also made itself politically felt. The policy of the Thatcher government sought to effect radical change of a structural kind in Britain, and the shock waves set alarm bells ringing in major national institutions, with the effect that the actual ideologies were forced to declare themselves. The radical drive forced opponents to reconsider the nature of the constitution, which all parties had generally tended to leave alone, on the grounds that this made manoeuvre easier. Anxiety about the effects of a truly determined radical political programme led to calls for constitutional reform to prevent extreme and sudden change: Mary Beard wrote in *The London Review of Books*, 26 October 1989, 'Westminster-style democracy has proved itself unable to protect central civil liberties – witness for example the recent erosion of the right to silence, the right to join a trade union, and the right to speak freely in the public interest... What the British have become accustomed to call their "parliamentary democracy" is merely... a reformation of sovereign power. Parliament is as illimitable and uncontrollable as the monarch once was.'

Attention was drawn to the position of the monarch, and it began to be asked what reserve powers the monarch in fact had, and when and why she might use them, and with what result. Commentators readily recognised that the monarchy is more than a residue of exhausted former real power, more than a convenient or, from an alternative point of view, a perniciously nostalgic and reactionary, signifier. What the commentators seem ready to admit is that the monarchy's power derives from the people's continuing readiness to grant it sacredness, and that the House of Windsor up to the beginning of the 1990s had most astutely seen to it that the territory of the sacred, though it might need shifting at its borders, could be maintained if the negotiation with present-day British culture were alertly, and also boldly, sustained.

The theatre makes a similar diagnosis, and witnesses to the same phenomenon. It was necessary for the satiric television cabaret, *Spitting Image*, routinely to represent the monarch, since the monarch was perceived as politically significant in a way which did not occur to previous generations of satirists during her reign. The reigning monarch was also impersonated in a stage play, Alan Bennett's *A Question of Attribution* (1988), something which has very rarely been done since 1603, when a play called *The Tragedy of Gowrie* presented the living monarch James I on stage, in the course of dramatising a recent attempt on his life. The play was promptly suppressed, and no copy of it has survived. As for the Church of England, David Hare's play *Racing Demon* (1989) focused on the Church's newly agitated situation. Despite the Church of England's tolerant doctrinal views and habitual interest in compromise, it nevertheless felt obliged to speak out against social hardship – and this at once involved it in political conflict. In *Racing Demon* the direct hostility of the government to such outspokenness produces an Establishment exercise in cynical *realpolitik*, a virtual inversion of the ending of *Measure for Measure*.

The sacredness of the monarchy today is not inevitable. Since the First World War the spread of democracy and the decline of the British aristocracy have required serious adjustment of the presentation of the monarchy, with the immensely important help of the media. A politically neutral and personally admirable monarchy was successfully presented as 'the rallying point of stability in this distracted age', the most effective aspect being 'its restrained, anachronistic, ceremonious grandeur'.[17] The first director general of the BBC saw to it that from the Duke of York's wedding in 1923 'audible pageants' made royal state occasions attractive to record-size audiences, with special microphones picking up the sound of bells, horses, and carriages; the fairytale mode of conveyance by gold coach grows increasingly popular in a mechanical age.[18] At the same time, the advent of television has been eagerly accommodated to such occasions, with the royal family learning its techniques, and today the royal family show an expert professional awareness of the whole television process; recent royal weddings, shown world-wide on television, seem to revive some of the raw assertion of the Jacobean court masque's mythopoeic celebration of the monarchy, combined with the older, medieval traditions of Lord Mayor's Show populism and the medieval feeling of royal entry pageants. The royal family present strict contracts before agreeing to collaborate on television films about themselves, retaining rights to approve the final version, to insist on cuts and changes, and generally to overrule directors, and they retain subsequent control of all copyrights of the material.[19] Film of the present monarch being actually crowned may not be shown without the Queen's permission, and this permission is rarely granted. The royal family and their advisers have ensured that the sacredness of these images is secured by law.

In the post-war world the tendency to elevate royalty as national prestige declines has been especially marked in Britain, and strikingly, the televised coronation of the present Queen has been called an 'act of national communion'.[20] The medium of television continues to convey the message that royalty is to be reverenced; it embodies a myth of unbroken tradition from medieval times imagined as chivalric and religious, and it simultaneously perpetuates the picture of the Queen and her family as quintessentially middle-class. However benevolent it may be in practice, it seems evident that this is a highly political myth, and one to which considerable thought and material resources are now devoted.

The more complex aspects of monarchy, its equivocal combination of the ordinary and the sacred, are much more important. However calculated the ordinariness of certain images of this family, there is never absent – and for safety's sake must never be absent – an element of difference marking out the line between sacred and non-sacred. The more subtle and flexible the distinction, the more effectively it functions. One small girl on a Christmas BBC television programme in 1989 asked the Queen what it was like to wear the crown, and the Queen replied that it was heavy, but then, it was meant to be. Here is that ambivalence, at once ordinary and remote, that interplay of the familiar and the other, which characterises this particular cultural phenomenon. Moreover, the metaphorical dimension is present whether consciously intended or not. The charisma is structural, not personal. Constructed within an evolving culture, it is susceptible to decay. It is particularly striking how presidents and premiers make an effort to try to invent sacredness. It is evidently elusive, but its power is undeniable.

CHAPTER 6

Amorous fictions in 'As You Like It'

While Shakespeare made limited use of pastoral elements in several early works, *As You Like It* is a full-scale pastoral comedy. Pastoral was generally popular in the 1590s: for instance the non-dramatic pastoral romances, Lodge's *Rosalynde* and Sidney's *Arcadia*, which were both first published in the same year, 1590, were reprinted (Lodge in 1592 and 1596, Sidney in 1593) and then in 1598 were both reprinted again. *As You Like It* appeared soon after, in 1599,[1] Shakespeare basing the narrative on Lodge. I take it, nevertheless, that it is to Sidney rather than Lodge that Shakespeare was more indebted in his thinking, and that the new pressure of intelligence to which Shakespeare subjects the pastoral mode in *As You Like It* owes more to the example of Sidney; and I certainly find that to return to *Arcadia* with *As You Like It* in mind sharpens response to Sidney's art.

In the space of two or three years from 1598 Shakespeare produced, in addition to the epic history, *Henry V*, and the pastoral comedy, *As You Like It*, two romantic tragicomedies, *Much Ado About Nothing* and *Twelfth Night*, a satiric history, *Troilus and Cressida*, a farce, *The Merry Wives of Windsor* (though this yet awaits satisfactory classification), and *Hamlet*. In a burst of such creative activity, in which he seems as a matter of deliberate decision to have chosen sharply contrasting kinds of play and several new modes (something which the old designation 'middle period' scarcely emphasises) – in a phase when, in short, Shakespeare's interest in the expressive resources and limitations of different kinds of theatre seems clearly to have been intense – it is entirely appropriate that he should decide to turn to pastoral, given that mode's particular reputation and particular traditions, its oblique treatment of its narrative subject, its invitation to the artist to reflect on his art, its prompting an audience to recognise his artistry. It may also be incidentally significant that 1599 is the year of Ben Jonson's first revolutionary experiment with metatheatrical comedy, *Every Man Out Of His Humour*. At any rate when, in *As You Like It*, Orlando interrupts a conversation between Jaques and Ganymede by making an exuberant entrance, exclaiming 'Good day and happiness, dear Rosalind' (4.1.30), Jaques reacts immediately to this as an unwelcome tone, lyric, and with it an alien mode, romance, to say nothing of the intolerable sense, simple well-being! He turns on his heel with the retort, 'Nay then God buy you, and you talk in blank verse.' In this collision between satire and romance the elaborate prose of the melancholy man is shown up as symptomatic of his vanity, while at the same time the open eager style of the lover, as we are amused to note, finds expression in less than artless metrical form. Here Shakespeare gets excellent comic effect by joining together what Ben Jonson held all men should keep asunder.[2]

At first sight Shakespeare's title for the play, *As You Like It*, emphasises style only to disarm critics as they enter the theatre. Here, it seems to say, shall you see only pleasure of a familiar kind in a well-tried style – and the seemingly over-simple art of the opening scenes may confirm such an impression. Yet pastoral is often mischievous in its manipulation of the reader or spectator, and *As You Like It* is almost studious in its adherence to the conventions of pastoral. We may well, on second thoughts, suspect ambiguity in the play's title, recognising it to be glancing outwards at the restrictions imposed by audience taste (what you like) and simultaneously glancing inwards at the author's attentiveness to decorum, pastoral being too dominant a genre, and too complete a system of construction, to permit more than variations on old themes. Shakespeare in the event takes the opportunity with both hands, finding in the theory and style of pastoral itself a fertile comic subject, and transforming its themes into dramatic poetry of a kind that honours the shade of Sidney.

If we accept that the Epilogue is an integral element in the play we must find it acting to reinforce this concern to stress the gap between literary fiction and physical immediacy of bodily life, asserting thereby a critical view of the audience's taste for mere fiction and false appearances. The boy-actor of Rosalind/ Ganymede, still in costume as a woman, steps forward for the Epilogue, half out of (yet still half in) the fictional frame, and asks the audience what they have earlier heard Ganymede ask Oliver in the play: was not this well counterfeited? This is just as piquant the second time, since we still do not have a real girl or real boy but yet another created dramatic part, this time of boy-actor half impersonating the play's heroine. This no-man's-land, so to speak, the obverse of a Jonsonian induction, this fictional representation of half-created fiction, corresponds to that other no-man's-land where pastoral is situated, between the present representation and the ideal world it strives to recover, to translate.

The play wilfully underlines the fact of its fictionality as Le Beau gives his news: 'There comes an old man and his three sons' (1.2.118): and Celia at once reacts to his style: 'I could match this beginning with an old tale.' In fact Shakespeare has done exactly that, matching the number of the old man's sons to those of Sir Rowland de Boys, as his source, Lodge, had not. So here *As You Like It* is even more like an old tale than is the prose narrative of *Rosalynde* on which it is based. But this is to anticipate. For the moment let it be enough to observe how Shakespeare's teasing Epilogue makes an audience recognise how readily, even at this moment after the play has ended, they would surrender to the counterfeit of art, even when its deceptions are half-exposed.

And this too is consistent with the treatment of pastoral as we find it in the non-dramatic writing of Shakespeare's contemporaries, who felt expected to include threads of reflective commentary in the fabric of their narratives, often teasingly playful in drawing the reader's attention to the artifice. Thus Sidney in his *Old Arcadia* [3] writes out for the reader a song which he says Cleophila sang, and then he remarks, 'I might entertain you, fair ladies, a great while, if I should make as many interruptions in the repeating as she did in the singing' (29). Sidney then gives a description of how much her sighing did interrupt the song, and this actually takes twice as long to read as the song itself did. Again, in Book 3, chapter 39 of The Countess of Pembroke's *Arcadia*, he begins: 'But Zelmane, whom I left in the cave hardly bestead … makes me lend her my pen awhile to see with what dexterity she could put by her dangers' (654). Sidney pretends whimsically to have no control at all over his narrative: he would have us imagine it unfolding in various strands simultaneously in separate places, only one of which can be recorded at any one time. More startling still for its playful and absurd disturbance of the reader who may have succumbed to the charm of the fiction is Sidney's description of one of the disguised princes taking his lady's hand, 'and with burning kisses setting it close to her lips (as if it should stand there like a hand in the margin of a book to note some saying worthy to be marked) began to speak these words' (176).

Sidney's humorous but also carefully self-conscious reference to his own act of writing paradoxically serves to win the centre of the stage for the events narrated. The lover's hand is given immediacy by contrast with the mere sign for a hand printed in a book's margin, and this immediacy of the narrated event over the act of describing is stressed when we read on: for as the lover begins poetically to lament love's power to change men's states and torture them, he is interrupted by a rather more urgent instance of inconstant fortune in the form of a real lion and a she-bear, ready to tear him (and his lady) limb from limb on the spot.

Such emphasis on the act of writing serves not only to foreground the events narrated but, more basically, to stress the gap between the verbal process of narration – the narrator's and the reader's time – and the time and place in which the narrated events occur. This is consistent with pastoral exactly because its whole cast is reflective, expressive of a longing for simplicity of life and of art, for simplicity of language to describe forms of life remote from a present perceived as more complex, confused or colourless. Pastoral laments the gap between representation and its imagined subject, and in a sense its subject is this gap. Situated between a fallen present and an imaginary place and time, persistently endeavouring and persistently failing to translate that remote subject into the here and now, pastoral creates its own provisional condition: its presence involves simultaneous awareness of the absent imagined subject, and its nature is hence reflective, its status paradoxical.

This is apparent, for instance, in the song of the young Prince Musidorus in *Arcadia* who, disguised as a shepherd, sings to the chaste Princess Pamela 'to show what kind of shepherd I was'. The kind of shepherd he was, as we see from the song, is a shepherd only in metaphor; he remains a prince, his shepherd's weeds a discardable disguise. In his song, the pastoral metaphors are only that. They can be simply removed to leave the decoded statement. The prince in his own condition is a complex figure, only one aspect of whom is apparent in shepherd's costume. His language here if shorn of its sheep's clothing, suddenly acquires the complexity of court poetry. The shapely closure of pastoral's decorum offers only illusory containment, as the adjectives 'fruitless' and 'endless', and the verb 'upholds' indicate:

> My sheep are thoughts which I both guide and serve,
> Their pasture is fair hills of fruitless love:
> On barren sweets they feed, and feeding starve:
> I wail their lot, but will no other prove.
> My sheephook is wanhope, which all upholds:
> My weeds, desire, cut out in endless folds.
> What wool my sheep shall bear, while thus they live,
> In you it is, you must the judgement give. (232)

To speak of Shakespeare 'translating' pastoral romance into a play, as I do, may serve to emphasise the nature and scale of the process, 'removing from one person, place or condition to another' and 'changing into another language while retaining the sense' (OED). Looking more closely at the idea of translation one sees that there is a qualification to be made to this sort of definition, since there is something ineffaceable in a work of art which will alter the native character of the language into which it is translated, thereby creating something new:

there inheres in a translation the shadow of the absent original which makes it a different thing from an independent work of art in either language. In fact Shakespeare seems to have wanted actually to stress the derivative literary model which he translated in *As You Like It*, and I hope to examine some of the ways in which he makes us aware of it. It is not only *As You Like It*, but also the preceding non-dramatic narratives *Arcadia* and *Rosalynde*, which stress their status as imitations, which call attention to the gap between themselves and antecedents with stronger claims to authenticity, being less veiled by repeated translations. Such purer narratives take the form of romance, an extended action whose configurations correspond to deep emotional patterns and whose process irresistibly absorbs the solitary reader. Secret hopes, desires, and dreams are represented there in forms which the conscious mind permits the reader to feed on uninhibitedly.

Sidney's *Arcadia* is a great work of literary imagination, whose power and wit must have influenced Shakespeare at levels deeper than most of the materials from which he borrowed his plots. To Sidney Shakespeare could look for subtle observation of the play of motive and counter-motive, for openness to the surprising mixtures of elements in intimate relationships developing – this above all – in time. The striking features of Shakespeare's romantic comedies are their depiction of major personal development in the chief protagonists, presented in a context of busy, diverse, humorous contrasts. I would not rule out the notion that *Arcadia* was used as a source (in the orthodox sense) in more places than Shakespeare-source-hunters have so far suggested, but here I am concerned with influence at a much more profound level. Sidney sets an example in depicting processes of change, of growth, and capacity for love, without protecting his characters from painful as well as ridiculous revelations about their personal inadequacy, and the mingled yarn from which experience is made; and Sidney continuously alters the degree of sympathy with which the narrative engages the reader, and the angle of vision from which it is recorded, so that his style enacts rather than simply conveys this incessantly dialectical record.

Sidney's narrator, and his characters in *Arcadia*, always speak, sing, and write within a decorum. In this sense there are no truly internal voices of self-communion. In place of a hesitant, erratic inner voice, Sidney presents one aspect of a character using oratorical means to address himself or herself.

Sidney makes distinct his frequent shifts from one style to another, and this sometimes has an abruptly dramatic effect. The reader, made conscious of the art of a particular style, becomes aware also of what its decorum excludes (this is comically evident in the speech of Miso, for instance). In style and in the narrative itself, Sidney makes outlines emphatic, but the eye is consequently drawn also to what lies beyond (or behind) the present subject, implied or as yet unseen or unsaid. This awareness of gap, of vacant space, is a characteristic feature of the pastoral mode: in defining the frame so consciously, Sidney ensures that we think also about what is precisely not said, so keeping us critically alert. In isolating and outlining an attitude or a group of figures, a detachable and summarisable meaning may be indicated, emblemising the speaking picture, yet this emblemising process is also resisted by the fluid current of dramatic action and the contrast and comparison of styles involved in it, making our assent to such emblems, when they seem too restricted or static, more than reluctant.

To approach Shakespeare by way of some detailed episodes from Sidney's *Arcadia* may serve to identify in the non-dramatic written mode, techniques and effects which Shakespeare translates into pastoral drama in *As You Like It*; for the process is much more thorough and complex than might be suggested by Duke Senior's speeches, which well merit the implied ironic criticism of his courtier, Amiens, that style alone is not enough:

> Happy is your Grace,
> That can translate the stubbornness of fortune
> Into so quiet and so sweet a style. (2.1.18–20)

In *As You Like It* Shakespeare employs the circumstances of stage performance to set the written in contrast to the spoken word. Episodes in verse are juxtaposed to prose; the revelation of character through realistic conversation is contrasted to formal emblematic descriptions of people (Jaques and the stricken deer, 2.1.25–66; or Ganymede's mock-portrait of the typical lover's 'careless desolation', 3.2.373–81). Written poems are brought on stage and pinned up, or read aloud to other characters and to the theatre audience in a critical spirit. Faultless songs are sung to musical accompaniment, creating emotion no mere words, spoken or written, can equal.

In terms of theatre spectacle, the physical charm of Ganymede, the strength and grace of Orlando, the mimic skill of Touchstone, the foulness of Audrey, make a direct impact on the audience's eyes and senses; but surprising emphasis is also placed on what is withheld from the audience's view, though described with literary art and having tantalisingly visual interest: the natural landscape; the weather; Orlando found sleeping under a tree, 'stretch'd along, like a wounded knight' (3.2.241); Oliver asleep and menaced by a green and gold serpent and a lioness; Orlando, bleeding, falling in a faint (only a shadow of this is seen on stage, when Ganymede faints on hearing of his wound).

Shakespeare not only reproduces the ingredients of non-dramatic pastoral as readers like it, he ensures also that the variety of ways of representing experience, which the contrasting styles afford, will constitute an implicit critical debate, to which nonsense and parody make telling contributions. While this is possible in non-dramatic narrative like Sidney's, it is stressed in the extra dimension of theatre in *As You Like It*, where Shakespeare's necessary concern with movement, and with time, sets against the writer's or painter's belief in the value of pattern the theatrical truth that a tableau is no sooner achieved than it must dissolve.

Sidney's account of the Princess Philoclea falling in love with a graceful Amazon (whom she fails to detect as a prince, Pyrocles, in disguise) begins apparently by chance; the narrator has been describing a day's hunting when he suddenly remembers the princess: 'And alas, sweet Philoclea,' he cries, 'how hath my pen till now forgot thy passions' (237). As he turns to tell her story, the day's hunting nevertheless lingers in his mind, yielding the brooding simile, 'she was like a young fawn who, coming in wind of the hunters, doth not know whether it be a thing or no to be eschewed' (238). We are told that Philoclea falls for the Amazon at first sight. She behaves exactly like a character in a stage play, miming the conventional signs of infatuation. Sidney presents this as a scene to be acted, and in a style visually reminiscent of the Commedia dell'Arte:

And if Zelmane sighed, she should sigh also; when Zelmane was sad, she deemed it wisdom and therefore she would be sad too. Zelmane's languishing countenance, with crossed arms and sometimes cast up eyes, she thought to have an excellent grace, and therefore she also willingly put on the same countenance, till at the last, poor soul, ere she were aware, she accepted not only the badge but the service, not only the sign but the passion signified. (239)

Sidney maintains a distance between tenor and vehicle in his own prose even if Philoclea cannot in reality. His own metaphors depict her susceptibility to signs and images, but though Sidney is not unsympathetic to the girl's tender pictorial fancies he makes clinically clear their graduated increase in sexual feeling, as he tells us how she progressed from emblematic frame to emblematic frame: 'First she would wish that they two might live all their lives together, like two of Diana's nymphs ... Then would she wish that she were her sister ... Then grown bolder, she would wish either herself or Zelmane a man, that there might succeed a blessed marriage betwixt them' (239). These brittle images disintegrate under pressure from below, where in her dreams Philoclea encounters self-begotten images that frighten her. Her whole personal development is presented in terms of her relation to images. Those of her secure childhood identity are reflected in her mother and sister. They become painfully defamiliarised as she acquires a separate selfhood through love for the Amazon, who at first seems an ideal female image, but very soon becomes disturbingly ambivalent.

Her sister Pamela, who reflects her childish self, repeats her own transformation into melancholy lovesickness. Her mother, who also falls for the Amazon, suddenly appears in the hostile role of sexual rival, presenting an image, distressingly close to

Philoclea, of lust and jealousy: adult sexuality at its most rank. So, torn by alienation, burned by desire for she knows not what, she feels as if, while acting a part (as we see she did when imitating the Amazon), the part has taken possession of her, and an alien person acts out a role through her own body: 'For now indeed love pulled off his mask and showed his face unto her, and told her plainly that she was his prisoner. Then needed she no more paint her face with passions, for passions shone through her face' (240).

We recognise that, viewed externally, this looks farcical, yet we sympathise with her inner dilemma. Sidney deploys metaphors drawn from the theatre – masks, costumes, disguises, expressive gestures and signs – and these we can see to be psychologically valid (as well as being appropriate to an intrigue plot, in which she finds herself). Philoclea's development proceeds from one imprinting (in the ornithological sense) to another, more appropriate to her maturation: she passes from a state of narcissism to the brink of love for the opposite sex, in the process discovering herself jealous of her own mother; and Sidney even intensifies the image of adolescent crisis by making her father also lust for the Amazon, so producing a situation claustrophobic and perverse as much as farcical. Philoclea is not willingly perverse; rather we recognise that she is undergoing a reorientation of the personality which is serious rather than ridiculous. Sidney's use of the analogy of stage comedy achieves, then, a double perspective, making the reader recognise two separate, opposed codes in the narrative: one detached, one sympathetic.

To depict the full onset of sexual love in Philoclea, Sidney creates a set of episodes, constructed in a subtly modified version of exemplary drama, in which setting, action and gesture are endowed with symbolic and emblematic visual meaning. Philoclea, suffering isolation 'by the smoke of those flames wherewith else she was not only burned but smothered', seeks comfort in a wood which was a favourite haunt in happier times; now, that familiar tuft of trees 'with the shade the moon gave through it, it might breed a fearful kind of devotion to look upon it' (240). In this place is 'a goodly white marble stone that should seem had been dedicated in ancient time to the Sylvan gods'. Sidney explains that only a short time before she first met the Amazon, Philoclea had taken her pen and written a poem on the white and smooth marble, praying that she might remain chaste. In the poem (which Sidney records for us to read) she makes the marble an emblem of her pure mind.

Though Philoclea does not know, apparently, what Sidney tells the reader about the place's dedication to the Sylvan gods, she does half-notice that the trees resemble a little chapel and that the place is half-concealed from Phoebus and Diana. Her poem may be addressed to chastity, but her attempt to dedicate the marble cannot succeed, cannot efface its more ancient consecration – to powers of which her immaturity makes her dangerously ignorant:

> Thou purest stone, whose pureness doth present
> My purest mind; whose temper hard doth show
> My tempered heart; by thee my promise sent
> Unto myself let after-livers know.   (241)

Now, returning to the marble stone at night in a state of emotional torment, she finds the moonlight will not allow her to read the words, and in any case the ink is now 'forworn and in many places blotted'. Although Philoclea sees at once how aptly the blotted lines reflect her present shame, she will not see her previous condition as other than pure. She composes new verses lamenting her shame, but this time she has no pen. These 'words unseen' thus represent her new discovery of mutability. Though she does not write them down, Sidney does do so. Though for Philoclea the words are ephemeral, as expressing a sense of futility, for Sidney they are to have a durable place in the larger frame of his narrative. Not for him, one sees, is a poetic truth ephemeral. We witness Philoclea's dilemma as tender rather than ridiculous, as the pictorial view by itself might suggest.

As readers, our perspective is via Sidney's text, in which everything is expected to yield to interpretation, rather than having the contingent tendency to randomness of real life, with which Philoclea is shown struggling. For her the clear marble's meaning has changed like the moon, and the sense of obscurity will never quite evaporate. To the reader, that poem written in ink on the marble perfectly defines a state of mind both deluded and ephemeral. In Sidney's text it is preserved, in Arcadia effaced.

When she returns to the lodge, she finds her sister Pamela also solitary and distraught, and reads in her appearance 'the badges of sorrow'. Pamela is discovered silent and motionless, not writing but reading: 'looking upon a wax candle which burnt before her; in one hand holding a letter, in the other her handkerchief which had lately drunk up the tears of her eyes' (244). Sidney presents a double image which refracts and clarifies, by subtle contrasts, the differences between two women so close, so very alike in all sorts of ways. We may well think of how Shakespeare uses pairs of lovers (Hermia–Helena and Rosalind–Celia, for example) in his comedies to present comparable effects. The sisters, lovelorn, console one another in a shared bed 'with dear though chaste embracements, with sweet though cold kisses' (245). Sidney makes the reader see in this the pictorial suggestion of Narcissus, but the dramatisation gives immediacy to the characters' emotion: for each sister longs for another mate in the phantom embrace here: and in the psychological sense, narcissism is waning. Philoclea's development, though repeatedly depicted in fixed emblematic images which suggest it is frozen, can yet be glimpsed and felt in motion in the underlying narrative current, which draws the reader expectantly beyond the frame of such tableaux. Sidney prompts the thought that the Narcissus story only begins with a mirror-image.

There is tension between the narrative's weaving process and the moments of stillness in which a framed scene is displayed. Sidney's characters are often composed in a scene which for a moment metamorphoses into a set-piece out of Ovid, making them mythological. This is clear in the episode where Philoclea, wandering alone, comes upon the Amazon, whose face is bent over a stream, weeping: 'one might have thought', Sidney says, that he 'began meltingly to be metamorphosed to the under-running river'. The Amazon composes poetry, writing with a willow stick in the sand of the river bank (one degree even more ephemeral than ink on marble) verses which emblemise the stream as mirror of his tearful eyes:

> In watery glass my watery eyes I see;
> Sorrows ill eas'd, where sorrows painted be. (326)

The Amazon unknowingly echoes Philoclea's second set of verses about the blotted marble, which (we recall) she did not write down at all. The Amazon's poem declares that the place has an echo, and as the poem ends Philoclea materialises in response to it by stepping into view (so neatly reversing the fate of Echo in Ovid). As the lovers begin to talk and the Princess Philoclea learns that her Amazon is really a prince, Sidney, with another neat reversal of Ovid, compares her to Pygmalion finding his beloved statue coming to life as a real woman. Sidney then dissolves the mythological tableau in order to foreground the Arcadian narrative once more, taking up a string of recapitulatory metaphors: Philoclea is like a 'fearful deer', though now a deer coming to the 'best feed' (329); she cannot resist revealing her heart to the prince, yet fears such boldness will provoke him 'to pull off the visor'; but for her part, she exclaims, 'Shall I labour to lay marble colours over my ruinous thoughts?' (330).

It is as if we are observing the aboriginal emergence of fables in the simple archetypal world of pastoral which precedes the codifying of Ovid – and so it is only natural that Ovidian translation of pastoral should fleetingly intervene between the simple story of Arcadia and the reader. In *As You Like It* the direct physicality of performance gives present tense to the pastoral action, sometimes stilled so that Ovidian allusion may be foregrounded. We see how in Sidney such shifts in narrative register create drama: so, in the episode between Philoclea and the Amazon, the Ovidian configuration is more restricted (as well as more faintly outlined) than the Arcadian frame in which the princesses are described, and the reader is made aware of the ceaseless movement between the text's surface and its remoter vales.

Sidney's writing has a limpid clarity and exactness, his

descriptions are focused, and the typically sharply etched
outlines make figures and signs stand out distinct and separate
from one another. We are aware of margins literally and
figuratively. Ultimately indeed it is a fastidious subtlety of mind
rather than eye to which his writing appeals, its system of
contrasts appealing to our judgement as spectators in a vivid
theatre of the mind. Yet, grounded as it is in scenic form, it must
give any dramatist reading it food for thought.

By contrast, Thomas Lodge in *Rosalynde*[4] requires caution. In
his opening pages (160–1) he almost falls over his own
metatextual conceits. After a formula from oral tradition,
disarmingly simple – 'There dwelled adjoyning to the citie of
Bourdeaux a Knight of most honorable parentage' – there
intervenes a rhetorical pattern: 'Whom Fortune had graced
with manie favours, and Nature honored with sundrie exquisite
qualities, so beautified with the excellence of both, as it was
question whether Fortune or Nature were more prodigal in
deciphering the riches of their bounties.' These personifications
prepare the reader for ever more bookish elements. The knight
is rapidly given attributes fitting a writer's hero in an Elizabethan prose fiction, 'the stroake of his Launce no less forcible,
than the sweetnesse of his tongue was perswasive'. Lodge insists
on the overwhelming importance of eloquence, as against
simple oral narration, because his work invokes the shade of
John Lyly in its preface; but this hardly excuses the ridiculous
lengths to which the narrative is pushed. The old knight Sir
John senses that he has not long to live and resolves to deliver a
speech, as well as his written will, to his three sons. Lodge says
that the old man is conscious of, and uses, the possibilities of his
aged face as a source of persuasion, since 'the map of age was
figured on his forehead: Honour sat in the furrowes of his face,
and many yeares were pourtraied in his wrinkled liniaments,
that all men perceive that his glasse was runne'.

Nevertheless, to take such a view of one's own features, as
adjuncts to one's rhetorical performance (old age as a visual aid,
so to speak), though it may possibly be allowable in a narrator,
appears ludicrous if not grotesque in a dramatic character

himself. The old man, however, Euphuist to the last, 'Having therefore death in his lookes to moove them to pitie, and teares in his eyes to paint out the depth of his passions', begins his oration to his three sons. Lodge sets the speech out on the page as an important textual event in its own right, with an upper-case title imitating the layout of a legal document or public proclamation:

SIR JOHN OF BORDEAUX
LEGACIE HE
GAVE TO HIS SONNES

We notice, however, that it is supposed to be delivered spontaneously.

Generally in *Rosalynde* stereotyped character and motive are baldly, explicitly accounted for in the authorial narrative. Scenes are staged in emblematic expository style. Action is held up while characters make formal orations for and against the alternative courses of action facing them, and their rhetoric is tediously elaborate, as when Rosader, coming upon his sleeping brother who lies in mortal danger from a lion, analyses the situation with all the restraint of a designer of mazes:

Now Rosader, Fortune that long hath whipt thee with nettles, meanes to salve thee with roses; and having crost thee with manie frownes: now she presents thee with the brightnesse of her favours. Thou that didst count thy self the most distressed of all men, maist accompt thy selfe now the most fortunate amongst men; if fortune can make men happie, or sweete revenge be wrapt in a pleasing content. (216)

This effusion is prefaced, according to Lodge's custom, with the upper-case, centred title

ROSADERS MEDITATION

and it is set out as an oration of (detachable) general interest.

Act 2, Scene 7 of *As You Like It* makes a striking contrast with Lodge's formal rhetorical mode. Orlando makes a heroic intrusion upon the courtly exiles as they are about to banquet. He draws his sword, and utters a suitably lofty command in keeping with his role: 'Forbear, and eat no more.' To his

audience on stage, his pose and style are all too familiar but
stagey, quite disjunct from this occasion. His melodramatic
claim 'I almost die for food, and let me have it' is answered with
the polite 'Sit down and feed, and welcome to our table', even
perhaps with an air of faintly amused condescension. This
sophisticated and subtle reaction to Orlando's speech becomes
unmistakable in the Duke's mock-solemn repetition, with slight
stylistic improvement, of Orlando's formal oration:

> If ever you have look'd on better days
> If ever been where bells have knoll'd to church
> If ever sate at any good man's feast,
> If ever from your eyelids wip'd a tear,   (2.7.113–16)

This, to someone who has recently been reading Lodge, if not
Sidney, parodies the typical procedure (and unintended absurdity) of romance, where formal rhetoric is utterly dissyn-
chronised from the situation, time and place of the narrative
action. Lodge does not provide Shakespeare with any central
informing poetic idea; that of Fortune, which some critics have
canvassed, is clumsily superimposed in Lodge and in *As You Like
It* serves as a butt of ridicule, parody and subversion from all
sides, particularly from the dramatist himself. But Lodge does
give Shakespeare one excellent thing, not to be found in Sidney:
a heroine with gaiety and sprightliness.

Critics sometimes describe the mode of *As You Like It* as if it
were anticipatory Chekhov. It may be worth recalling how
different it is. Here is an intelligent comment on Chekhov's
dramatic style in *The Cherry Orchard*:[5]

the call of the business to be done behind the scenes is almost more
insistent than the call of what is to be enacted by the footlights; the
stage is not so much a point or a focus as a passage over which his
personages drift or scurry, a chance meeting place where we hear only
fragments of their talk and see less important moments of their action.

The same critical view sees much of the dialogue as elliptical,
more important for its subtextual content than its overt function
as exchange between characters. Compared with this, it is
obvious that the structure of *As You Like It* foregrounds positively
competitive encounters between contrasting characters, making

dialogue often exciting as debate, in a manner Shaw himself, but for his determined obtuseness towards *As You Like It*, would have had to find congenial.

Viewed analytically, this play's style is indeed so far from Chekhov that it shows significant affinities with the technique of Shakespeare's late romantic tragicomedies, where Shakespeare exploits sudden changes in style and even mode as part of an overall dramatic strategy, awaking surprise, shock and wonder in the audience. In these plays certain episodes are presented with a realism of social and psychological observation which would be congenial to a George Eliot; then suddenly a medieval rhyming Chorus-figure will take over, insisting on the simple primitive folk-tale level of the narrative, or highly self-conscious and mannered allusions to acting, to the technique of spectacular staging, or to the openly acknowledged presence of the audience, will insist that the entrances and exits and dialogue are recognised as artifice. Then, without warning, an irresistibly powerful dramatic illusion will be restored to seize the audience's full imaginative concentration.

In *As You Like It* many passages of dialogue present an illusion of lifelike spontaneous conversation, even in characters given to oratorical flights or witty repartee; particularly naturalistic are the conversations which, so far from being lively, animated and competitive, reveal one or both speakers to be dull in mood and halting in speech, as when Rosalind confesses she has not one word to throw at a dog (1.3.3), or Jaques says to Orlando 'Let's meet as little as we can' (3.2.257). Yet such episodes of naturalism are embedded in a plot whose overall shape is determined by the inexplicable and astonishing: at the beginning, the sudden and violent malevolence of Duke Frederick; at the very last moment, the sensational news delivered by a messenger who is in himself surprising – he is Jaques de Boys:

> Let me have audience for a word or two.
> I am the second son of old Sir Rowland
> That bring these tidings to this fair assembly.
> Duke Frederick, hearing how that every day
> Men of great worth resorted to this forest,
> Address'd a mighty power, which were on foot

> In his own conduct, purposely to take
> His brother here, and put him to the sword;
> And to the skirts of this wild wood he came;
> Where, meeting with an old religious man,
> After some question with him, was converted
> Both from his enterprise and from the world   (5.4.151–62)

This announcement generates wonder; there is wonder, too, for this third de Boys brother, discovering he is just in time for the weddings of both his brothers as well as two other couples; the sending-in of this forgotten third brother at the last moment seems deliberately to exaggerate the plot's artifice and the contrived tying up of all loose ends. Its chief effect is comic wonder and explicitly theatrical delight, but it reminds an audience of sensational moments elsewhere in the play: Frederick's anger, Orlando demanding food for his dying old servant at sword point, not to mention the heroine's dead faint, and the epiphany of Hymen, elements which seem clearly to anticipate *Cymbeline* and *The Tempest*.

What is alien to the theatre of Chekhov here is the use of the style which states nothing obliquely, leaves nothing to be inferred, which employs expository soliloquies or asides, clearly announces entrances and exits, makes spectators expressly aware of the reasons for stage action, formally patterns language so that its structures are brought to the surface, supporting other patterned codes.

The very beginning of *As You Like It* is a dialogue between an auspiciously named young man, Orlando, and an old man, Adam – a little reminiscent, in this, of an Elizabethan pastoral eclogue. The name Adam might make an audience notice that the dialogue contains Biblical as well as folk-tale resonances. Orlando stresses his plight in physical terms, born gentle but stalled like an ox (1.1.10), denied education while even his brother's horses are 'bred better; for besides that they are fair with their feeding, they are taught their manage' (1.1.11–13); nourishment for the mind we take for granted as essential to a hero of literary romance, but it is striking that equal stress is here placed on nourishment for the body. Adam, though aged and virtually worn out in body, is sustained by spiritual vigour. We recognise in this pair Youth and Age, and an emblem of the interplay of body and spirit. Shakespeare then adds to the group the lonely saturnine figure, Oliver, of whom Orlando has been speaking. Oliver's perfectly stereotyped cold villainy awakes instantly the hot resentment of his younger brother, who seizes him and proves the better wrestler. The tableau which results has the eloquence of antique sculpture as Adam, fatherly spectator, intervenes to stop the potential fratricide.

The extensive space and emphasis Lodge gives to the description of fights, roistering and general violence on a larger scale, is reduced in narrative terms and focused in the two violent wrestling bouts performed before the audience's eyes, making a shocking physical impact extremely early in the play. This, the first bout, between Orlando and Oliver (1.1.52–4) is violent, however short and inconclusive; the second (1.2.212–15) is violent, complete and very conclusive indeed: Charles, the professional, having to be carried away speechless.

Once the impact of the violent wrestling bout is made directly on stage, and the literal meaning of 'a fall' in wrestling is demonstrated, the word can become metamorphosed in the dialogue as a term for falling in love, and verbal wrestling, wit combats, many of which are vigorously competitive, can become the prevailing sport for everyone in Arden.

The repercussive shock-waves from the initial physical violence persist throughout the play, mainly below the surface of explicit action but glimpsed in the verbal account of the stricken deer, and again in the entry of the deer-slayers, before making one more direct impact when Rosalind falls unconscious on hearing of Orlando's wound as she looks at the bloody napkin.

The emotional malevolence of the wicked brothers Oliver and Duke Frederick is an indirect expression of violence and persists through the action. It propels the lovers into exile: their journeys are identified with the body and physical hardship, but the 'desert inaccessible' (2.7.110) is soon reached, and is a place full of civilised people, whose hunting, before being a brute necessity for physical survival, is first of all a cultural rite, inspiring poetry and music. From the play's outset, then, such archetypes, directly shown or formally described, secure for the play a deep structure in fable and keep the audience subliminally in touch with the primitive sources of the narrative's power. The basic dramatic structure maintains a naive expository attitude against which the varied display of fashionable literary manners, of wit and nonsense, is set in contrast.[6]

In his consistent change of emphasis from his source, Lodge's *Rosalynde*, Shakespeare can be seen emphasising a central theme of transformation through love which is very reminiscent of Sidney, while at the same time calling persistent attention to the effect upon pastoral themes and styles of their translation into dramatic form. In the play hunting has a double value, as reality and as metaphor: in pastoral Arden, hunting is as much an embodiment of literary love imagery and a metaphor for political tyranny as it is the real thing from which metaphors are created. In the same way physical exile is a fact of the narrative but also a metaphor for spiritual freedom.

The equal status of thing signified and sign is a feature of pastoral writing; so Shakespeare insists on recognition of the imperatives of the body as an essential precondition for true wit, and insists, remarkably, that the body's irrationality is essential as an informing substance for true style. In translating pastoral he gives pronounced emphasis through the language of the theatre to this literary and dramatic judgement.

Self-consciousness in the writer of Elizabethan pastoral is, as we have seen, a constituent feature of the mode; in *As You Like It* Shakespeare begins to draw the audience's attention to style, in a spirit of playfulness, extremely early on. In 1.1.85–7, Shakespeare gives the villainous Oliver a moment alone on stage so that he can tell the audience directly and simply of his feelings and plots. He calls for Charles the wrestler, to whom he puts a series of abrupt questions, making no comment whatever on the long and rather surprising answers. The overall dramatic style seems to be expository: the questions are not revelatory of Oliver's character or state of mind, they are merely a dramatist's device: 'what's the new news at the new court? ... Can you tell if Rosalind, the Duke's daughter, be banish'd with her father? ... Where will the old Duke live?' On the other hand, considering the muscle-bound masculinity presumably to be ascribed to a wrestler, the answers are so unexpectedly polished in their eloquence, and so romantically idealistic in feeling, that the incongruity must surely be deliberate and the audience is invited to savour the effect. Even though Charles, it could be argued, may be supposed to be partly protected by the obvious expository form, his effusions on the tenderness of feminine affection, or on the merry men who flock to Arden where they fleet time carelessly as they did in the golden world, seem altogether too improbable to explain away, and furthermore invite us to make an ironic reassessment of Orlando himself, who speaks uncommonly well for one who has been, as he claims to have been, starved of education.

Soon after, in staging which has a hint of allegorical stiffness, young Orlando enters exile accompanied by the faithful servant Adam, and the two young ladies take as their companion Folly, in the shape of Touchstone. They are all received by a Duke-in-exile presiding over a no-Court in which everybody habitually translates their surroundings, nature and the elements, into consciously elaborated metaphor and allegory. (For the audience this is more complex, since the natural world they inhabit can also be recognised as having pastoral, literary–fictional status.) The 'moralising' of the natural world produces a bizarre reversal: courtiers in Arden, supposedly a 'desert', read it as an allegory of civilisation, finding 'books in the running brooks' (2.1.16) exactly like characters in *Arcadia*.

Such details amount cumulatively to a thorough-going stylistic subversion which Shakespeare seems wilfully to encourage, and later this has become quite explicit, when in an exchange which is Shakespeare's invention, Orlando tells Ganymede that he finds it surprising Ganymede should speak so well: 'Your accent is something finer than you could purchase in so remov'd a dwelling' (3.2.341–2). To the audience (including Celia, an on-stage spectator) who are here enjoying Rosalind's first moments in the riskily improvised part of 'saucy lackey', Ganymede's momentary embarrassment at this question is comic, but so also is Orlando for asking it, in a pastoral. Such a matter-of-fact attitude looks even more ridiculous, too, when he swallows Ganymede's explanation, which is as highly improbable as the purest traditions of pastoral fiction allow.

When the ladies begin their first scene, Rosalind idly proposes, as a sport, falling in love. Given the self-conscious dramatic style Shakespeare creates here, the prompt appearance of the Fool is partly a comment on her flippancy. A moment or two later there is another interruption, this time the sophisticated courtier Le Beau (presumably he is supposed to live up to his name in dress and manner). This event the ladies treat as a frankly artificial bit of theatre, and Le Beau is to be put out of his part with mockery. Indeed the ladies' attitude does invite us to question such stagecraft, sending in this courtier, so conventional a stage type, in this perfunctory way, in order to get the story going.

Le Beau begins his tale with a sentence startlingly incongruous for a sophisticate: 'There comes an old man, and his three sons' (1.2.118). Is this conscious parody? Celia is amused by its predictable and childish quality and mocks it (purely from the point of view of style) with flippant indecency: 'I could match this beginning with an old tale.' All the same, Le Beau's words might well serve to begin a non-dramatic version of *As You Like It* itself, and a moment later the ladies, despite themselves, do in fact become gripped by the tale when they realise that while they have been exchanging melancholy and silly remarks three young men have fallen to Charles the wrestler and now lie with little hope of life. The words Le Beau uses give way to the physical reality they describe: in confronting that, Rosalind can say no more than 'Alas'. Words fail her on the first of three memorable occasions in the play (1.2.133, 1.3.1–3, 4.3.156). Presumably the number is not a coincidence.

For the climax of physical action Shakespeare shows tension building up for Rosalind (4.3), although he does not build it up in the same degree for the audience. Rosalind notes Orlando's lateness with evidently real impatience. When someone does enter it is not he but only Silvius. Then, when the next person enters, it is still not the expected Orlando but his brother Oliver, whom neither lady has ever before seen. Oliver, taking his time, delivers his fabulous report of having just been saved from two mortal dangers, a golden and green serpent as well as a nursing lioness (Lodge could only manage a lion). This speech, climaxing in the announcement that the bloody napkin which he brandishes is 'Dy'd' in Orlando's blood, has two simultaneous effects: it makes Celia fall in love, and Rosalind fall in a dead faint. In telling his tale Oliver demonstrates with his own body the physical wound Orlando suffered, to positively gruesome effect:

> and here upon his arm
> The lioness had torn some flesh away,
> Which all this while had bled; and now he fainted
> (4.3.146–8)

This whole on-stage episode is Shakespeare's invention; Lodge offers no parallel to the meeting, the direct report, the falling in love at first sight of Celia, or the dead faint of Rosalind–Ganymede. Shakespeare gives pronounced visual and physical emphasis to this reception on stage of off-stage events, the romantic nature of which Shakespeare makes even more fantastic as he takes them over from Lodge. The pronounced extravagance of Oliver's tale is made evident to the audience by the sharp contrast of the matter-of-fact style in which it is delivered, by the very unexpected absence of witty raillery by the ladies, and by their completely unquestioning acceptance of it: indeed Rosalind's anxious impatience to hear what the bloody napkin has to do with Orlando makes her oblivious to everything except that one thing. The existential fact of the bloody cloth before her eyes blinds her to the tale's blatant romantic incredibility. Certainly, we can say that Love triumphs literally in her fall, but the literalness is not without absurdity, as she half-acknowledges when she revives: the cloth, a sign for passion, has exposed the actual passion she was concealing under the sign of a boy. To put it another way, Oliver's role as messenger is obvious to the audience, and the highly artificial tale he tells endows the napkin with a degree of unreality, as a stock stage property, to be recognised as a literary motif in the same breath as the literary lion and literary serpent, whose actual presentation on stage would be an absurdity too heavily distracting from Shakespeare's chief purpose here. The normally witty Rosalind's reaction exposes the gap between the pastoral fiction in which Ganymede figures and the dramatic present of *As You Like It* where Rosalind is to be found.

Our response to her faint is sympathetic, but also amused. Her reaction of fainting betrays intense emotion, acute vulnerability, and gives the lie to Ganymede's mockery of love's ideals, thereby honouring the shades of Ovid and of Marlowe, the 'dead shepherd'. Anticipating Orlando, Rosalind here finds she 'can live no longer by thinking' (5.2.50), cannot suppress or disguise her serious emotion. Yet at the same time the self-conscious theatricality of the episode's style is given almost as much prominence, for the audience: Oliver's matter-of-fact tone contrasts with the extraordinary story he relates in a manner so extreme as to appear absurd. The audience finds comedy in his assumption, when he addresses Ganymede, that he is talking to a fellow male and so perhaps should emphasise his stiff-upper-lip attitude. His brisk thrusting forward of the bloody napkin is, again, as the audience see, bound to give Ganymede an unintended violent shock.

All these details help to give comic momentum to his speech and to his splendidly unimpressed (and wonderfully incurious) comment on Ganymede's dead faint: 'Many will swoon when they do look on blood' (4.3.158). The further reflection an audience may make, that the attractive presence of Celia acts as a stimulus to Oliver's boastfully manly attitude adds an even more Sidneian complexity to a complex comedy of mistaken identity, already reminiscent of Sidney in the sense that it is precisely through this mode that Shakespeare expresses the profounder theme, of self-discovery in love for another.

The pleasures and perils of eloquence are given pronounced critical attention in this play, as they are in *Much Ado* and *Twelfth Night*, but unhesitating eloquence as a value in itself appears suspect. Many forms of utterance, copious, curt, artless, elaborate, fantastic, curmudgeonly, formally oratorical or nonsensical, are displayed for their delightfulness and variety, but each is subjected to the process of contrast and comparison which informs Shakespeare's whole idea of theatre in *As You Like It*.

Sidney, it will be remembered, juxtaposes, as stuff for low comedy and caricature, the unself-conscious human animal in Miso, Mopsa and Dametas, against those who have the breeding and education to set their erected wit against their infected will. In 3.3.17–18, Audrey's remark to Touchstone, 'I do not know what "poetical" is. Is it honest in deed and word? Is it a true thing?' summons unwittingly the shade of Sidney in *An Apologie for Poetrie*, where the relation between decorum of behaviour and decorum of speech is affirmed, and their status as arts is basic to the discussion. That Touchstone, doughty defender of the claims of the body, should be provoked to some of his greatest exertions of wit by the basic Audrey and the plain Corin, is characteristic of the play's *faux-naïf* working; indeed Corin's simplicities – for example 'I know the more one sickens the worse at ease he is; and that he that wants money, means, and content is without three good friends' (3.2.23–5) – are so accurate as criticism of Touchstone's situation as to seem like urbane irony, or even flat parody of one of the Fool's habits of wit, as when he responds to Rosalind's 'O Jupiter, how weary are my spirits!' with the remark, 'I care not for my spirits, if my legs were not weary' (2.4.1–3).

It is true that in Rosalind–Ganymede Shakespeare presents speech which might be thought to approach an ideal of artifice fused with spontaneity, but this is rather a reader's than a playgoer's judgement. It is certainly true that Rosalind's key qualities of nerve, of risk-taking and vitality, springing from acute, quick response to the moment, live in her eloquent speech; but in a performance of the play it is when she shows herself ready in her double self to immerse in nonsense, self-contradiction, parody, incoherence, and, climactically, speechlessness, that the play's and her most important moments come.

So Shakespeare stresses the practical physical hardship, the physical risk, and the physical pleasures which a real journey, real countryside, and real sexual feeling must involve, and he has of course real physical actors to perform the play. Nevertheless, and wholly consistent with pastoral's ambiguity, he keeps this sense of practical experience in tension with artifice and reflection. His basic style in *As You Like It* is by no means to be described as realism.

As You Like It is remarkable for containing a very rare and absolutely unmistakable allusion by Shakespeare to his greatest contemporary and rival, Marlowe, together with a direct quotation from his *Hero and Leander*:

> Dead shepherd, now I find thy saw of might,
> 'Who ever lov'd that lov'd not at first sight?' (3.5.81–2)

Yet this is not the only allusion to versions of the Hero and Leander story in *As You Like It*, and the other reference seems equally topical (though it has gone unremarked). The year *As You Like It* appeared, 1599, was also the year of Nashe's *Lenten Stuff*,[7] with its exuberant, dizzyingly playful prose version of the Hero and Leander story; and Rosalind-as-Ganymede, the pretty youth, speaks in an accent very reminiscent of Thomas Nashe. Nashe cheerfully admits that Hero and Leander are the merest literary clichés: 'Two faithful lovers they were, as every apprentice in Paul's churchyard will tell you for your love, and sell you for your money'. Nashe stresses the English cultural impact of Marlowe's version, making Hero a sonneteer's image, an Elizabethan poet's 'Mistress or Delia', though Marlowe even at his most boisterous is outdone by Nashe's extremes of Elizabethan slang: 'she was a pretty pinkany and Venus' priest' – 'the toothless trot, her nurse, who was her only chat-mate and chambermaid' – 'he sprawled through the brackish suds to scale her tower' – 'This scuffling or bo-peep in the dark they had a while'. Nashe's overall scheme is rhetorically sanctioned, as an exercise in the mock-heroic, in which the fame of the tragic lovers is owed solely to their association with the epic of 'how the herring first came to be a fish, and then how he came to be king of fishes'. Rather than give this theme full epic treatment, which would 'require as massy a tome as Holinshed', Nashe will invent new mythology and a new allegorical signification for the ancient fable, exactly as Marlowe does, in mock-heroic: 'Small things we may express by great, and great by small, though the greatness of the red herring be not small (as small a hop on my thumb as he seemeth)'.

Nashe's version, in accordance with this burlesque approach, values the lovers fishily: Leander in the storm-tossed sea is like a fish cooking in a boiling broth – indeed *primarily* of interest for this resemblance to a fish, which must be the highest theme for the poet of a herring-epic! The sea is miniaturised to a soup-tureen or wash-tub, the heroic lover to a red herring, the personified elements become squabbling kitchen-maids, but the violence remains a constant, however farcical:

> the wind and the Hellespont contended which should howl louder; the waves dashed up to the clouds, and the clouds on the other side spit and drivelled upon them as fast.

> Hero wept as trickling as the heavens, to think that heaven should so divorce them. Leander stormed worse than the storms, that by them he should be so restrained from his Cinthya. At Sestos was his soul, and he could not abide to tarry in Abidos. Rain, snow, hail, or blow it how it could, into the pitchy Hellespont he leaped, when the moon and all her torch-bearers were afraid to peep out their heads; but he was peppered for it, he had as good have took meat, drink, and leisure, for the churlish frampold waves gave him his bellyful of fish-broth, ere out of their laundry or wash-house they would grant him his coquet or *transire*, and not only that, but they sealed him his *quietus est* for curveting any more to the maiden tower, and tossed his dead carcase, well bathed or parboiled, to the sandy threshold of his leman or orange, for a disjune or morning breakfast.

And now here, for comparison, is Rosalind-as-Ganymede in *As You Like It*:

> Leander, he would have lived many a fair year though Hero had turned nun, if it had not been for a hot midsummer night; for, good youth, he went but forth to wash him in the Hellespont, and being taken with the cramp he was drown'd; and the foolish chroniclers of that age found that it was – Hero of Sestos. (4.1.100–6)

It is not just the parallel between 'wash him in the Hellespont' and Nashe's account of the 'churlish frampold waves' that kept Leander in their 'laundry or wash-house'; the whole movement of the prose recalls Nashe's energetic, off-hand, throwaway style; his way with colloquialisms – 'many a fair year', 'turned nun', 'went but forth to wash him' – abruptly juxtaposed to the immortal names – Leander, Hero, Hellespont, Sestos.

As You Like It makes explicit allusion to Marlowe – the 'dead shepherd' – as the poet of love's absolute irrationality and suddenness, and it presents the theme of love at first sight from multiple perspectives, as did Marlowe. If Orlando and Rosalind fall in love with one another at first sight in 1.2 (an event mirrored at the end when Oliver and Celia first set eyes on each other in 4.3), we should also note the case of Phoebe, who falls for Ganymede at first sight (although Ganymede is for no woman). Then there is Touchstone, who falls for Audrey, gives her poems, and (in a ludicrous parallel with Romeo) even hastily finds a priest to marry her, and all this before his first scene with her on stage in 3.3! And while Phoebe's love for Ganymede is entirely engendered in the eyes (those eyes which gave Silvius 'invisible wounds'), Touchstone, on the other hand, falls for Audrey without even the excuse of Audrey's looks; Touchstone is entirely at a loss to explain it, as is Audrey, who imperturbably remarks 'I thank the gods I am foul' (3.3.39). Touchstone as, in a sense, the most extreme and paradoxical case of love's folly and rashness, is therefore right to allude with feeling to Marlowe: 'it strikes a man more dead than a great reckoning in a little room' (3.3.14–15).

At the centre of *As You Like It* Rosalind, in the guise of Ganymede, watched by a usually silent Celia, performs a translation of herself as she projects for Orlando a delicious dream-courtship, controlled and devised according to the rules of romance. Neither Orlando nor Ganymede makes love in his own person, exactly; that is deferred by the rules of the game. In the contemplation of this 'fiction' Celia too is silently trans-formed in unconscious preparation for meeting the transformed Oliver, Orlando's brother. The persona of Ganymede is an uncertain entity, insisting that all things are provisional, including the fiction in which he himself exists, a pretty youth in a *paysage moralisé* which is realised only by the play's language and which, on the Elizabethan stage, can only be distinguished (if at all) from the court, or from nowhere (an unlocalised playing space) by at most a few token property-trees.

Rosalind appears 'in her own person' again at the end of the play, but here she is translated anew, being no longer the Rosalind of the beginning of the play but now a Rosalind in whom the shadow of the absent Ganymede remains, making her now different from either the one or the other. She introduces a classical deity: Hymen is a mythological, if not a magical, figure, and in his actual appearance on stage a new kind of theatre supervenes. In Lodge there is a real priest who conducts a real marriage service. Elizabethan law forbade the presentation of a marriage service in a play, thus posing an obvious technical problem for the Globe playwright. Shakespeare's solution is to bring on stage this mythological deity to stand beside the play's familiar human characters, effecting a transformation of the dramatic decorum. The theatrical artifice of the episode is qualified by the highly ritualised staging and music, which translate initial disbelief among the characters on stage into wonder, while leaving the audience still partly conscious of an element of trickery.

Hymen has several simultaneous meanings. He is pure theatrical surprise, a 'happening' inducing wonder. He is an evident metaphor for Christian marriage, devised to evade Elizabethan censorship. He is a fashionable Renaissance theatre figure, from the court masque. Finally, he is literally and simply the ancient god of marriage, truly at home in Arden and the remote world of pastoral. Through Rosalind the equivocal relation of trickery to magic, of theatrical to spiritual wonder, is evoked, and through Jaques, with his disenchanted realistic voice and presence, a double view of this ending is indicated, bringing an audience to a new sense of ending and unending. Hymen exists in the true dimension of pastoral, between here and there, dialectically: a place of the mind, and of the theatre, in Shakespeare's translation.

CHAPTER 7

Unstable Proteus: Marlowe and 'Antony and Cleopatra'

In *Hero and Leander* and *The Tragedy of Dido Queen of Carthage* Marlowe is lyrical and heroic, yet indulges in wilful exuberance. He is playfully and recklessly indecorous, he wittily elicits latent – and often unexpected – energies. In this he is anticipated by Arthur Golding, his precursor in the art of Englishing Ovid. In Golding there is a delight in multiplicity, not only as an informing aesthetic, but as a continuous local effect in the tone, texture, and manner of poetry. The Elizabethans admired Ovid for his 'unclassical' qualities – 'his lack of reticence, his copiousness, his facile wit, his command of a polished and complex surface texture and of an easily imitable rhetoric'.[1]

Golding is full of pre-echoes both of *Hero and Leander* and *The Tragedy of Dido*. His translation[2] of the story of Phaeton, from the second book of the *Metamorphoses*, begins in simple declamatory terms:

> The princely palace of the sun stood gorgeous to behold
> On stately pillars builded high of yellow burnish'd gold,
> Beset with sparkling carbuncles that like to fire did shine. (1–3)

This scene comes to life with Vulcan's picture, wrought on the silver doors, of the sea and sea gods:

> Loud sounding *Tryton* with his shirl and writhen trump in hand:
> Unstable *Protew* changing aye his figure and his hue,
> From shape to shape a thousand sithes as list him to renew:
> *Aegeon* leaning boistrously on backs of mighty whales
> And *Doris* with her daughters all: of which some cut the wales
> With splayed arms, some sate on rocks and dried their goodly hair,
> And some did ride upon the backs of fishes here and there. (12–18)

Golding turns the picture into an Elizabethan Renaissance masque or water-pageant,[3] with music and action – the shrill trumpet, Proteus changing shapes and colours, '*Aegeon* leaning boistrously', and the humorously observed antics of the girls. Hyperbole, wit, self-conscious sophistication, a keen sense of irony, geniality – in short a mercurial sensibility – such are the qualities which the poet as Elizabethan spectator identifies with court art.

The feelings of gods and the heroic scale of their powers are represented with due dignity: here Golding describes the horses of Phoebus being bridled:

> His fiery-foaming steeds full fed with juice of ambrosie
> They take from manger trimly dight: and to their heads do tie
> Strong reined bits   (160–2)

And they can haul the chariot of the sun at a gallop faster than the east wind (210). The narrative offers continuous modulations: the story of Phaeton is one of violent tragedy, but there are light moments, as when the father, Phoebus, is reduced to a domestic scale in replying to his son's entreaties:

> Thou fondling thou, what dost thou mean with fawning arms about
> My neck thus flatt'ringly to hang? Thou needest not to doubt.
> I have already sworn by *Styx*, ask what thou wilt of me
> And thou shalt have.   (135–8)

For the fateful moment when Phaeton – 'the wilful lad' - mounts the chariot, Golding is equal to the poetic challenge: his tone, his choice of verb, exactly catch the irony that so much pent-up violence can be sprung by so slight an act:

> for *Phaeton* both young in years and wit,
> Into the chariot lightly leapt   (97–8)

In *Hero and Leander* Marlowe compares young Leander to a horse, a conventional enough heroic simile, except that the narrator exults in the runaway, uncontrollable energy and destructiveness of the powerful animal, so that youthful human passion, represented in such exaggerated terms, looks in contrast ridiculous:

> as a hot proud horse highly disdains
> To have his head controll'd, but breaks the reins,
> Spits forth the ringled bit, and with his hooves
> Checks the submissive ground   (2.141–4)

The tone anticipates Shakespeare's Mercutio, welcoming any chance to release over-charged energy, however violent: as when he mocks Romeo's love-lorn state by ebulliently cavorting with the old trope of the danger of Venus to Mars:

Alas, poor Romeo, he is already dead, stabbed with a white wench's black eye, run through the ear with a love-song, the very pin of his heart cleft with the blind bow-boy's butt-shaft   (2.4.13–15)

Unconsciously, Mercutio here anticipates his own death, run through when fighting in Romeo's cause. In Marlowe's *Hero and Leander* the fateful act of Leander – plunging into the Hellespont – is described in a memorable couplet:

> With that he stripp'd him to the ivory skin,
> And crying, 'Love, I come', leapt lively in.   (2.153–4)

Contrasting ideas are simultaneously conveyed: the narrator registers Leander's physical thrill as he dives in, his heady impetuousness, the hidden tragic irony of his death (hinted at in 'ivory') and also the spectator's erotic pleasure at his young naked body.

The Tragedy of Dido deliberately provokes ironic interpretations. Dido and her court could be understood as a flattering mirror of the much-courted, husbandless, imperious Queen Elizabeth, just as the tragic story of love denied by destiny might seem at once prudent and piquant as an equivocal allusion to Elizabeth. In the play's final scene Dido is granted tragic status at the last, stabbing herself and leaping into the flames of her funeral pyre with the cry 'Live, false Aeneas, truest Dido dies.' A fate like mythical Semele's, consumed by the flames of the sun's embrace, seems to Dido a consummation devoutly to be wished, but she cannot wait passively for 'flaming Jupiter'. She is as rash as Phaeton, and in her ardent imagination transforms Icarus into a symbol of supreme erotic ecstasy:

> I'll frame me wings of wax like Icarus,
> And o'er his ships will soar unto the sun
> That they may melt and I fall in his arms   (5.1.243-5)

In *Romeo and Juliet*, these are lines recalled in Juliet's passionate impatience for her wedding night:

> Gallop apace, you fiery-footed steeds,
> Towards Phoebus' lodging; such a waggoner
> As Phaeton would whip you to the west,
> And bring in cloudy night immediately.
> Spread thy close curtain, love-performing Night,
> That runaways' eyes may wink, and Romeo
> Leap to these arms   (3.2.1-7)

Yet however fierce the erotic aspiration in Juliet or in Dido, the tragic consequence of the myth reasserts itself in both cases. Juliet falls in love with Romeo at first sight, before learning his name is that of her family's mortal enemies. Dido's love for Aeneas is enforced by a divine scheme (Venus exchanges Cupid for the child Ascanius, so that, as Marlowe shows in 3.1, Dido unknowingly takes Cupid on her lap, and he touches her breast with love's golden arrow). When Jupiter intervenes, Aeneas leaves Dido at once and for ever. Dido is then free, but free only to make her destiny of tragic love her choice. In the bitterest sense her fate recalls lines from *Hero and Leander*:

> It lies not in our power to love, or hate,
> For will in us is over-rul'd by fate.   (1.167-8)

Although there is no record of a performance of *The Tragedy of Dido* in Marlowe's lifetime, the title-page of the first edition of 1594 announces that it was 'Played by the Children of her Maiesties Chappell'. This company acted at the so-called 'private', indoor theatre at Blackfriars until 1584, and *The Tragedy of Dido* is full of evidence that Marlowe designed it for performance by boy-actors. The part of Dido herself is a most demanding one and the actor must be able to rise to the challenge of the final act, with its magnificent female passions. Elsewhere in the play, though she can be loftily regal, her moods are varying: she displays anger at a messenger, changes her mood unpredictably with Iarbas (3.1.1-55), is angry with

Anna for speaking his name – 'Yet must I hear that loathsome name again?' (3.1.77) – and vacillates in nervous passion with Aeneas: 'I love thee not – / And yet I hate thee not' (3.1.170–1). Marlowe also subjects her to a degree of burlesque when, after she consummates her love with Aeneas in a cave, Anna and Achates exchange notes on the extraordinary accompanying storm:

> ANNA It hail'd, it snow'd, it lighten'd, all at once.
> ACHATES I think it was the devils' revelling night,
>   There was such hurly-burly in the heavens;
>   Doubtless Apollo's axle-tree is crack'd,
>   Or aged Atlas' shoulder out of joint,
>   The motion was so over-violent.   (4.1.8–13)

As a mock-heroic analogy this burlesques the physical act of love; yet it also – again without the speakers realising it – registers the fact that the storm is supernatural and the union fateful. A taste for ironic wit in the audience is no disadvantage.

Dido and Aeneas, like Tamburlaine and Zenocrate and Antony and Cleopatra, are continually invested with epic proportions by the dramatic poetry and the stage imagery. When Dido appears in the costume of Diana, in which Venus herself has already appeared, the exaltation is made emblematic, and later in the play Aeneas is enthroned as splendidly as Jupiter in the opening scene, and doubtless on the same throne. The opportunities for extravagant display with rich costumes are alone almost enough to explain why Marlowe turned his attention to this mode of theatre with its sophisticated courtly taste, 'feigning bawdy fables gathered from the idolatrous heathen poets'. When Aeneas first enters, he is dressed 'like a fisher swain' (Dido's description, 5.1.162). He and his men meet Illioneus and his companions; they have been given fine new clothes by Dido (2.1.65) and Dido's first act on meeting Aeneas is to dress him splendidly:

> Warlike Aeneas, and in these base robes?
> Go fetch the garment which Sicheus ware   (2.1.79–80)

The hunting costumes of Venus and Dido are emphasised; Venus has a purple costume and a bow and quiver, and describes her sisters as dressed in leopard skins. When Dido gazes in wonder at Aeneas after endowing him with 'the imperial crown of Lybia' and the golden 'Punic sceptre', she cries in joy,

> Now looks Aeneas like immortal Jove (4.4.45)

(This confirms the splendour of the play's opening scene, where Jove is enthroned with Mercury at his feet.) Dido goes on with an enticing speech which in its hyperbolic fantasy is a pre-echo of Shakespeare: we might associate it not only with Enobarbus' description of Cleopatra at Cydnus (2.2.191 ff.) but with the first entrance of Cleopatra in *Antony and Cleopatra*, '*with eunuchs fanning her*':

> Ten thousand Cupids hover in the air
> And fan it in Aeneas' lovely face!
> O that the Clouds were here wherein thou fled'st,
> That thou and I unseen might sport ourselves!
> Heaven, envious of our joys, is waxen pale,
> And when we whisper, then the stars fall down,
> To be partakers of our honey talk. (4.4.48–54)

There are suggestive anticipations of the sensuous language and sensuous personality of Shakespeare's Cleopatra in Marlowe's Dido, and, in an in-joke, Shakespeare's Egyptian queen (played by a boy-actor in whom Shakespeare thereby displays complete confidence) disparagingly alludes to a boy-actor's impersonation of her as a 'squeaking Cleopatra'. The part of Marlowe's Dido is a demanding one by comparison with female roles in plays of the 1580s. It would have been an education in itself for a boy-actor to learn to play this role, as it must have been to those who created leading female roles in Shakespeare. By 1595 Shakespeare had enough confidence in the actors' abilities to write the part of Juliet for a boy-actor, and the subsequent women's parts in Shakespeare's plays extend even today's professional women actors, however gifted they may be. It has been argued by Ernst Honigmann[4] that Shakespeare demands virtuoso brilliance from the boy-actor who played

Cleopatra, as when she stages a fainting spell, threatens the
messenger, dances, hops, skips, pants, yawns, bites, pinches, and
– rather than body contact between her and Antony being
minimised – kisses and embraces and caresses Antony.

What little can be inferred from the plays written for the so-
called 'children's' companies in the 1580s, indicates that the
boys were emphatically not amateur, their style was disciplined,
formal, and elegant. Their youth – some of them at least must
have been of rather diminutive stature – has led to speculation
that they were suited to perform plays in which there was
parody, comic pastiche, where their appearance expressed the
drama's concern with simultaneously heroic and mock-heroic
effects. These are certainly effects intended in the stage direction
in *The Tragedy of Dido*:

> *Here the Curtains draw. There is discovered* JUPITER *dandling* GANYMEDE
> *upon his knee, and* MERCURY *lying asleep.*

Marlowe can take for granted the spectacular impact of
costume and tableau, the whole stage image, here, and can set
up a counterpoint of comic derision. So Ganymede complains of
the 'shrewish blows' given by jealous Juno, in terms which
deftly parody the 'mighty line' yet express direct physical
shock:

> She reach'd me such a rap for that I spill'd
> As made the blood run down about mine ears.   (1.1.7–8)

Jupiter's reassurance to Ganymede reveals simultaneously the
absurdity of the god's subjection to erotic needs and the
awesome rashness of his divine power:

> I vow, if she but once frown on thee more,
> To hang her meteor-like 'twixt heaven and earth   (12–13)

The emotions of the gods are extreme, sudden, and volatile; in
their lives hyperbole is the normal mode, as paranoia is the
appropriate and usual condition; and Marlowe's emphasis in
this opening scene prepares us for wider themes in the play. This

is a Jupiter who for his sport plucks a feather from Hermes' wing and in his turn is twitted by Venus for his lechery – he, a middle-aged married god!

The staging requirements for *The Tragedy of Dido* are practical, and highly artificial, a *décor simultané*:[5] one side being *en pastorale*, representing the wood, and also the cave, and with space for Jove's throne and its curtain, while the other side, representing Carthage, evidently had a 'house' – an open loggia – a wall and gate. It would appear that the centre of the stage was clear, and backed by trees. The play begins with curtains being drawn to reveal the throne of Olympus.

Shakespeare in *Antony and Cleopatra* concentrates on the figures of his actors, not on elaborate scenery. Rome and Alexandria are apparent in triumphal processions and monumental stage-groupings: Egypt and Rome are differentiated by costume, including the no doubt spectacular robes of a queen of Egypt and her female attendants and her eunuchs; the contrast with the Roman armour of Antony's group makes a continuous visual emphasis on the play's themes of Mars and Venus, Europe and Asia; but only in the monument scenes is there spectacular use of stage action, as Antony, wounded, is hoisted aloft by the women. Elsewhere the impression of great battles by sea and land, of royal barges, vast armies and navies on the move, is confined to verbal description – as are smaller but equally vivid images, Cleopatra hopping forty paces through the public street (2.2.238–9), or fishing, playing billiards, or Antony enthroned in a marketplace. Cleopatra may say she has given someone a suit of solid gold armour, but we do not see this happen; she describes Antony on horseback, but we have to imagine it with her:

> O happy horse, to bear the weight of Antony!
> Do bravely, horse, for wot'st thou whom thou mov'st?
> The demi-Atlas of this earth, the arm
> And burgonet of men. (1.5.22–5)

It was left to the Victorian historical genre-painters, the scene-painters and carpenters of the nineteenth-century theatre and of Hollywood,[6] to give negative confirmation of Shakespeare's wisdom in evoking much of the spectacular activity in *Antony and Cleopatra* in verbal terms alone. There is a more important reason for this than the limitations of staging: as Marlowe showed by example in the *Tragedy of Dido*, it is the power of what is imagined that makes a great poetic tragedy, and compelling images in the *Tragedy of Dido*, like many in *Antony and Cleopatra*, are powerful because their significance is more than literal. Dido's exalted erotic invitations to Aeneas could have been enhanced by the setting of her royal palace, since at court performances scenery, costume, and lighting effects were elaborate[7] – but Marlowe takes no chances on the quality of the scene-painters; he creates in his dramatic poetry alone a powerful imaginative world: so Dido woos Aeneas:

> I'll give thee tackling made of rivell'd gold
> Wound on the barks of odoriferous trees;
> Oars of massy ivory, full of holes,
> Through which the water shall delight to play
>
> (3.1.115–18)

Even the sails are to be of 'folded lawn' (123). Dido's female sensuousness encloses the manly warrior Aeneas: one might recall Cleopatra's memory of drinking Antony to his bed and dressing him in her 'tires and mantles' while she wore his 'sword Philippan' (2.5.21–3). Like Cleopatra, Dido does not sympathise with the warrior who is honoured by men for heroic exploits, she wants all that to be forgotten, she wants an Aeneas new-made as part of her overwhelmingly soft, sensuous and luxurious world. Marlowe shows Aeneas recounting to her the terrible price he and his men have paid in escaping Troy. Dido says very little in response: her thoughts and feeling are of the future, yet the compelling force of Aeneas' memories suggest that forgetting is easier said than done; as he describes his experience of the Fall of Troy, Aeneas relives the terror:

> 'kill, kill!' they cried.
> Frighted with this confused noise, I rose,
> And looking from a turret might behold
> Young infants swimming in their parents' blood,
> Headless carcases piled up in heaps   (2.1.190–4)

Aeneas cannot forget how the 'frantic' queen hung by her nails
in Neoptolemus' eyelids until

> the soldiers pull'd her by the heels,
> And swung her howling in the empty air,
> Which sent an echo to the wounded King:
> Whereat he lifted up his bed-rid limbs,
> And would have grappled with Achilles' son,
> Forgetting both his want of strength and hands
>
> (2.1.247–52)

The description is both compassionate and alienated by
hysteria. Aeneas confesses that he failed to protect first his wife,
then Cassandra, then Polixena, who, he relates,

> Was by the cruel Mirmidons surpris'd
> And after by that Pyrrhus sacrific'd.   (2.1.287–8)

We learn that Aeneas, when he saw this happen, 'swum quickly
back' to the ship. The apparent hero, ancestor of the British
race, loyal defender of Troy, founder of Rome, guilty of
cowardice: it is, we may think, characteristic of Marlowe to
treat Aeneas, a very type of the Renaissance hero, with sardonic
irreverence; but this is not mere gratuitous caricature. Aeneas'
account of the Fall of Troy combines Virgilian grandeur and
range with medieval details of horror and violence which derive
from popular romances, especially the well-known *Troy Book* of
Lydgate; and this must remind the audience that the Aeneas of
medieval legend was a notorious villain not an epic hero.
Aeneas knows the frightful details of Priam's death because he
and Antenor had led Pyrrhus to the king's place of refuge and
stood by, consenting, as he was murdered.[8] By interweaving
Virgil and Lydgate, Marlowe fuses contradictory attitudes to
Aeneas, and Aeneas himself is consequently radically unstable,
Protean: a hero, a traitor, a great lover, a wretched and
impotent coward, a tragic victim of destiny.

This dialectical manner of dramatic composition, of generating debate between contrasting interpretations of character
and event, is something which Marlowe and Shakespeare have
in common, but which Marlowe explored first. In *The Aeneid* the

importance of Dido is reduced in the larger story, which concerns the hero Aeneas and his destiny, the founding of Rome. Marlowe, however, gives extraordinary emphasis to the heroine, and this puts the manly concept of the heroic life which Aeneas obeys in question. In this sense *The Tragedy of Dido* is complementary to *Tamburlaine*, in which Marlowe explores the idea of one man's success in breaking all limits, except those of his body's physical time-span, to impose his vision on the world, and with complete impunity, rewriting, as it were, the concept of heroism to exclude every kind of moral sanction.

In *Romeo and Juliet* (1595) the civil war between the Montagues and Capulets is presented as a relatively small-scale affair, all the more ironic therefore in proving fatal to the two lovers. What is interesting is Shakespeare's decision in his later love tragedies *Othello* and *Antony and Cleopatra* to expand the public theme of war and politics and ennoble it to heroic scale, and here the contribution of *Tamburlaine* to Shakespeare's conception of the heroic is worth assessing. What had been new, and extremely important, in *Tamburlaine* (1587–8) was the attention to political and strategic issues, and to the detailing of many real geographical locations and nations. This gives an air of authentic worldliness that counters the impression usual in pre-Marlovian heroic drama or romance that ordinary time, place, and causality are suspended or reordered. The re-orientation of interest may partly be due to Marlowe's source, George Whetstone.[9] It was he who presented Tamburlaine's career plainly as that of a ' poore labourer, or in the best degree a meane souldiour, descended from the Partians: notwithstanding the povertyie of his parents: even from his infancy he had a reaching & an imaginative minde', and a 'ruling desire'.

Marlowe's *Tamburlaine* has no scenes utilising a stage-heaven or hell, there are no supernatural characters, nor are there presenters to guide the audience in interpreting the events or to provide moral guidance. The audience instead must draw its own conclusions from the speech and action and visual spectacle. The hero, moreover, is himself an active and self-conscious deviser of self-aggrandising pageants, and Marlowe places great importance on Tamburlaine's will to create his own role. Thus, where in earlier romance or heroic plays a character simply presents his fictional self to an audience, in *Tamburlaine* the audience is required to notice that a heroic self is being created before their eyes. Tamburlaine may use brutality and ruthless harshness as he proceeds, but he is from the first a skilled orator as well as effortlessly generating instinctive animal attraction towards himself.

The analogy between theatrical and actual role-play is raised in the opening scenes, and its implications lead to the very centre of the dramatic conflict, on the one hand serving to display the operation of power in terms recalling Machiavelli (politics as deceit), on the other hand showing how powerful imagination can wield the systems of rhetoric, the arts of language, to make real changes in the real world, as well as to dissolve limits hitherto supposed fixed.

Tamburlaine is endowed with a great range of cultural reference. Western classical mythology is at his command, and is disconcertingly defamiliarised in the mouth of this 'Scythian shepherd', especially when the audience finds itself irresistibly drawn by his astonishing language and exciting presence:

> Ye petty kings of Turkey, I am come
> As Hector did into the Grecian camp
> To overdare the pride of Graecia,
> And set his warlike person to the view
> Of fierce Achilles, rival of his fame –
> I do you honour in the simile: (Part 2, 3.5.64 ff.)

Tamburlaine's vast conquests confront the audience with uncomfortable new perspectives – with views of the world different from that which the Christian West promotes. In place of absent divinities Tamburlaine presents himself as a scourge of God, and towards the end of Part 2 an audience may be reminded of apocalyptic images from the Book of Revelation; but the play's narrative cannot easily be accommodated to a Christian scheme. Perhaps the idea is, precisely, too conventional, as Marlowe would have found it in Richard Knolles, who explained the victories of the Turks as 'the just and secret judgement of the Almightie'.[10] Montaigne notes in his essay *Of Prognostications* that in public disorders men stunned by their fate will throw themselves back, as on any superstition, on seeking in the heavens the ancient causes and threats of their misfortune.[11] Marlowe's way of involving an audience in a process of critical thinking by frustrating stock responses can be illustrated in his shaping of the episodes in Part 2 concerning the Christians under Sigismond. Having made a pact, sworn on oath, with the Turk Orcanes, the Christian general Sigismond reluctantly gives way to his Christian comrades' argument that a treacherous attack on the Turk would be 'necessary policy'; in addition they argue that oaths sworn with unbelievers are not binding; but Sigismond is defeated and interprets his defeat as God's vengeance, while the Turk, musing on his own survival, remarks 'Now Christ or Mahomet hath been my friend'. Was the outcome a sign of the Christian God's justice? His comrade drily answers

> 'Tis but the fortunes of the wars, my lord,
> Whose power is often proved a miracle.
>
> (Part 2, 2.4.31–2)

The invocation of a specifically Machiavellian perspective exposes the audience to issues of 'Ragion del Stato', rule as art, not as inherited mystery: a thing separate from religion, morality, or national custom; instead secular, international, impersonal. Machiavelli, who had himself meditated on the career of Tamburlaine, concedes in chapter 15 of *The Prince* that fortune is of great importance to princes; but he ascribes equal importance to the possession of free will, and notes that fortune favours impetuosity, especially in young men, who are more ardent and audacious. In *Antony and Cleopatra*, it is these daunting truths, embodied in the young Caesar, that relentlessly pursue Antony and give tragic impetus to his decline. By contrast, it is Tamburlaine's unhesitating certainty which marks his first appearance, discarding his shepherd's clothes and assuming armour before the eyes of the captured Princess Zenocrate and his own men, with the loads of treasure serving as a portable display of triumph. Tamburlaine accepts the adulation of his men, who amplify his impressive show with epic similes:

> As princely lions when they rouse themselves,
> Stretching their paws and threat'ning herds of beasts,
> So in his armour looketh Tamburlaine:
> Methinks I see kings kneeling at his feet,
> And he with frowning brows and fiery looks
> Spurning their crowns from off their captive heads.
>
> (Part 1, 1.2.52–7)

This is hyperbole, the figure appropriate for the extreme. In *Antony and Cleopatra* there are many exalting hyperbolic images of the hero and heroine – Cleopatra and her barge which 'like a burnish'd throne / Burned on the water' (2.2.201–2), or Antony visualised by Cleopatra,

> His legs bestrid the ocean; his rear'd arm
> Crested the world; his voice was propertied
> As all the tuned spheres, and that to friends;
> But when he meant to quail and shake the orb,
> He was as rattling thunder (5.2.81–5)

but repeatedly the play separates the hyperbolic from the mundane – as in this instance, indeed, where Cleopatra asks Dolabella: 'Think you there was or might be such a man / As this I dreamt of?' and he replies, 'Gentle madam, no' (5.2.92–3). It is otherwise in Marlowe's *Tamburlaine*. Tamburlaine's seemingly fantastic imaginary spectacle of kneeling kings becomes actualised later in the play as Tamburlaine strives to realise his wildest imagining; but when the audience does see it, then, they have no precedents for how to react. In Act 4 a white-robed Tamburlaine uses a captured king, Bajazeth, as a footstool to his throne, from where he declares:

> So shall our swords, our lances and our shot
> Fill all the air with fiery meteors;
> Then, when the sky shall wax as red as blood,
> It shall be said I made it red myself,
> To make me think of naught but blood and war.
>
> (Part 1, 4.2.51–5)

To turn the sky itself red to suit a mood (as the stage was hung with black when a tragedy was acted) becomes actual in Tamburlaine's mind even as his imagination creates the metaphor. Expanding from his poetic conceit in which the flashing blades and glinting lances suggest lightning, the cannon shot become actual meteors, supernatural omens: these disorders become apocalyptic, seemingly instantaneously, 'then' as in the Book of Revelation:

And I beheld when he had opened the sixth seal, and lo, there was a great earthquake, and the sun was as black as sackcloth of hair, and the moon was like blood.   (Geneva version of 1602: 6.12)

Tamburlaine is full of injunctions to look, to admire, or to be horrified by the expressions of the human face, the posture, costume, and gesture of its characters; Marlowe certainly seeks to exploit the differences between language and show, and he makes Tamburlaine's refusal or inability to distinguish between what can be imagined and what can be actualised a central issue in the play's exploration of the heroic. Tales about the hero, writes Eugene M. Waith,[12] do not so much excuse his moral defects as point to a special morality: 'What matters most is something difficult to define, which pushes the hero to the outermost reaches of the human and even beyond.' It is a greatness that has less to do with goodness than 'with the transforming energy of the divine spark'. Marlowe's Tamburlaine pursues a career of sustained expansion, enlarging our sense of what it means to be without limits; it is not only that he makes actual what he imagines, but that he dares to imagine on so grand a scale, whereas in Shakespeare's *Antony and Cleopatra* the world of the imagination is steadily set in opposition to the material world, time, and history, in a movement recalling *Romeo and Juliet*.

A link between *The Tragedy of Dido* and *Antony and Cleopatra* which seems of particular importance is that both make carnal sexuality a heroic value, something very rare in Renaissance plays.[13] Shakespeare's Enobarbus tells how Cleopatra's sheer erotic power is inexhaustible, and makes desire in Antony inexhaustible, too – she makes hungry where most she satisfies (2.2.247–8). She says herself she is eroticism incarnate, 'with Phoebus' amorous pinches black' (1.5.29).

So, as the pressure of desire mounts, Dido exalts Aeneas to divine proportions:

> Prometheus hath put on Cupid's shape,
> And I must perish in his burning arms. (3.4.20–1)

In her erotic hyperbole, Dido also unconsciously predicts her own tragic destiny in the flames of her funeral pyre. Cleopatra meets the same fate as Dido, not in real flames but in sublime metaphor:

> I am fire and air; my other elements
> I give to baser life. (5.2.283–4)

Cleopatra's real tragic destiny is unconsciously predicted also, in the imagery associating her with the serpent. The lines

> He's speaking now,
> Or murmuring 'Where's my serpent of old Nile?'
> For so he calls me. Now I feed myself
> With most delicious poison. (1.5.25–8)

are recalled in the final moments of the play when a real serpent feeds her its poison, and the experience is turned into a moment of carnal sexuality:

> The stroke of death is as a lover's pinch,
> Which hurts, and is desired. (5.2.289–90)

Thus Dido's bitter image of disappointment and rejection:

> O Serpent that came creeping from the shore
> And I for pity harbour'd in my bosom,
> Wilt thou now slay me with thy venomed sting (5.1.165–7)

is absorbed into an image in which the serpent, the lover, and the baby are merged, each state implying the other, inviting dream of the other:

> Peace, peace!
> Dost thou not see my baby at my breast,
> That sucks the nurse asleep? (5.2.302–4)

This snake-bite on the breast is not from North or Plutarch, where the bite is on the arm. Of the sources for Shakespeare's version the closest and likeliest seems to be Nashe in *Christ's Tears over Jerusalem*.[14] It seems to me likely that a memory of Nashe would fuse in Shakespeare's mind with a memory of Marlowe, both of whom were vivid in his imagination when writing his first *Liebestod* tragedy, *Romeo and Juliet*. Cleopatra's final attitude, lying in regal majesty as if alive, is also not in North, but is Shakespeare's invention, a climax to the sequence of actually shown or verbally described statue-images in the play. It accords, too, with Marlowe's dramatic emphasis on sculptural and monumental groupings of figures in the *Tragedy of Dido*, and it constitutes a private allusion to Juliet, who lies unconscious, sculpture-like, on her tomb, awaking only to find Romeo newly dead beside her. Like Cleopatra, she turns her death into an act of love: 'This is thy sheath' she exultantly cries as she stabs herself with his dagger. Earlier Romeo, in a strange anticipation of Antony, and echo of Aeneas, dreams

> my lady came and found me dead
> (Strange dream that gives a dead man leave to think!)
> And breathed such life with kisses in my lips
> That I revived and was an emperor.   (5.1.6–9)

Like Dido, Cleopatra achieves finally a state of peace, yet during the play often appears comic and ludicrous in her emotional instability, while Antony can be compared to the watery Aeneas, for Shakespeare's hero is shown in dissolution, which contradicts his original Roman essence. The ironic relationship between the storms at sea, the storms of war, and the stormy force of passion, is apparent in the personal confession Aeneas makes to Dido, when he tells her his ships are unrigged, his sails all rent in sunder, oars broken, tackling lost, 'Yea, all my navy split with rocks and shelves' (3.1.107). Dido takes up these implicit metaphors of Aeneas' sense of physical and sexual dereliction, and transforms them with fresh erotic energy: 'I'll give thee tackling made of rivell'd gold' (3.1.115). The consummation of their love is symbolised by an enchanted storm which enriches the harmony: 'The air is clear, and southern winds are whist' (4.1.25). Hence, later, Aeneas embraces Dido with the cry

> This is the harbour that Aeneas seeks,
> Let's see what tempests can annoy me now.   (4.4.59–60)

and Dido magnificently recalls it with the lines

> O that I had a charm to keep the winds
> Within the closure of a golden ball,
> Or that the Tyrrhene sea were in mine arms,
> That he might suffer shipwrack on my breast
> As oft as he attempts to hoist up sail!   (4.4.99–103)

Antony, as he prepares for suicide, senses his very body as if turning to water, to vapour, with the loss of his Roman honour, his bronze heroic resolution:

> ANTONY Sometime we see a cloud that's dragonish,
> A vapour sometime like a bear or lion,
> A towered citadel, a pendent rock,
> A forked mountain, or blue promontory
> With trees upon't that nod unto the world
> And mock our eyes with air…
> That which is now a horse, even with a thought
> The rack dislimns and makes it indistinct
> As water is in water.
> EROS   It does, my lord.
> ANTONY My good knave Eros, now thy captain is
> Even such a body. Here I am Antony,
> Yet cannot hold this visible shape
>   … I, that with my sword
> Quartered the world, and o'er green Neptune's back
> With ships made cities, condemn myself to lack
> The courage of a woman.   (4.14.2–14, 57–60)

Antony believes the messenger who tells him that Cleopatra has committed suicide – he is tragically deceived for taking her to be as resolute as Dido. Cleopatra's unreliability, her unpredictably alternating warmth and coldness to Antony, recalls Dido's behaviour to Aeneas. Cleopatra may finally hold Antony in her arms as he dies, but in the play she is remarkable rather for her instability. The fact that it is only at the last that Cleopatra commits herself to suicide, after scheming calculation of the odds of doing a deal with Caesar, keeps an audience in suspense about how to judge her – as a subtle deceiver who is secretly true to Antony, or as shamelessly unscrupulous. Dido's response to Cupid's stimulus suggests the cruelty of her subjection to a divine plan, as well as the folly of her own hubris.

In *The Tragedy of Dido*, images of the sea and ship's tackling, of storm and fire, have a central dramatic function as leitmotivs; it is a characteristic Marlovian paradox that Dido's tragic love for the mariner Aeneas associates her with fire, and Aeneas with the element of water, a fit emblem for his unmanliness and inconstancy. Yet, at another level of the play, Aeneas cannot but be passive because he must suffer at the command of the gods and as part of a much wider drama in which his true heroic role is confirmed. Marlowe, in selecting from Virgil's *Aeneid* only the Dido episode, makes the doubleness inevitable. Shakespeare, in focusing in *Antony and Cleopatra* only on the final phase in Antony's career, achieves the same result by the same means. In similar terms, if Marlowe's Aeneas is the prisoner of the fates, we cannot ignore his more personal passivity in his relations with Dido. There is something shocking in Aeneas' abrupt, immediate, and total capitulation to the command of the gods to leave Carthage (4.3) and on this and the later occasion (5.1) his radical change of tone, his cynical indifference to Dido, make him contemptible. Indeed there is pathos, but also Marlovian mockery, in presenting Aeneas as seeking in Dido's arms an escape from destiny; once more destiny calls him and once again he capitulates. Dido subjects him to the full fury of her passion – which she expresses in metaphors of sea-tempest – the waves crash over Aeneas, and then she offers herself up to him:

> if thou wilt stay,
> Leap in mine arms: mine arms are open wide.
>
> (5.1.179–80)

Without a word Aeneas leaves, in implicitly ironic contrast to the aspiring leaps of Phaeton, or Leander, or Romeo, and the choice of Antony.

Tamburlaine takes as its theme the imperial dominion of Asia as it threatens to engulf Europe. *The Tragedy of Dido* dramatises the tragic love of Africa and Europe, the contradictions between the exceptional human individual and the pitiless imperatives of imperial rule. In *Antony and Cleopatra* Rome, though European, threatens to possess Asia and Africa, the two remaining parts of the known world in the T-in-O maps which Tamburlaine would re-draw.[15] Marlowe multiplies associations, historical and mythological, in expanding the significance and scale of *Tamburlaine*.[16] Though sixteenth-century European knowledge of Asia was imperfect in substance and muddled in method, the colossal scale and importance of this background was obvious. Tamburlaine asserts that he will make all the maps of the world obsolete by discovering new regions, and his new map of the world will have his conquest, Damascus, at its meridian. He is neither European nor Christian, but stands above mere national significance: what is focused in him is a question as applicable to Asia as to the Mediterranean, located in the historical past but illustrative of the avant-garde thought of Machiavelli, immediately applicable, moreover, in late sixteenth-century England to dangerously near events in the Netherlands or Ireland as well as to Peru or the colony of Virginia.

Shakespeare's protagonists in *Antony and Cleopatra*, themselves both imperial figures, and often indeed referred to simply as 'Rome' and 'Egypt', confront one another in a portentous moment of world history, the last age before the birth of Christ.[17] They face a situation resembling that of Dido and Aeneas, and Antony recognises Aeneas as his rival in heroic love, not Roman history, when (in 4.14.50–4) he boasts that in the Elysian fields Dido and her Aeneas shall want troops, and all the haunt be his and Cleopatra's (he forgets that in Virgil Dido rejects Aeneas when they meet again after death in Hades).

The imperial theme exalts Antony and Cleopatra to a heroic scale, in struggles to master empires and nations, and the direction of armies in war, but also involves them in bitter Machiavellian politics, so that they are degraded and soiled by ugly and sordid personal and public actions. The sublime heroic rhetoric and mythological imagery of Antony, and of Cleopatra, owe much to *Tamburlaine*; but the relation of Shakespeare's tragedy to Marlowe's *Tragedy of Dido* is perhaps more decisive for its depiction of the multiple textures of experience in its dramatic narrative. It was natural for Shakespeare to remember Marlowe's play among other versions of the Dido and Aeneas story because Marlowe's was already designed for performance on an Elizabethan stage, but there was another important reason too: in the treatment of the Antony and Cleopatra story before and after Shakespeare it was the classically 'correct' Senecan versions which dominated.[18] Shakespeare constructed his play according to his native dramatic tradition. Among the few Elizabethan models for classical love tragedy in that native tradition, *The Tragedy of Dido* stands out. It had clearly impressed Shakespeare deeply before he wrote *Romeo and Juliet*; and he never forgot it.

CHAPTER 8

Multiplicity

Shakespeare in his last phase from *Antony and Cleopatra* to *The Tempest* shows dazzling stylistic virtuosity, and an uninhibited readiness to manipulate his audiences through surprise, thrill and shock; yet a readiness to do the unexpected, boldly breaking with established dramatic conventions, is not something he only developed late in his career – on the contrary, it is a consistent feature of his work, apparent from his earliest comedies, not only in the extraordinary Act 5 of *Love's Labour's Lost*, culminating in the entry of Marcade, but even in the ostensibly classical confines of *The Comedy of Errors*, and in its opening moments, which present the most solemn and gloomy occasion, as old Aegeon is condemned to death and faces his last few hours on earth.

By beginning with the romance plot Shakespeare teases an audience that he is going to break the non-classical rules of the three unities, which the educated element in the public would have been taught to respect. The classic Elizabethan statement of these rules is Sir Philip Sidney's in his essay *An Apology for Poetry* (1581 – though only actually published in 1595). Sidney ridicules early Elizabethan drama's readiness to represent directly on stage ' story which containeth many places and many times'; he impatiently points out that such material should be relegated to a reporter's account. He sketches a lively caricature of a typical Elizabethan 'mongrel' dramatic plot: 'two young Princes fall in love. After many traverses, she is got with child, delivered of a fair boy; he is lost, groweth a man, falls in love, and is ready to get another child, and all this in two hours space'. Sidney insists that everything – common sense, the example of ancient drama, the present-day 'ordinary players in Italy' – prescribes that the performance time of a play should be 'fitted to the time it set forth'. He warns English dramatists, 'if they will represent an history they must not (as Horace saith) begin ab ovo, but they must come to the principal point of that one action which they will represent'. Sidney cites the example of how Euripides, dramatising the story of Hecuba, begins with her discovery of Polydorus' murdered body, not where an Elizabethan would begin, with the whole life story of Polydorus beginning with his birth.

It might be no coincidence – it might indeed be consistent with Shakespeare's whole attitude to Sidney the dramatic theorist – that Sidney's mocking description of 'mongrel' tragicomedy may be suspected as the root provocation which Shakespeare eventually answered with *The Winter's Tale* and *Cymbeline*. Certainly, as far as the early Shakespeare's practice is concerned, Sidney had the role of provocative agent. The overall design in *The Comedy of Errors*, no less than *The Tempest*, may be seen as a witty and satiric response to dogmatic defenders of the unities such as Sidney, with their anxiety about plausibility. In *The Comedy of Errors* Shakespeare chooses a dramatic action which emphatically conforms to the unities: confined in time, between dawn and sunset, and place, Ephesus, and the mode of comedy. Shakespeare chooses as a main source one of the Renaissance's favourite plays, Plautus' comedy about a pair of twins, *Menaechmi*. Shakespeare's adaptation is perfectly plotted, and no event goes unaccounted for; but by the one act of doubling the pairs of twins Shakespeare foregrounds the elaborate artifice of Plautus: for now the audience's pleasure is unmistakably based on the cumulatively extreme absurdities which 'logically' result from the situation. By then adding a romance frame-plot, he combines this strict exercise in the three unities with a romance story. The fact that this story is presented in a reporter's speech by old Aegeon in the play's first scene, might be taken as studious obedience to academic rules (Sidney: 'Again, many things may be told which cannot be showed, if they know the difference betwixt reporting and representing'), except that it is a monologue unvarying in its gloominess, excessive in length, and placed right at the beginning of the play, exactly where a comic dramatist is supposed to seize the audience's attention at once, awaken their expectations and get the action going. It tells, moreover, of a separation lasting twenty-three years, of extravagant geographical wandering, some excessively improbable coincidence, and a miserably pointless end. It is a studious compendium of romance motifs, each of which is taken to an extreme: it begins, not with his sons' but with his own birth – 'ab ovo' indeed – and there is much more absurdity besides.

The rhetoric Aegeon uses tends to the stiff and pedantic, so that the tale itself, highly conventional in content, is made even more artificial in the telling. It is like versified Thomas Lodge. The family of father, mother, and twin sons is augmented by the second set of twin boys, and this doubling tends to make an already far-fetched tale top-heavy with implausibility. They are threatened with shipwreck: the mother binds herself with two boys at one end of a mast, the father with the matching pair of boys at the other. They outlast the storm, and two far-off ships are sighted; but at once their own ship and mast are split in half by a rock. Each half-mast, bearing one parent and two boys apiece, floats away, and each is picked up by a different ship, 'Of Corinth that, of Epidaurus this'. The narrative's structural rhythm of combining and separating is given a comically exaggerated regularity.

Aegeon's narrative rivals any Tudor romance in highly conventionalised and derivative form and content, in slow pace and clumsy artifice. Yet, as the interruptions remind us, this long, slow narrative is in starkest contrast to the urgent crisis Aegeon faces. The discrepancy between style and situation is extreme to the point of absurdity. For Shakespeare to begin with such a gloomy situation might make spectators who have come to see a 'comedy of errors' wonder if they are in the right playhouse (they will soon enough discover what a feast of comedy is in store); while for brighter audiences at the time, such as that at the Gray's Inn Revels, with their classical education and literary pretensions, this beginning offered wonderfully straight-faced burlesque of romance and at the same time an oblique dialogue with Sidney, playful but acute in its engaging crucial questions confronting the playwright: to obey or ignore the dramatic unities, to separate or combine tragedy and comedy, to report or represent narrative material. As in other early comedies, Shakespeare's interest seems at its most acute precisely when such issues are made a focus – as they seem inescapably to be here – for parody and burlesque.

Shakespeare's early work as a whole presents an incomparably ambitious range of dramatic kinds and styles, yet he approached the particular area of lyrical romance with the greatest care; the advances in technical complexity no less than imaginative power greatly accelerate towards 1595–6 with *A Midsummer Night's Dream* and *Romeo and Juliet*. Shakespeare's early explorations of romance indicate that he thought such material very challenging: he deploys a wide variety of styles, including various kinds of parody and burlesque, and the special quality of *A Midsummer Night's Dream* is his creation of a composite context for the intense ideal aspiration of the lovers, and their lyricism.

Before writing *Romeo and Juliet* Shakespeare composed a shorter and structurally simpler romantic comedy, *The Two Gentlemen of Verona*, in which lyrical idealism (precisely the special quality which supremely characterises *Romeo and Juliet*) is persistently betrayed by the behaviour, speech and attitudes of the very young principal characters. The cumulative effect is to expose their highly artificial romance codes of honour, friendship and love to the charge that they are impossible and absurd except when confined to the pages of a book. An intelligent audience which did not know what Shakespeare's future development was to be might have supposed, judging by the end of *The Two Gentlemen of Verona*, that here the playwright is debunking Petrarchan idealism as a feasible subject for future serious drama, so acute is his identification of its inherent weaknesses. Modern critics have dismissed the play as a failed attempt at romantic comedy, not being ready to suppose – indeed not even asking themselves whether – Shakespeare was using parody, burlesque and comedy to explore in controlled circumstances, subjects to which he was profoundly drawn, but for which he had yet to evolve fully expressive means. My own direct practical experience in a stage-production convinced me that Shakespeare's sophistication and wit here have been underestimated. A few years after the stage-production I came upon a similar view presented in a lively essay by William Rossky, arguing for ' *The Two Gentlemen of Verona* as Burlesque '.[1]

I believe that the more sophisticated *The Two Gentlemen of Verona* is taken to be, the better: the play then at once comes alive as recognisably kin to its Shakespearean contemporaries; and does it really seem plausible that the Shakespeare who created the young lords in *Love's Labour's Lost* would wish to present the likes of Proteus and Valentine as subjects of serious imaginative concern? It would certainly be much more consistent to read *The Two Gentlemen of Verona* as working in the same spirit as the opening of *The Comedy of Errors*, as intelligent, critical burlesque; and this would take account of the broader pattern of Shakespeare's career. With the germ of *Romeo and Juliet* and *A Midsummer Night's Dream* in his mind, Shakespeare must have been acutely anticipating the difficulties in making new plays which accepted, head on, the challenge of bringing both Petrarchan love-idealism and romance-narrative home to London audiences in direct, convincing, contemporary terms. In *Romeo and Juliet* and *A Midsummer Night's Dream* this most notoriously difficult aim is successfully achieved through the integration of the vital elements of burlesque, mockery and parody; and these become, from *Love's Labour's Lost* to *Antony and Cleopatra*, essential components in Shakespeare's dramatic presentation of lyricism; they are used as mechanisms to prepare an audience's receptivity and to develop dialectic in which an extreme ideal is confronted by rival energies, rival ideas, and rival senses of experience.

It remains uncertain whether Shakespeare wrote *A Midsummer Night's Dream* before *Romeo and Juliet* or after it, and although there is the evident possibility that he conceived and wrote both together, commentators are reluctant to think that Shakespeare could be so assured as to have ridiculed in advance, in the Pyramus and Thisbe episode of *A Midsummer Night's Dream*, the lyric mode of *Romeo and Juliet*. Yet that Shakespeare was thoroughly at home with multiple presentation of the love-death motif ought to seem only predictable when one takes account of the full Elizabethan literary context, and one needs only to consider his design of *As You Like It* to see how he will, characteristically, grant ecstatic lyricism its full aesthetic rights while ensuring, with no less even-handedness, that the voice of humorous or grave disbelief is given a hearing. Thus, because Rosalind-as-Ganymede has so sparkling a set-piece on the absurdity of imagining that a man could die for love, it is hard to remember that this Rosalind-as-Ganymede is the same one who later in the play falls in a dead faint just at the sight of a cloth stained with Orlando's blood. Yet Shakespeare's play takes a flexible, paradoxical, multiple view for granted; it was his inheritance.

It is awareness of multiple aspects of the central theme which informs *As You Like It*. Before *As You Like It*, in *Romeo and Juliet* (four years before, in fact), Shakespeare had set the young lovers' dedication to a shared, absolute idea of love in a context of multiple mirrors, and if Mercutio stands out in opposing the tender lyricism of Romeo by adopting now the voice of Nashe, now that of the ironic narrator of Marlowe's *Hero and Leander*, there are more extreme diverging voices still, such as Juliet's father and, most graphically of all, the aged Nurse, who suggests Juliet forget she has become Romeo's wife (it is a secret, after all):

> I think it best you married with the County.
> O, he's a lovely gentleman!
> Romeo's a dishclout to him.   (3.5.217–19)

Shakespeare in *Romeo and Juliet* recalled not only the Marlowe of *Hero and Leander* but also of the *Tragedy of Dido Queen of Carthage*, and it is in *Dido*, *par excellence*, that the various Elizabethan modes of multiplicity offered to Shakespeare a model in dramatic form, one that can be seen influencing not only *Romeo and Juliet* (which contains a number of direct echoes and general parallels) but which also informs Shakespeare's later, extraordinary work of multiplicity, *Antony and Cleopatra*.

In *Romeo and Juliet*, the background of vendetta between the Capulets and Montagues had been presented as a small-scale affair, although in Chaucer's *Troylus and Criseyde*, which influences the play's deep structure, the setting is the Trojan war. It is all the more ironic therefore that a family feud in Verona should prove fatal to Shakespeare's lovers. In Shakespeare's later love tragedies *Othello* and *Antony and Cleopatra*, perhaps partly because they follow *Troilus and Cressida*, the background is ennobled to the heroic scale and greatly expanded to the realms of war and national politics. There is also, progressively, a change in the age of the central characters: in place of Romeo's youthful and therefore natural rashness, Othello, when he first appears in the play, makes an impression of mature authority: his poise, his stillness, is indeed somewhat unexpected after the play's first scene where Iago causes uproar over Othello's secret and bold elopement, in the night, with Desdemona. In *Antony and Cleopatra* Shakespeare goes a stage further, making both hero and heroine middle-aged; yet precisely because the central protagonists have so much experience of the world, know themselves to have 'declin'd /Into the vale of years', their dedication to love must seem a more extreme idealism even as it must also seem foolish and degrading: the decay of powers always seeming sordid, where as yet undeveloped power is permitted some indulgence.

In his later plays Shakespeare's developing arts of characterisation make the dramatic texture more complex, so much so indeed that in the plays from *King Henry IV* onwards the action is often discussed by critics as if it arose not from the overall plot so much as from the psychological interplay of virtually autonomous individual characters. Yet Shakespeare does not reduce the importance of his general design, indeed quite the reverse, he amplifies its scope as a means of manipulating the audience in increasingly complex ways. He chooses stories which already incorporate discrepant awareness and manipulation as key elements in the fiction. The idea of manipulation is shown up as dangerous even in the comedies, and darkens the conception of such roles as Falstaff, Parolles, Don Pedro. Shakespeare gives emphatic visual emphasis to the theme in the scenic form of key episodes – to take some instances, the gulling of Benedick in *Much Ado About Nothing* (2.3), the nunnery scene in *Hamlet* (3.1), the letter scene in *Twelfth Night* (2.5), the whole of Act 5 of *Measure for Measure*, the episode in *Troilus and Cressida* (5.2) when Thersites watches Troilus watching Cressida yield to Diomed, or in *Othello* (4.1), when Othello watches Iago question Cassio.

The sense of the instability of perspective is from the beginning significant in Shakespeare's work; in *Macbeth* and *The Tempest* he invents new expressive means for the theme of imagination's trickery of the senses. The characters are confronted by shapes so strange they seem imaginary, yet for that reason having their own compelling power. It is no insignificant matter that the audience is repeatedly drawn in to this experience: the stage history shows that the banquet scene in *Macbeth* can be played with no actor to impersonate Banquo's ghost. Macbeth's reaction is so powerful it can summon up for an audience an invisible Banquo as an undeniable presence on stage; similarly, the image of Duncan murdered remains in the memory, even though Shakespeare never stages it. In these plays visual events on stage may paradoxically be less powerful than verbal description. The experience of the spectators parallels that of the characters in being perplexed in their effort to disentangle themselves from delusion, to find bearings on events seen now from this angle, now from that, or events physically verifiable though they defy explanation or belief. Shakespeare presents this in parodic terms in Act 2, Scene 2 of *The Tempest*, when Stephano encounters the strange monster with four legs and two mouths. An audience may be amused to notice that for once there is a perfectly simple explanation for this, it is only Trinculo and Caliban under the gaberdine – a perfectly simple explanation, until they realise that they have no certainty about the nature of Caliban himself. Through Caliban Shakespeare reflects many kinds of contradiction in Prospero's culture: above all Caliban is both monster and poet, and in him two contradictory ideas of drama are shown ironically united – a medium with dark origins, in which the creative spirit must struggle with its physical incarnation, with its bodily and visual sign-systems which, at their worst, produce such clumsy and crude effects as to 'make nature afraid', in Ben

Jonson's contemptuous phrase – yet also a medium in which the imagination may be freed, with the whole of nature for its province.

Shakespeare's plays are so charged with matter that they can seem just as full of unrealised potential after a fine performance as before one. The majority of the plays – including the most laughter-provoking ones – have a more intellectually ruthless zest than seems consistent with any natural or assumed desire, on the part of their author, for conformity. Successful modern stage productions, furthermore, would seem to support the idea that this richness of material and design, this enquiring, zestful spirit, so far from being bad box-office may actually be a key to their power to entertain, despite the modern proverbial wisdom that nobody ever lost money by underestimating the intelligence of the public. Shakespeare is usually treated alone – 'sheer off, disseveral, a star' – but in this book I explore instances where he is intimately involved with his contemporaries Sidney, Spenser, Marlowe, Nashe or Jonson, and then we can read him in their light and also – I think refreshingly – read them in his. In this approach to the plays the concept of the artist's critical intelligence remains useful; it emphasises the play of mind as an aesthetic pleasure in itself, and as a source of Shakespeare's power to keep generating new interpretations, and new life in the theatre.

Notes

1. INTRODUCTION

1 Louise George Clubb's *Italian Drama in Shakespeare's Time* (New Haven, Conn., 1990) offers new light on this subject.

2 For these preferences see, respectively, Ernst Honigmann, *Shakespeare, the Lost Years* (Manchester, 1985), pp. 128–9; Brian Morris, ed., *The Taming of the Shrew, The Arden Shakespeare* (London, 1981); Alfred Harbage (rev. Samuel Schoenbaum and Sylvia Wagonheim), *Annals of English Drama 975–1700* (London, 1989); S. Wells and G. Taylor, *William Shakespeare, The Complete Works* (Oxford, 1986).

3 Samuel Johnson, *Proposals for Printing the Dramatic Works of Shakespeare*, 1756. I quote from the edition of W. K. Wimsatt, *Dr Johnson on Shakespeare* (Harmondsworth, 1969).

4 David Hare writes memorably on the unpredictability of audiences: 'As I sought to surprise them, so, endlessly, the audience has surprised me. The experience of this, the direct experience of people's response to my work, makes me not a better writer than a poet or novelist of my same temperament and ability, nor even, God knows, a wiser one. But it makes me a different kind of writer. It makes me one who is at home with risk.' *Writing Left-Handed* (London, 1991), p. 50.

5 Shakespeare quotations are mainly from *The New Cambridge Shakespeare*. For plays which have not yet appeared in that series I quote from G. Blakemore Evans, ed., *The Riverside Shakespeare* (Boston, 1974). In chapter 4, *King Lear* is quoted from Jay Halio's forthcoming edition of the 1608 Quarto text in *The New Cambridge Shakespeare* (Cambridge, 1994).

6 William B. Long, 'Stage Directions', *TEXT* 2, 1985, 121–37, and '*John a Kent and John a Cumber*: an Elizabethan playbook and its implications', in W. R. Elton and William B. Long, eds., *Shakespeare and Dramatic Tradition: Essays in Honor of S. F. Johnson* (Newark, Del., 1989) pp. 125–43.

7 See R. A. Foakes, *Hamlet Versus Lear. Cultural Politics and Shake-speare's Art* (Cambridge, 1992), chapter 4.

8 See the stimulating discussion by Christopher Hill, *The Intellectual Origins of the English Revolution* (Oxford, 1965), chapter 4.

9 See Robert Speaight, *Shakespeare on the Stage* (London, 1973), p. 256.

10 See Charles H. Shattuck, *Shakespeare on the American Stage* (Washington, D. C., 1976), pp. 145–7.

11 See Glynne Wickham, *Early English Stages 1300–1660* (3 vols. in 4, London, 1959–81), vol. II, part 1, pp. 16–17.

12 For instance I myself, as a schoolboy, first saw the play in Tyrone Guthrie's Edwardian-dress production at the Old Vic in 1956, and I vividly recall Pandarus, dressed as for the Royal Enclosure at Ascot in grey top-hat and morning-coat, using his racing binoculars to give Cressida a running commentary on the heroes.

13 George Lukacs, *The Historical Novel*, Peregrine edn. (Harmondsworth, 1969), pp. 57–8.

14 Hayden White, *Tropics of Discourse* (Baltimore, Md., 1978), p. 69. This position is of importance in the new historicist studies of Stephen Greenblatt, and underpins his procedure, to make fluid interdisciplinary relations between history, cultural anthropology, and literary studies in the discussion of Renaissance texts.

15 For an admirable discussion of this and other features of post-modernism see Linda Hutcheon, *A Poetics of Postmodernism* (New York, 1988). As her choice of authors implies, by her account post-modernism views history critically not nihilistically, it does not see history as merely textual and therefore fictive, not as always and only a function of the will to power. Christopher Norris, on the other hand, in *Uncritical Theory: Postmodernism, Intellectuals and the Gulf War* (London, 1992), does firmly associate post-modernism with such writers as Foucault, Fish, Baudrillard and Lyotard, with the more extremist assertions – which he powerfully attacks – that realist epistemologies are a thing of the past and that truth values are merely a figment of bourgeois ideology.

16 The interview was with David Brooks, *Helix* 19, 1984. See also Lloyd Grove's interview with Rushdie in *International Herald Tribune* 27 May 1986. I owe these references to my student Silvia Maag, in her admirable University of Zürich Lizentiatsarbeit, 1991, 'Salman Rushdie's *Midnight's Children*: The Chutnification of Time or the Stuff That History is Made Of'.

17 Wölfflin's proposition is developed with singular subtlety and sophistication by E. H. Gombrich, in his meditations on the schema in art: see his *Art and Illusion* (London, 1960, and many later editions).

18 In *Image Music Text* (London, 1977), p. 160; see also his *S/Z*, translated by Richard Miller (New York, 1974). It goes without saying that the polemical, playful manner has tended to harden in the hands of other deconstructionist writers.

19 See Richard S. Peterson, *Imitation and Praise in the Poetry of Ben Jonson* (New Haven, Conn., 1981), and, more generally, Thomas M. Greene, *The Light in Troy: Imitation and Discovery in Renaissance Poetry* (New Haven, Conn., 1982).

20 The more general emergence of originality as a valued quality, in relation to respect for classical sources, is discussed by David Quint, *Origin and Originality in Renaissance Literature, Versions of the Source* (New Haven, Conn., 1983). His account of Ariosto and Rabelais is particularly pertinent.

21 This is discussed and illustrated in Marion Trousdale, *Shakespeare and the Rhetoricians* (Chapel Hill, N. C., 1982). Of related interest is Terence Cave, *The Cornucopian Text, Problems of Writing in the French Renaissance* (Oxford, 1979). See also Brian Vickers's recent wide-ranging work, *In Defence of Rhetoric* (Oxford, 1988).

2 FABLED 'CYMBELINE'

1 Christopher Hill, *The Intellectual Origins of the English Revolution* (Oxford, 1965), p. 139. He refers to Vico, *La Scienza Nuova*, 3rd edn, 1744, Bk I, sec. iii, para. 337.

2 I am very grateful to Leo Salingar for privately pointing out two instances where Jacobean writers defend the colonising efforts of the British in Virginia by referring to the historical benefits conferred on Britain by Roman colonisation. In 1609 the Virginia Company published a tract, *Nova Britannia*, in which the charge that the Virginia colonisers aimed to supplant the Red Indians is refuted: the writer asserts that, on the contrary, God has reserved to 'us' the task of converting the Indians, and in doing so 'we' shall do them good – as 'will easily appeare, by comparing our present happinesse with our former ancient miseries, wherein we had continued brutish, poore and naked Britanes to this day, if *Iulius Caesar* with his Roman Legions (or some other) had not laid the ground to make us tame and civill'. Peter Force, ed., *Tracts... relating... to... the Colonies in North America* (Washington, 1836, reprinted New York, 1947), vol. I. The second quotation has overtones of *Cymbeline*, as Salingar says: William Strachey in 1612–13 wrote of the Roman colonisation of Britain: 'Had not this violence... bene offred to us by the Romans..., even by Julius Caesar himself, then by the emperor Claudius... who reduced the conquered parts of our barbarous iland into provinces, and

established in them colonies of old souldiers ... we might yet have lyved overgrowen satyrs, rude and un-tutred, wandring in the woodes, dwelling in caves, and hunting for our dynners, as the wyld beasts in the forrests for their praye'. *A History of Travaile into Virginia Britannia*, cited in Howard Mumford Jones, *O Strange New World* (London, 1965), p. 165.

3 Arthur B. Ferguson, *Clio Unbound* (Durham, N. C., 1979), p. 381. See also Andrew Hadfield, 'Briton and Scythian: The Representation of the Origins of Tudor Ireland', *Irish Historical Studies* (forthcoming). I am very grateful to Dr Hadfield for allowing me to see this excellent essay.

4 Written in 1596 but not published until 1633 and then not in London but Dublin. Quotations from the edition by W. L. Renwick (Oxford, 1970), pp. 39–40.

5 English translation in *Works*, ed. Spedding, Ellis and Heath (7 vols., London, 1857–74), vol. vi, p. 697. Bacon is discussing mythological fables here, not a specific treatment of them by particular writers or artists.

6 That criticism of the play generally assumes it to be a romance is attested by the fact that Geoffrey Bullough in his *Narrative and Dramatic Sources of Shakespeare* (8 vols., London, 1957–75) places it in the same volume as *The Winter's Tale* and *The Tempest*, and not in the volume devoted to 'Later English History Plays'. Dr Johnson's hostile view of the play's mode succinctly summarises the critical issues: 'To remark the folly of the fiction, the absurdity of the conduct, the confusion of the names and manners of different times, and the impossibility of the events in any system of life, were to waste criticism upon unresisting imbecility, upon faults too evident for detection, and too gross for aggravation.' The publications which most convincingly deal with the play as historical are G. Wilson Knight, *The Crown of Life* (London, 1947); Philip Brockbank, 'History and Histrionics in *Cymbeline*', *Shakespeare Survey* 11, 1958; Emrys Jones, 'Stuart *Cymbeline*', *Essays in Criticism* 11, 1961.

7 See Emrys Jones, 'Stuart *Cymbeline*'.

8 See Marion Lomax, *Stage Images and Traditions: Shakespeare to Ford* (Cambridge, 1987). I owe stimulus in thinking about *Cymbeline* to discussion with Marion Lomax when she was working with me on her thesis, which is the basis of her book.

9 See Bullough, vol. viii, pp. 10–11. 'Innogen' is the name given in the stage direction in the First Quarto of *Much Ado* for the wife of Leonato, but she has no speaking part. It is possible that in *Cymbeline* the name should be spelt 'Innogen', as G. Blakemore Evans notes in his *Riverside Shakespeare* (Boston, 1974), p. 1561.

10 The topicality of the play is succinctly pointed to by Emrys Jones, in the article cited above.

11 See Bullough, *Narrative and Dramatic Sources of Shakespeare*, vol. VIII, pp. 11–12 for full details.

12 Jonson was summoned before the Privy Council after *Sejanus* was performed to answer a charge of writing treason. He was not proceeded against. The play was published in 1605, and later became applied to the career of George Villiers, Duke of Buckingham, which Jonson could not possibly have foreseen. On topicality of this kind see the recent book by Annabel Patterson, *Censorship and Interpretation* (Madison, Wis., 1984). One might also recall the observation of Francis Bacon published in 1609 in *De Sapientia Veterum*: 'Not but I know very well what pliant stuff fable is made of, how freely it will follow any way you please to draw it, and how easily with a little dexterity and discourse of wit meanings which it was never meant to bear may be plausibly put upon it.' English translation in *Works*, ed. Spedding, Ellis and Heath (London, 1857–74), vol. VI, p. 695.

13 See Emrys Jones, 'Stuart *Cymbeline*'.

14 Roy Strong, *Henry, Prince of Wales* (London, 1986), p. 149. The heir to the throne, Prince Henry, was dressed as a Roman emperor in the masque *Oberon*, the next year, 1611, as shown in Strong, illustration 78, and in John Harris, Stephen Orgel and Roy Strong, *The King's Arcadia, Inigo Jones and the Stuart Court*, Catalogue of the Arts Council Exhibition (London, 1973), pp. 45–51.

15 J. M. Nosworthy, editor of *Cymbeline*, *The Arden Shakespeare* (London, 1955, revised edn, 1960), regards the choice of the romance material in the following terms: 'he was indebted to Holinshed's *Chronicles*, but the debt is a relatively slight one, for the historical matter serves merely to round off a play that is mainly concerned with specifically comic or romantic themes'.

16 *Shakespeare and the Traditions of Comedy* (Cambridge, 1974), pp. 45–59, especially p. 57. I have found this study by Salingar exceptionally illuminating.

17 Spenser is quoted from the Penguin edition by T. P. Roche and C. P. O'Donnell (Harmondsworth, 1978).

18 Salingar, *Shakespeare and the Traditions of Comedy*, p. 59, suggests a memory of Plautus, *Amphitryon*, the noted tragicomoedia, known to Shakespeare since using it in *The Comedy of Errors*. Salingar persuasively argues against the influence of *Love and Fortune*, which the Arden editor, Nosworthy, canvasses. It is characteristic of Shakespeare's manner in *Cymbeline* that one suspects an ironic allusion to Aristotle, who in the *Poetics* 15 objected to the use of the

deus ex machina. A similar conscious allusion to dramatic criticism has been detected in *The Winter's Tale* by Andrew Gurr: see his article, 'The Bear, the Statue, and Hysteria in *The Winter's Tale*' in *Shakespeare Quarterly* 34, 1983, 420–5.

19 I am not aware that this point has been explored by other critics, but I would acknowledge the discussion about 'apparel' in *Much Ado* by Arthur C. Kirsch, in his *Shakespeare and the Experience of Love* (Cambridge, 1981), where Kirsch relates the topic to its treatment in the scriptures.

20 See Richard Marienstras, *New Perspectives on the Shakespearean World*, trans. Janet Lloyd (Cambridge, 1985, first published in French, 1981). Marienstras offers an analysis of the action of *Mucedorus* in terms of structural anthropology (pp. 11–15) which stresses the use of the wild man's own club to brain him. Marienstras is reluctant to grant the Welsh sequences in *Cymbeline* the status of aboriginal 'wildness', to judge by a comment he makes on p. 36, but this is made in passing, and he does not consider the relation between *Cymbeline* and *Mucedorus* with which I am concerned.

21 Shakespeare's *Cymbeline* (like *Antony and Cleopatra* and *The Winter's Tale*) in its design might almost be seen as offering a good-natured ironic tribute to Sidney, who meant to mock early Elizabethan heroical romances but also commemorated their vitality: 'where you shall have Asia of the one side, and Afric of the other, and so many other under-kingdoms, that the player, when he cometh in, must ever begin with telling where he is, or else the tale will not be conceived. Now ye shall have three ladies walk to gather flowers and then must we believe the stage to be a garden. By and by we hear news of a shipwreck in the same place, and then we are to blame if we accept it not for a rock. Upon the back of that comes out a hideous monster with fire and smoke, and then the miserable beholders are bound to take it for a cave. While in the meantime two armies fly in, represented with four swords and bucklers, and then what hard heart will not receive it for a pitched field?' *Sir Philip Sidney, An Apology for Poetry*, ed. G. Shepherd (Manchester, 1973), p. 134.

22 Further Spenserian elements may be seen when Shakespeare immediately follows the bedchamber scene with Cloten. It turns out that Cloten has been playing cards all night, and has lost – thus while Iachimo was winning a wager, Cloten was losing one. Iachimo and Cloten both serve as doubles of Posthumus, though it is when he is headless that Cloten has his most substantial significance. Then, minus his 'clotpoll' and with Posthumus' suit

upon his back, he does prove a torment to Imogen – though not quite as he had visualised. Cloten is a character deployed in Spenser's manner, from one aspect stiffly allegorical, from another an occasion for mocking humour, from a third an obscure projection of the dreamer's own subconscious. Cloten's wicked mother loses all substance at the moment when renewal and reconciliation dawns for Cymbeline's true family.

23 The whole sequence from Iachimo's seductive conversation with Imogen to the description of her bedchamber and its ornate decoration may be compared with the strongly scenic account of Britomart's experiences in Castle Ioyeous in *The Faerie Queene* Book 3, 1. (I would not wish to press a comparison too strongly: it is the general affinity, not any precise similarity, which seems to me interesting here.) Britomart, Spenser's chaste heroine, in male warrior guise, is invited to stay at the castle of Lady Malecasta. The evening entertainment takes place in a chamber decorated with a large tapestry depicting Venus and Adonis in a number of amorous scenes. In Spenser's narrative description of this tapestry the dimension of time is added by the medium of poetry, and the reader is prompted to recreate the pictures in imagination: Spenser's poetry controls the viewer's/voyeur's eye, which is moved with kindled erotic interest from image to image, as the tapestry Venus makes love to Adonis:

> And whilst he slept, she ouer him would spred
> Her mantle, colour'd like the starry skyes,
> And her soft arme lay vnderneath his hed,
> And with ambrosiall kisses bathe his eyes;
> And whilest he bath'd, with her two crafty spyes,
> She secretly would search each daintie lim   (3.1.36)

Because this is not painting but poetic narrative, the imagination of the reader must be excited to summon up these images: the scene becomes to an extent the reader's own fantasy, seeking to stir the imagination erotically, although it may also make the reader self-conscious of this temptation. In *The Rape of Lucrece* Shakespeare describes how deliberately Lucrece views a painting of the Fall of Troy to find images which can arouse her feelings: 'She throws her eyes about the painting round, / And who she finds forlorn, she doth lament' (1499–1500). She selects images of grief to arouse her passion: 'She lends them words, and she their looks doth borrow' (1488). The corollary is that the figures contemplated are unaware of being viewed, they are passive reflectors of the viewer's state of mind. This seems to be equally true of Imogen in the Iachimo scenes in *Cymbeline*. In the Britomart episode in Spenser the company of knights and ladies, duly influenced by the erotic surroundings, indulge in love-making, whereas Britomart stays aloof and keeps on her armour and even her helmet. Lady Malecasta finds the idea of the man concealed by this armour erotically irresistible and in the middle of the night she slips into Britomart's chamber. It is too dark to see: she gets into bed, trembling with desire, 'Of euery finest fingers touch affrayd'. Beside the calm, unconscious Britomart now lies an ironic mirror-self, a self burning with conscious lust. Britomart wakes, leaps out of bed, seizes her sword. The lady shrieks. Knights rush to the chamber and find an unknown young woman wearing nothing but her smock, her long golden hair disshevelled, but 'Threatning the point of her auenging blade' (63) at an equally scantily clad Lady Malecasta, who now lies fallen in a faint from their disarranged bed. For the reader there is humour in recognising the paradoxical pattern which is so confusing to the participants. The knights must think Britomart to be the aggressor, but her golden hair contradicts this; Malecasta seems the victim, but what is she doing in someone else's bed? The reader sees how Britomart's disguise as a man has betrayed the intimate feelings both of Malecasta and herself, while on the other hand the real differences between them are disguised by their both being near-naked: Malecasta is really guilty; Britomart is genuinely heroic as a defender of truth – Truth is traditionally naked – and chastity – which is her real, but spiritual, armour. Comparison of this episode with the bedchamber scene in *Cymbeline* shows, perhaps surprisingly, how strong is the scenic and dramatic nature of Spenser's writing.

3. A SPEECHLESS DIALECT: INTERPRETING THE HUMAN
BODY IN SHAKESPEARE'S PLAYS

1 I owe general debts in this chapter to E. H. Gombrich, *Symbolic Images*, 2nd edn (Oxford, 1978); Rudolf Wittkower, *Sculpture* (Harmondsworth, 1977), and Arthur C. Danto, *The Transfiguration of the Commonplace* (Cambridge, Mass., 1981). The general question of the representation and understanding of the body in the Shakespeare period is discussed in Leonard Barkan, *Nature's Work of Art* (New Haven, Conn., 1975), and Lucy Gent and D. Llewellyn, eds., *Renaissance Bodies* (London, 1990). For discussion of conventional signals on the Elizabethan stage see Bernard Beckerman, *Shakespeare at the Globe* (New York, 1962), John Russell

Brown, *Shakespeare's Plays in Performance* (London, 1966), John
Russell Brown, *Free Shakespeare* (London, 1974), J. L. Styan,
Shakespeare's Stagecraft (Cambridge, 1967), G. K. Hunter, 'Flatcaps
and Bluecoats: Visual Signals on the Elizabethan Stage', *Essays &
Studies* 33, 1980, 16–47; Michael Hattaway, *Elizabethan Popular
Theatre* (London, 1982), Ann Pasternak Slater, *Shakespeare the
Director* (Brighton, 1982); David Bevington, *Action Is Eloquence*
(Cambridge, Mass., 1984); Alan Dessen, *Elizabethan Stage Con-
ventions and Modern Interpreters* (Cambridge, 1984). Reviews of
Shakespeare productions are regularly published in *Shakespeare
Survey* and *Shakespeare Quarterly*.

2 Especially in the work of Erwin Panofsky, *Studies in Iconology* (New
York, 1939) and *Meaning in the Visual Arts* (Garden City,
N.Y., 1955). See also Edgar Wind, *Pagan Mysteries in the Renaissance*
(New Haven, Conn., 1958), and Roy Strong, *The English Icon*
(London, 1969).

3 For the learned application of emblem to court masques see D. J.
Gordon, *The Renaissance Imagination*, ed. Stephen Orgel (Berkeley,
1975). See also the diversity of interesting approaches in David
Lindley, ed., *The Court Masque* (Manchester, 1984).

4 See J. G. Nichols, *The Progresses ... of Queen Elizabeth* (3 vols.,
London, 1823); E. K. Chambers, *The Elizabethan Stage* (4 vols.,
Oxford, 1923), Alice Venesky, *Pageantry on the Shakespearean Stage*
(New York, 1951), David M. Bergeron, *English Civic Pageantry
1558–1642* (London, 1971), Andrew Gurr, *The Shakespearean Stage
1574–1642*, 3rd edn (Cambridge, 1991).

5 See my Introduction to *Romeo and Juliet*, *The Arden Shakespeare*
(London, 1980) pp. 36–77.

6 See Terence Spencer, 'The Statue of Hermione', *Essays & Studies*
30, 1977, 39–49; David M. Bergeron, 'The Wax Figures in *The
Duchess of Malfi*', *Studies in English Literature* 18, 1978, 331–9;
Leonard Barkan, '"Living Sculptures": Ovid, Michaelangelo,
and *The Winter's Tale*', *English Literary History* 48, 1981, 639–67;
Marion Lomax, *Stage Images and Traditions: Shakespeare to Ford*,
chapter 6.

4 SHAKESPEARE'S 'ROAD OF EXCESS': 'THE TAMING OF THE
SHREW', 'TITUS ANDRONICUS', 'KING LEAR'

1 John C. Bean in *The Woman's Part: Feminist Criticism of Shakespeare*,
ed. C. R. Lenz, G. Greene and C. T. Neely (Urbana, Ill., 1980),
p. 66. Quotations from *King Lear* in this chapter are from the
edition by Jay Halio of the 1608 Quarto (*The New Cambridge*

Shakespeare, forthcoming, 1994). For structural approaches to the plays discussed in this chapter see Emrys Jones, *Scenic Form in Shakespeare* (Oxford, 1971), G. K. Hunter, 'Shakespeare's Earliest Tragedies', *Shakespeare Survey* 27, 1974, 1–10, Stanley Wells, '*The Taming of the Shrew* and *King Lear*, A Structural Comparison', *Shakespeare Survey* 33, 1980, 55–66.

2 The sub-plot involving Edmund is the basis for the satiric tragedy of 1606, *The Revenger's Tragedy*, a play in which comic plotting and farce give a cruel twist to the revenge theme. See *The New Mermaid* edition of *The Revenger's Tragedy*, ed. Brian Gibbons (London, 1991).

3 The old play *King Leir* was performed by the Queen's Men before 1594 but not published until 1605, the year of Shakespeare's *King Lear*. Shakespeare took the story of the Paphlagonian king from Sidney, *Arcadia*, as the basis for the story of Gloucester and his sons. A further significant source, Spenser, *The Faerie Queene*, Book 3, canto 10, 56–7 (the Malbecco episode), is discussed by J. J. M. Tobin, *Notes and Queries*, Dec. 1985, 478.

4 This idea of carnival refers to the theory set out in several works by Bakhtin, the first published in English in 1968 being *Rabelais and his World*. See also François Laroque, *Shakespeare's Festive World* (Cambridge, 1991).

5 See Richard Marienstras, *New Perspectives on the Shakespearean World*, trans. Janet Lloyd (Cambridge, 1985), pp. 1–72.

6 In Virgil's *Aeneid* a storm overtakes Dido and her guest Aeneas when out hunting and they shelter in a cave, where they make love. Marlowe dramatises the episode in his *The Tragedy of Dido Queen of Carthage* (1584?). See my discussion in chapter 7 below.

7 See D. H. Madden, *The Diary of Master William Silence* (1897, reprinted New York, 1969), chapters 1–5.

8 See René Girard, *La Violence et le Sacré* (Paris, 1972), trans. P. Gregory (Baltimore, 1977).

9 Terence Spencer, 'Shakespeare and the Elizabethan Romans', *Shakespeare Survey* 10, 1957.

10 Brian Morris, ed., *The Taming of the Shrew* (London, 1981), pp. 129 ff.

11 René Girard, *La Violence et le Sacré*.

12 See Eugene M. Waith, ed., *Titus Andronicus*, The Oxford Shakespeare (Oxford, 1984) p. 85, note to 1.1.35.

13 *La Violence et le Sacré*, passim.

14 See Joseph Wittreich, '*Image of that Horror*': *History, Prophecy and Apocalypse in 'King Lear*', (San Marino, Calif., 1984). An interesting discussion which I came upon after completing this chapter is in

William C. Carroll, '"The Base Shall Top th'Legitimate": The Bedlam Beggar and the Role of Edgar in *King Lear*', *Shakespeare Quarterly* 38, 1987, 426–41.

15 See M. C. Bradbrook, 'Marlowe's *Dr Faustus* and the Eldritch Tradition' in R. Hosley, ed., *Essays on Shakespeare and Elizabethan Drama in Honour of Hardin Craig* (Columbia, Mo., 1962), pp. 83–90.

16 For a discussion of Shakespeare's use of the 'presentational' mode in his late plays see Barbara Mowat, *The Dramaturgy of Shakespeare's Romances* (Athens, Ga., 1976).

17 See Bernard Spivack, *Shakespeare and the Allegory of Evil* (New York, 1958).

18 This differs in significant respects from the text in the First Folio of 1623; the equivalent passage from the Folio version reads:

> And my poore Foole is hang'd: no, no, no life?
> Why should a Dog, a Horse, a Rat have life,
> And thou no breath at all? Thou'lt come no more,
> Never, never, never, never, never.
> Pray you undo this Button. Thanke you Sir,
> Do you see this? Looke on her? Looke her lips,
> Looke there, looke there.

The Quarto version of *King Lear* appeared in 1608 and it is with this, the earlier version of the play, that I am concerned here. The changes evident in the text printed in the First Folio of 1623 are certainly interesting and significantly alter certain features of the play, although to what extent the changes represent a coherent and systematic revision, and to what extent they are authorial, remains contentious.

19 See *The Faerie Queene*, Book 2, canto 10, and the discussion in chapter 2 above.

20 Emrys Jones, *The Origins of Shakespeare* (Oxford, 1976).

5 ALWAYS TOPICAL: 'MEASURE FOR MEASURE'

1 There is a graphic review of this production at Stratford-upon-Avon by Peter Thomson in *Shakespeare Survey* 28, 1975, 137–49.

2 Cinthio's version is in *Hecatommithi* (1565, reprinted for the fifth time in 1593, earlier translated into French in 1583–4 and Spanish in 1590). I have discussed the nature of Shakespeare's use of tragicomedy in my edition of *Measure for Measure*, *The New Cambridge Shakespeare* (Cambridge, 1991), pp. 18–20 and 48–51; quotations from the play in this chapter are also from this edition. For wider discussion of tragicomedy in the period see also Arthur Kirsch, *Jacobean Dramatic Perspectives* (Charlottesville, 1972), and

more recently, Louise George Clubb, 'Shakespearean Comedy and Late Cinquecento Mixed Genres', in *Shakespearean Comedy*, ed. Maurice Charney (New York, 1980), pp. 129–39.

3 Quotations from Whetstone's *Promos and Cassandra* in this chapter are from Mark Eccles, ed., *Measure for Measure, The New Variorum Shakespeare* (New York, 1980).

4 See Giorgio Melchiori, ed., *The Second Part of King Henry IV, The New Cambridge Shakespeare* (Cambridge, 1989), pp. 15–17, and Alan C. Dessen, *Shakespeare and the Late Moral Plays* (Lincoln, Nebr., 1986), and David M. Bevington, *From Mankind to Marlowe* (Cambridge, Mass., 1962). On Tudor interlude staging, T. W. Craik, *The Tudor Interlude* (Leicester, 1958), is indispensable.

5 *King Henry IV, Part 2*, ed. Melchiori, p. 17.

6 *Ben Jonson*, ed. C. H. Herford and P. and E. Simpson (11 vols., Oxford, 1925–52), vol. IV.

7 Dekker, *The Shoemaker's Holiday* (1599), has several scenes in which shops feature, where either a counter hinged to a window or a movable work table represented the shop. Elizabethan shop-windows had wooden shutters hinged at the top and bottom. The stage doors might have been fitted with such practicable shutters: see *The Revels Plays* edition by R. L. Smallwood and Stanley Wells (Manchester, 1979), pp. 45–6.

8 Glynne Wickham, *Early English Stages 1300–1600* (3 vols. in 4, London, 1963), vol. I, p. 110.

9 Thomas Dekker, *The Magnificent Entertainment* (1604), in Fredson Bowers, ed., *The Dramatic Works of Thomas Dekker* (4 vols., Cambridge, 1953–61), vol. II, pp. 253–303.

10 For a useful comparison of Chettle's pamphlet with Nashe, see Lorna Hutson, *Thomas Nashe in Context* (Oxford, 1989), pp. 139–40.

11 See Brian Gibbons, ed., *Measure for Measure* (Cambridge, 1991), pp. 21–4.

12 Ibid., pp. 2–3.

13 When James became King of England new editions of *Basilikon Doron* were brought out in London: the number of copies was dramatically high – between thirteen thousand and sixteen thousand, according to the estimate of P. W. M. Blayney: see Jenny Wormald, '*Basilikon Doron* and *The Trew Law*' in Linda Levy Peck, ed., *The Mental World of the Jacobean Court* (Cambridge, 1991), p. 51.

14 Thomas Nashe, *The Anatomie of Absurditie* (1589) in *Works*, ed. R. B. McKerrow (5 vols., 1904–10), revised by F. P. Wilson (Oxford, 1958), vol. I, pp. 20–22.

15 See the stage history in recent editions by Brian Gibbons, *The New*

Cambridge Shakespeare and N. W. Bawcutt, *The Oxford Shakespeare* (Oxford, 1991), and Mark Eccles, *The New Variorum Shakespeare*.

16 James I inherited from Elizabeth I the status of supreme head of the Church in an independent sovereign Protestant monarchy. There were many in the population who retained Catholic beliefs despite the official status of the Protestant religion. On the other hand, some extreme Puritans demanded reform of the Protestant Church of England on a 'pure' primitive pattern, and the abolition of all distinctive ecclesiastical dress. Their hostility centred on the bishops who, under pressure from Elizabeth I, suppressed demands for such changes. Strict Puritans and Presbyterians believed the key to the establishment of a godly nation was the enforcement of an effective Church discipline. The ecclesiastical courts of the Church of England were, they maintained, unable to enforce moral discipline, for their sanctions were too easily evaded. Hooker had pleaded for the view that Church and nation should be one: he thought most of the Puritan arguments were about matters not essential to salvation and not as important as a united Church of England.

In the view of recent 'revisionist' historians, such as J. P. Kenyon, *The Stuart Constitution* (Cambridge, 1969), Englishmen in the early years of the seventeenth century shared a belief that the English common law, consisting of ancient custom, defined the rights of the king and the liberties of subjects, and although James I might have made absolutist statements, these were confined to theory, and in practice he was careful to operate within the framework of common law – even, in his later years, abandoning the theory of absolutism. In a recent essay J. P. Somerville disputes this view. He asserts (and illustrates his case) that there were several ideologies current in early Stuart England: 'the climate was not one of unity and harmony' ('James I and the Divine Right of Kings: English Politics and Continental Theory', in Linda Levy Peck, *The Mental World of the Jacobean Court*, p. 57). Somerville argues that James I's thinking was scarcely if at all influenced by the common law, whereas he was decidedly influenced by the fact that the Scottish Presbyterian Church used its power to depose his own mother from her throne, and by continental assertions that kings derived their power from the people, or that the pope could use his spiritual power to intervene in secular affairs and depose Protestant rulers. James I believed that 'however monarchs had at first acquired their crowns, their authority was derived from God alone' (p. 63). Subjects derived political privileges only from the king, and the exemption of the clergy from civil jurisdiction existed because the king had willed it, not in virtue of any law independent of the monarch. This applied to *all* groups within the realm, parliament included. See also J. P. Somerville, *Politics and Ideology in England 1603–1640* (London, 1986), Patrick Collinson, *The Elizabethan Puritan Movement* (London, 1967), and 'The Jacobean Religious Settlement: The Hampton Court Conference' in H. Tomlinson, ed., *Before The English Civil War* (London, 1983), A. G. Dickens, *The English Reformation* (New York, 1964), William Haller, *Foxe's Book of Martyrs and the Elect Nation* (London, 1963), Peter Lake, *Moderate Puritans and the Elizabethan Church* (Cambridge, 1982). For allusions to James I in the play see Brian Gibbons, ed., *Measure for Measure*, pp. 12–15 and 21–4.

17 Elizabeth Longford, *The Royal House of Windsor* (London, 1976), p. 91, cited by David Cannadine, 'The British Monarchy c. 1820–1977' in Eric Hobsbawm and Terence Ranger, eds., *The Invention of Tradition* (Cambridge, 1983), p. 141.

18 Cannadine, *The Invention of Tradition*, pp. 142–3.

19 The director of a film about Princess Anne said in an interview in April 1991, on Channel 4, that he was astonished to discover this, when he began work on the film.

20 E. Shils and M. Young, 'The Meaning of the Coronation', *Sociological Review* n.s. i, 1953, 80, cited by Cannadine, *The Invention of Tradition*, p. 158.

6 AMOROUS FICTIONS IN 'AS YOU LIKE IT'

1 According to some scholars it was a revival of Lyly's pastoral comedies by the Children's companies that gave an immediate incentive to Shakespeare and his company, with their new theatre, the Globe, to respond to the revived fashion for pastoral comedy. See Agnes Latham, ed., *As You Like It, The Arden Shakespeare* (London, 1975), p. xxvi. It is my conviction that what we know of the circumstances of Shakespeare's company in 1599, and of Shakespeare's work of the time, makes his decision to turn to pastoral more than opportunist. I should like to record my debt to Hans-Jost Frey, in his article on translation in *Colloquium Helveticum* no. 3 (Bern, 1986). General discussions of pastoral include William Empson, *Some Versions of Pastoral* (London, 1935), Frank Kermode, ed., *English Pastoral Poetry from the Beginnings to Marvell* (London, 1952), Renato Poggioli, 'The Oaten Flute', *Harvard Library Bulletin* 11, 1957, 147–84, A. Bartlett Giamatti, *The Earthly Paradise and the Renaissance Epic* (Princeton, 1966), Harry Levin, *The Myth of the Golden Age in the Renaissance* (London, 1970),

Helen Cooper, *Pastoral: Mediaeval into Renaissance* (Ipswich, 1977), Peter Lindenbaum, *Changing Landscapes* (Athens, Ga., 1987).

2 See *Every Man Out Of His Humour*, 3.6.191–212.

3 Quotations from Sidney are from Jean Robertson, ed., *The Old Arcadia* (Oxford, 1973), a work not published in Shakespeare's lifetime; and the version known as The Countess of Pembroke's *Arcadia* – the episodes discussed in the present chapter appeared in the 1590 edition and subsequent editions. The 1590 edition consisted of Sidney's revised version of *The Old Arcadia*: Books 1, 2, and part of 3, ending in mid-fight and mid-sentence. I give page references for the reader's convenience to Maurice Evans's Penguin edition (Harmondsworth, 1977).

4 Quotations from Lodge's *Rosalynde* are from Geoffrey Bullough, ed., *Narrative and Dramatic Sources of Shakespeare*, vol. II.

5 George Calderon, writing in 1911, quoted by Jan McDonald, 'Productions of Chekhov's Plays in Britain before 1914', *Theatre Notebook* 44, 1980.

6 By changing Lodge's story so that the usurper Duke becomes brother of the exiled Duke, and by excluding the third de Boys brother, Shakespeare contrives a highly symmetrical pattern, the function of which is expository, presenting the characters as paired: indeed they are bound either by close kinship or by love. Shakespeare adds a bond of love between the exiled Duke and Orlando's dead father, which completes the pattern of strong ties between all the main characters. In reducing the vague supporting cast of *Rosalynde* he gives each Duke one leading courtier: Le Beau is discreetly disloyal to Frederick, Amiens is discreetly ironic in flattering Senior's stylish pose of literary stoicism. If these courtiers are instances of equivocal service, then Shakespeare's important new characters Touchstone and Jaques present, as marginal figures, more detached questioning of the pastoral and social ties between human beings. Even the wrestler Charles is shown to be honourable (accepting no bribes as he does in Lodge), despising Orlando only after being made to believe him to be 'a secret and villainous contriver' against his elder brother. Shakespeare drastically abbreviates, reduces, and concentrates Lodge's story to give central emphasis to love's power, and juxtaposes clearly contrasted groups in highly symmetrical patterns of twos and threes to generate a visual, and then a more general, dialectic of contrast and comparison. The prolonged bad relations between the brothers in Lodge are telescoped by Shakespeare and simplified, so that Orlando goes directly into exile, with Rosalind fresh in his mind. When she arrives in Arden, with a Celia who has come with

her out of pure love (not as in Lodge banished like Rosalind), the poems they find on trees and shrubs are by Orlando himself not, as in Lodge, by a minor character, Montanus. Orlando, arriving in Arden, interrupts the ducal banquet with sword drawn and heroic martial challenge, although in Lodge Rosader shows only polite civility.

7 Quotations are from the first edition: I have modernised the spelling.

7 UNSTABLE PROTEUS: MARLOWE AND 'ANTONY AND CLEOPATRA'

1 G. K. Hunter, *John Lyly* (London, 1962), p. 142.

2 Quotations from *Arthur Golding, The XV. Bookes of P.Ouidius Naso, entytuled Metamorphosis, translated* (1567; reprinted and corrected W. H. D. Rouse, London 1961); I have modernised the spelling. Quotations from Marlowe are from *The Revels Plays*: *The Tragedy of Dido Queen of Carthage* ed. H. J. Oliver (London, 1968), *Hero and Leander* in *The Poems*, ed. Millar McClure (London, 1968), and *Tamburlaine*, ed. J. S. Cunningham (Manchester, 1981). The present chapter began life as an article, 'Unstable Proteus: Marlowe's *The Tragedy of Dido Queen of Carthage*' in *Christopher Marlowe, Mermaid Critical Commentaries*, ed. Brian Morris (London, 1968). I had not then read T. P. Harrison, 'Shakespeare and Marlowe's *The Tragedy of Dido Queen of Carthage*', *University of Texas Studies in English* 35, 1956, 57–63, but I did know J. B. Steane, *Marlowe: A Critical Study* (Cambridge, 1964). Since 1968 there has appeared a further book-length study, Janet Adelman, *The Common Liar* (New Haven, Conn., 1973), with its appendix on *The Tragedy of Dido Queen of Carthage* and *Antony and Cleopatra*.

3 *The Entertainment at Elvetham*, a water-pageant performed for Elizabeth I in 1591, is described in David M. Bergeron, *English Civic Pageantry 1558–1642* (London, 1971), pp. 58–9.

4 Ernst Honigmann, *Shakespeare, Seven Tragedies* (London, 1976), pp. 155–6.

5 E. K. Chambers, *The Elizabethan Stage* (4 vols., Oxford, 1923), vol. III, pp. 35–6.

6 See Margaret A. Lamb, *Shakespeare's 'Antony and Cleopatra' on the English Stage* (London, 1980).

7 See G. K. Hunter, *John Lyly*, pp. 112–13, for contemporary accounts of performances before Elizabeth I in the hall of Christ Church, Oxford, of Edwardes's *Palamon and Arcite* in 1566 and in 1583 of William Gager's *Dido*. In the latter there was a kennel of

real hounds, Mercury and Iris 'descending and ascending from and to an high place, the tempest wherein it hailed small comfits, rained rosewater and snew an artificial kind of snow: all strange, marvellous and abundant'.

8 See Ethel Seaton, 'Marlowe's Light Reading', in Herbert Davis and Helen Gardner, eds., *Elizabethan and Jacobean Studies Presented to Frank Percy Wilson in Honour of his Seventieth Birthday* (Oxford, 1959), p. 27.

9 J. S. Cunningham, ed., *Tamburlaine*, p. 113.

10 *The General Historie of the Turkes* (1603), cited by Cunningham, p. 80.

11 Cited by Judith Weil, *Christopher Marlowe, Merlin's Prophet* (Cambridge, 1977), p. 200, n. 15.

12 Eugene M. Waith, *The Herculean Hero* (New York, 1962), p. 16.

13 R. J. Dorius, cited in David Bevington, ed., *Antony and Cleopatra*, *The New Cambridge Shakespeare* (Cambridge, 1990), p. 26, n. 2.

14 The Nashe reads 'At thy breasts, asps shall be put out to nurse'; see Nashe, *Works*, ed. R. B. McKerrow, with corrections by F. P. Wilson (5 vols., Oxford, 1958), vol. II, p. 140. David L. Frost, *The School of Shakespeare* (Cambridge, 1968), p. 144, points out that an emblem for lechery depicted a woman suckling a snake, and argues that the shockingly unnatural aspects of the tableau should be fully recognised.

15 The archaic T-in-O maps divided the known world into three parts, Europe, Asia and Africa (probably referred to in Marlowe's phrase 'the triple region') with Jerusalem at the centre. In devising the geographical action of the play Marlowe made extensive use of the atlas by Abraham Ortelius, as Ethel Seaton in 'Marlowe's Light Reading' notes. See Cunningham's note to *Tamburlaine*, Part 1, 4.4.77–84, which suggests that Tamburlaine plans to replace Jerusalem with Damascus.

16 Timur the Lame was the last great nomad Mongol Khan. His predecessor Chingis (Ghengis) Khan had used his swift and devastating cavalry to win an empire embracing China and nearly all of Asia. The Ottoman Turks themselves had been horsemen from the steppes before converting to Islam and mounting a holy war against Christendom. The actual military campaigns dramatised in *Tamburlaine* concern Timur the Lame's defeat of the two Muslim states which menaced Christian Byzantium. Although in the short term this brought the Christians relief, in the long term it worked to their disadvantage. See J. H. Parry, *The Age of Reconnaissance* (London, 1963, new edn 1981), pp. 22–4.

17 Herod of Jewry is named at 3.5.73 and 4.6.12, and Caesar declares

that 'The time of universal peace is near'. The historical Caesar, later to be known as the Emperor Augustus, was praised by St Augustine as having been specially chosen by Providence to reign at the time of Christ's birth (as Bevington notes in his *New Cambridge Shakespeare* edn, p. 5).

18 Geoffrey Bullough, ed., *Narrative and Dramatic Sources of Shakespeare* vol. v, (London, 1964), pp. 229–39.

8 MULTIPLICITY

1 *English Literary Renaissance*, 1982, 210–19. For an up-to-date critical history and stage history of the play see Kurt Schlueter, ed., *The Two Gentlemen of Verona, The New Cambridge Shakespeare* (Cambridge, 1990).

Bibliography

Adelman, Janet. *The Common Liar*, New Haven, Conn., 1973.

Amussen, Susan. *An Ordered Society. Gender and Class in Early Modern England*, Oxford, 1988.

Auster, Paul. *The New York Trilogy*, New York, 1987.

Bakhtin, Mikhail. *Rabelais and his World*, trans. Helene Iswolsky, Cambridge, Mass., 1968.

　The Dialogic Imagination: Four Essays by M. M. Bakhtin, ed. Michael Holquist, trans. Caryl Emerson and Michael Holquist, Austin, Tex., 1981.

Banfield, Ann. *Unspeakable Sentences: Narration and Representation in the Language of Fiction*, Boston, Mass., 1982.

Barkan, Leonard. *Nature's Work of Art*, New Haven, Conn., 1975.

　'"Living Sculptures": Ovid, Michelangelo, and *The Winter's Tale*', *English Literary History* 48, 1981, 639–67.

Barker, Francis. *The Tremulous Private Body*, London, 1984.

Barroll, Leeds. *Politics, Plague, and Shakespeare's Theater*, Ithaca, N.Y., 1991.

Barthes, Roland. *Mythologies*, trans. Annette Lavers, London, 1973.

　S/Z, trans. Richard Miller, New York, 1974.

　The Pleasure of the Text, trans. Richard Miller, New York, 1975.

Bate, W. J. *The Burden of the Past and the English Poet*, Cambridge, Mass., 1970.

Beckerman, Bernard. *Shakespeare at the Globe*, New York, 1962.

Benjamin, Walter. 'The Work of Art in the Age of Mechanical Reproduction' in *Illuminations*, ed. Hannah Arendt, trans. Harry Zohn, New York, 1968, 217–51.

Bennett, Josephine Waters. *'Measure for Measure' as Royal Entertainment*, New York, 1966.

Bentley, Eric. *The Playwright as Thinker*, New York, 1946.

Bergeron, David M. *English Civic Pageantry 1558–1642*, London, 1971.

　'The Wax Figures in *The Duchess of Malfi*', *Studies in English Literature* 18, 1978, 331–9.

Bevington, David M. *From Mankind to Marlowe*, Cambridge, Mass., 1962.

Action Is Eloquence, Cambridge, Mass., 1984.

Bloom, Harold. *The Anxiety of Influence*, New York, 1973.

Bloomfield, M. W. (ed.). *The Interpretation of Narrative: Theory and Practice*, Cambridge, Mass., 1970.

Bluestone, M. *From Story to Stage*, The Hague, 1974.

Bradbrook, M. C. 'Marlowe's *Dr Faustus* and the Eldritch Tradition' in Richard Hosley (ed.), *Essays on Shakespeare and Elizabethan Drama in Honour of Hardin Craig*, Columbia, Mo., 1962, 83–90.

Shakespeare the Craftsman, London, 1969.

Braudy, Leo. *Narrative Form in History and Fiction: Hume, Fielding, and Gibbon*, Princeton, N.J., 1970.

Braunmuller, A. R., and Michael Hattaway. *The Cambridge Companion to English Renaissance Drama*, Cambridge, 1990.

Brennan, Anthony. *Shakespeare's Dramatic Structures*, London, 1986.

Bristol, Michael D. *Carnival and Theater*, New York, 1985.

Shakespeare's America, America's Shakespeare, London, 1990.

Brockbank, Philip. 'History and Histrionics in *Cymbeline*', *Shakespeare Survey* 11, 1958, 42–9.

Brooke, Nicholas. 'Marlowe as a Provocative Agent in Shakespeare's Early Plays', *Shakespeare Survey* 14, 1961, 34–44.

Brooks, David. 'An Interview with Salman Rushdie', *Helix* 19, 1984, 55–69.

Brown, John Russell. *Shakespeare's Plays in Performance*, London, 1966.

Free Shakespeare, London, 1974.

Bullough, Geoffrey (ed.). *Narrative and Dramatic Sources of Shakespeare*, 8 vols., London, 1957–1975.

Burke, Peter. *The Renaissance Sense of the Past*, London, 1969.

Cannadine, David. 'The British Monarchy c. 1820–1977' in Eric Hobsbawm and Terence Ranger (eds.), *The Invention of Tradition*, Cambridge, 1983, 101–64.

Caroll, David. 'The Alterity of Discourse: Form, History, and the Question of the Political in M. M. Bakhtin', *Diacritics* 13, 1983, 65–83.

Cave, Terence. *The Cornucopian Text: Problems of Writing in the French Renaissance*, Oxford, 1979.

Chambers, E. K. *The Elizabethan Stage*, 4 vols., Oxford, 1923.

Churchill, Caryl. *Top Girls*, London, 1982.

Clubb, Louise George. 'Shakespeare's Comedy and Late Cinquecento Mixed Genres' in Maurice Charney (ed.), *Shakespearean Comedy*, New York, 1980, 129–39.

Italian Drama in Shakespeare's Time, New Haven, Conn., 1990.

Colie, Rosalie, and F. T. Flahiff (eds.), *Some Facets of 'King Lear'*, Toronto, 1974.

Collingwood, R. G. *The Idea of History*, Oxford, 1946.

Collinson, Patrick. *The Elizabethan Puritan Movement*, London, 1967.
'The Jacobean Religious Settlement: The Hampton Court Conference' in Howard Tomlinson (ed.), *Before the English Civil War*, London, 1983.

Cooper, Helen. *Pastoral: Mediaeval into Renaissance*, Ipswich, 1977.

Craik, T. W. *The Tudor Interlude*, Leicester, 1958.

Culler, Jonathan. *On Deconstruction: Theory and Criticism after Structuralism*, Ithaca, N.Y., 1982.

Danto, Arthur C. *Analytical Philosophy of History*, New York, 1968.
The Transfiguration of the Commonplace, Cambridge, Mass., 1981.

Davis, Lennard J. *Factual Fictions: The Origins of the English Novel*, New York, 1983.

Derrida, Jacques. *Writing and Difference*, trans. Alan Bass, Chicago, 1978.

Dessen, Alan. *Elizabethan Stage Conventions and Modern Interpreters*, Cambridge, 1984.
Shakespeare and the Late Moral Plays, Lincoln, Nebr., 1986.

Dickens, A. G. *The English Reformation*, New York, 1964.

Doebler, J. *Shakespeare's Speaking Pictures: Studies in Iconic Imagery*, Albuquerque, N. Mex., 1974.

Eagleton, Terry. *Literary Theory: An Introduction*, Oxford, 1983.

Eco, Umberto. *Postscript to 'The Name of the Rose'*, trans. William Weaver, San Diego, Calif., 1983.

Empson, William. *Some Versions of Pastoral*, London, 1935.

Ferguson, Arthur B. *Clio Unbound*, Durham, N.C., 1979.

Ferguson, Margaret *et al. Rewriting the Renaissance*, Chicago, 1986.

Fletcher, Anthony, and John Stevenson (eds.). *Order and Disorder in Early Modern England*, Cambridge, 1985.

Frost, David L. *The School of Shakespeare*, Cambridge, 1968.

Fussner, F. S. *The Historical Revolution*, London, 1962.

Genette, Gérard. *Narrative Discourse: An Essay on Method*, trans. Jane E. Lewin, Ithaca, N.Y., 1980.

Gent, Lucy, and D. Llewellyn (eds.). *Renaissance Bodies*, London, 1990.

Giamatti, A. Bartlett. *The Earthly Paradise and the Renaissance Epic*, Princeton, 1966.

Gibbons, Brian. *Jacobean City Comedy*, 1968, new edn., London, 1980.

Girard, René. *La Violence et le Sacré*, Paris, 1972, trans. P. Gregory, Baltimore, 1977.

Gombrich, E. H. *Art and Illusion*, London, 1960.
Meditations on a Hobby Horse, 2nd edn, London, 1971.

Symbolic Images, 2nd edn, Oxford, 1978.

Gordon, D. J. *The Renaissance Imagination*, ed. Stephen Orgel, Berkeley, 1975.

Greenblatt, Stephen. *Shakespearean Negotiations*, Berkeley, 1988.

Learning to Curse, New York, 1990.

Greene, Thomas M. *The Light in Troy: Imitation and Discovery in Renaissance Poetry*, New Haven, Conn., 1982.

Greenwood, John. *Shifting Perspectives and the Stylish Style – Mannerism in Shakespeare and his Jacobean Contemporaries*, Toronto, 1988.

Griffin, Alice V. *Pageantry on the Shakespearean Stage*, New Haven, Conn., 1951.

Gurr, Andrew. 'The Bear, the Statue, and Hysteria in *The Winter's Tale*', *Shakespeare Quarterly* 34, 1983, 420–5.

Playgoing in Shakespeare's London, Cambridge, 1987.

The Shakespearean Stage: 1574–1642, 3rd edn, Cambridge, 1991.

Hadfield, Andrew. 'Briton and Scythian: The Representation of the Origins of Tudor Ireland', *Irish Historical Studies* (forthcoming).

Haller, William. *Foxe's Book of Martyrs and the Elect Nation*, London, 1963.

Hamilton, A. C. *et al.* (eds.). *The Spenser Encyclopedia*, Toronto, 1990.

Hapgood, Robert. *Shakespeare the Theatre-Poet*, Oxford, 1988.

Harbage, Alfred (revised Samuel Schoenbaum and Sylvia Wagonheim). *Annals of English Drama 975–1700*, London, 1989.

Hare, David. *Writing Left-Handed*, London, 1991.

Harris, John, Stephen Orgel, and Roy Strong (eds.). *The King's Arcadia, Inigo Jones and the Stuart Court*. Catalogue of the Arts Council Exhibition, London, 1973.

Hassan, Ihab (ed.). *The Dismemberment of Orpheus: Toward a Postmodern Literature*, 2nd edn, Madison, Wis., 1982.

Hattaway, Michael. *Elizabethan Popular Theatre*, London, 1982.

Hill, Christopher. *The Intellectual Origins of the English Revolution*, Oxford, 1965.

Hill, Geoffrey. *Mercian Hymns*, London, 1971.

Honigmann, Ernst. *Shakespeare, Seven Tragedies*, London, 1976.

Shakespeare, The Lost Years, Manchester, 1985.

Howard, Jean E. *Shakespeare's Art of Orchestration*, Chicago, 1984.

Hunter, G. K. *John Lyly*, London, 1962.

'Shakespeare's Earliest Tragedies', *Shakespeare Survey* 27, 1974, 1–10.

'Flatcaps and Bluecoats: Visual Signals on the Elizabethan Stage', *Essays & Studies* 33, 1980, 16–47.

Hutcheon, Linda. *Narcissistic Narrative: The Metafictional Paradox*, Waterloo, Ont., 1980.

A Poetics of Postmodernism: History, Theory, Fiction, New York, 1988.

Hutson, Lorna. *Thomas Nashe in Context*, Oxford, 1989.

Jameson, Fredric. *The Political Unconscious: Narrative as a Socially Symbolic Act*, Ithaca, N.Y., 1981.

Jencks, Charles. *The Language of Post-Modern Architecture*, London, 1977.

Jones, Emrys. 'Stuart *Cymbeline*', *Essays in Criticism* 11, 1961, 84–99.

Scenic Form in Shakespeare, Oxford, 1971.

The Origins of Shakespeare, Oxford, 1976.

Josipovici, Gabriel. *Writing and the Body*, Princeton, N.J., 1982.

Kermode, Frank (ed.). *English Pastoral Poetry from the Beginnings to Marvell*, London, 1952.

The Sense of an Ending, London, 1966.

The Genesis of Secrecy: On the Interpretation of Narrative, Cambridge, Mass., 1979.

Kirsch, Arthur C. *Jacobean Dramatic Perspectives*, Charlottesville, Va., 1972.

Shakespeare and the Experience of Love, Cambridge, 1981.

Knight, G. Wilson. *The Crown of Life*, London, 1947.

LaCapra, Dominick. *History and Criticism*, Ithaca, N.Y., 1985.

Lake, Peter. *Moderate Puritans and the Elizabethan Church*, Cambridge, 1982.

Lamb, Margaret A. *Shakespeare's 'Antony and Cleopatra' on the English Stage*, London, 1980.

Laroque, François. *Shakespeare et la Fête*, Paris, 1988, English version *Shakespeare's Festive World*, Cambridge, 1991.

Leggatt, Alexander. *Shakespeare in Performance: 'King Lear'*, Manchester, 1991.

Lenz, C. R., G. Greene and C. T. Neely (eds.). *The Woman's Part: Feminist Criticism of Shakespeare*, Urbana, Ill., 1980.

Levin, Harry. *The Myth of the Golden Age in the Renaissance*, London, 1970.

Levin, Richard, *The Multiple Plot in English Renaissance Drama*, Chicago, 1971.

Levy, F. J. *Tudor Historical Thought*, San Marino, Calif., 1967.

Lindenbaum, Peter. *Changing Landscapes*, Athens, Ga., 1987.

Lindley, David (ed.). *The Court Masque*, Manchester, 1984.

Linthicum, M. C. *Costume in the Drama of Shakespeare and His Contemporaries*, Oxford, 1936.

Lomax, Marion. *Stage Images and Traditions: Shakespeare to Ford*, Cambridge, 1987.

Longford, Elizabeth. *The Royal House of Windsor*, London, 1976.

Lukacs, Georg. *The Historical Novel*, Harmondsworth, 1969.

Marienstras, Richard. *New Perspectives on the Shakespearean World*, trans. Janet Lloyd, Cambridge, 1985.

Marowitz, Charles. *Recycling Shakespeare*, Houndmills, 1991.

Márquez, Gabriel García. *One Hundred Years of Solitude*, trans. G. Rabassa, London, 1970.

McGuire, Philip C. *Speechless Dialect: Shakespeare's Open Silences*, Berkeley, 1985.

McHale, Brian. *Postmodernist Fiction*, London, 1987.

McPherson, David C. *Shakespeare, Jonson, and the Myth of Venice*, Newark, Del., 1990.

Mebane, John S. *Renaissance Magic and the Return of the Golden Age: The Occult Tradition and Marlowe, Jonson, and Shakespeare*, Lincoln, Nebr., 1989.

Miller, J. Hillis. 'Narrative and History', *English Literary History* 41, 1974, 455–73.

Morris, Brian (ed.). *Christopher Marlowe, Mermaid Critical Commentaries*, London, 1968.

Nichols, J. G. *The Progresses ... of Queen Elizabeth*, 3 vols., London, 1823.

Norris, Christopher. *The Contest of Faculties: Philosophy and Theory after Deconstruction*, London, 1985.

   Uncritical Theory: Postmodernism, Intellectuals and the Gulf War, London, 1992.

Orrell, John. *The Human Stage: English Theatre Design, 1567–1640*, Cambridge, 1988.

Panofsky, Erwin. *Studies in Iconology*, New York, 1939.

   Meaning in the Visual Arts, Garden City, N.J., 1955.

Parry, J. H. *The Age of Reconnaissance*, London, 1963, 2nd edn, 1981.

Patterson, Annabel. *Censorship and Interpretation*, Madison, Wis., 1984.

Pocock, J. G. A. *The Ancient Constitution and the Feudal Law*, New York, 1967.

Poggioli, Renato. 'The Oaten Flute', *Harvard Library Bulletin* 11, 1957, 147–84.

Pope, Nancy P. *National History in the Heroic Poem: A Comparison of the 'Aeneid' and ' The Faerie Queene'*, New York, 1990.

Portoghesi, Paolo. *Postmodern: The Architecture of the Postindustrial Society*, New York, 1983.

Powell, Jocelyn. 'Marlowe's Spectacle', *Tulane Drama Review* 8, 1964, 195–210.

Praz, Mario. *The Flaming Heart*, Gloucester, Mass., 1966.

Pynchon, Thomas. *The Crying of Lot 49*, New York, 1965.

Quint, David. *Origin and Originality in Renaissance Literature – Versions of the Source*, New Haven, Conn., 1983.

Raab, Felix. *The English Face of Machiavelli*, London, 1964.

Rabkin, Norman. *Shakespeare and the Common Understanding*, New York, 1967.

Rackin, Phyllis. *Stages of History*, London, 1990.

Ricoeur, Paul. *Interpretation Theory: Discourse and the Surplus of Meaning*, Fort Worth, Tex., 1976.

Riffaterre, Michael. 'Intertextual Representation: On Mimesis as Interpretive Discourse', *Critical Inquiry* 11, 1984, 141–62.

Ripley, John. '*Julius Caesar*' *on Stage in England and America, 1599–1973*, Cambridge, 1980.

Roberts, Jeanne Addison. *The Shakespearean Wild – Geography, Genus, and Gender*, Lincoln, Nebr., 1991.

Rose, Mark. *Shakespearean Design*, Cambridge, Mass., 1972.

Rushdie, Salman. *Midnight's Children*, London, 1981.

  'Angel Gabriel', *London Review of Books*, 16 September–6 October 1982.

Said, Edward W. *The World, the Text, and the Critic*, Cambridge, Mass., 1983.

Sales, Roger. *Christopher Marlowe*, Houndmills, 1991.

Salingar, L. G. *Shakespeare and the Traditions of Comedy*, Cambridge, 1974.

Schmidgall, Gary. *Shakespeare and Opera*, New York, 1990.

Seaton, Ethel. 'Marlowe's Light Reading' in Herbert Davis and Helen Gardner (eds.), *Elizabethan and Jacobean Studies Presented to Frank Percy Wilson in Honour of His Seventieth Birthday*, Oxford, 1959, 17–35.

Sharpe, J. A. *Early Modern England: A Social History, 1550–1760*, London, 1987.

Shattuck, Charles H. *Shakespeare on the American Stage*, Washington, D.C., 1976.

Slater, Ann Pasternak. *Shakespeare the Director*, Brighton, 1982.

Slights, Camille. *The Casuistical Tradition*, London, 1981.

Smidt, Kristian. *Unconformities in Shakespeare's Tragedies*, Basingstoke, 1989.

Spencer, Terence. 'Shakespeare and the Elizabethan Romans', *Shakespeare Survey* 10, 1957, 27–38.

  'The Statue of Hermione', *Essays & Studies* 30, 1977, 39–49.

Spivack, Bernard. *Shakespeare and the Allegory of Evil*, New York, 1958.

Steane, J. B. *Marlowe: A Critical Study*, Cambridge, 1964.

Stevenson, David L. 'The Role of James I in Shakespeare's *Measure for Measure*', *English Literary History* 26, 1959, 188–208.

  The Achievement of Shakespeare's 'Measure for Measure', Ithaca, N.Y., 1966.

Stoppard, Tom. *After Magritte*, London, 1971.
   Travesties, London, 1975.
Strong, Roy. *The English Icon*, London, 1969.
   Henry, Prince of Wales, London, 1986.
Styan, J. L. *Shakespeare's Stagecraft*, Cambridge, 1967.
   The Dark Comedy, 2nd edn, Cambridge, 1968.
Thomson, Peter. *Shakespeare's Theatre*, London, 1983.
Tompkins, Jane P. (ed.). *Reader-Response Criticism: From Formalism to Post-Structuralism*, Baltimore, Md., 1980.
Trousdale, Marion. *Shakespeare and the Rhetoricians*, Chapel Hill, N. C., 1982.
Underdown, David. *Revel, Riot and Rebellion, Popular Politics and Culture in England 1603–1660*, Oxford, 1985.
Vaughan, Alden T. and Virginia Mason Vaughan. *Shakespeare's Caliban*, Cambridge, 1991.
Waith, Eugene M. *The Herculean Hero in Marlowe, Chapman, Shakespeare, and Dryden*, New York, 1962.
Warren, Roger. *Staging Shakespeare's Late Plays*, Oxford, 1990.
Weil, Judith. *Christopher Marlowe, Merlin's Prophet*, Cambridge, 1977.
Wells, Stanley. '*The Taming of the Shrew* and *King Lear*: A Structural Comparison', *Shakespeare Survey* 33, 1980, 55–66.
White, Hayden. *Metahistory: The Historical Imagination in Nineteenth-Century Europe*, Baltimore, Md., 1973.
   Tropics of Discourse: Essays in Cultural Criticism, Baltimore, Md., 1978.
Wickham, Glynne. *Early English Stages 1300–1660*, 3 vols. in 4, London, 1959–81.
Williams, Raymond. *Keywords: A Vocabulary of Culture and Society*, 2nd edn, London, 1983.
Wilson, F. P. *Marlowe and the Early Shakespeare*, Oxford, 1953.
Wind, Edgar. *Pagan Mysteries in the Renaissance*, New Haven, Conn., 1958.
Wittkower, Rudolf. *Sculpture*, Harmondsworth, 1977.
Wittreich, Joseph. '*Image of that Horror*': History, Prophecy, and Apocalypse in '*King Lear*', San Marino, Calif., 1984.
Wrightson, Keith. *English Society 1580–1680*, New Brunswick, N.J., 1982.

Index

Wagonheim, Sylvia, 212
Waith, Eugene, M., 51, 53, 196, 221, 228
Warner, Deborah, 51, 53
Webster, John, 63–4
Weil, Judith, 228
Wells, Stanley, 212, 221, 223
Whetstone, George, 15, 120–8, 131–6, 139, 146, 192, 223
White, Hayden, 10, 213
White, John, 19
Whitman, Walt, 12
Wickham, Glynne, 128, 213, 223

'The wife lapped in Morel's skin', 81
William of Normandy, 29
Wilson, F. P., 223, 228
Wimsatt, W. K., 212
Wind, Edgar, 47, 220
Wittkower, Rudolf, 219
Wittreich, Joseph, 221
Wölfflin, Heinrich, 12
Wormald, Jenny, 223

Yeats, William Butler, 45, 107
York, Duke of, 151
Young, M., 225